hotels • resorts • therapies • cuisine

spachic asia

For regular updates on our special offers, register at
www.thechiccollection.com

hotels • resorts • therapies • cuisine

■ asia

spachic

text kate o'brien • brandon lee

thechiccollection

managing editor
francis dorai

editors
laura dozier
valerie ho

assistant editor
josephine pang

studio manager
annie teo

designer
joanna poh

production manager
sin kam cheong

sales and marketing director
antoine monod

sales and marketing managers
rohana ariffin
catherine gay paras

sales and marketing consultants
tanya asavatesanuphab
carolyn bickerton

editions didier millet pte ltd
121 telok ayer street, #03-01
singapore 068590
telephone : +65.6324 9260
facsimile : +65.6324 9261
enquiries : edm@edmbooks.com.sg
website : www.edmbooks.com
www.thechiccollection.com

first published 2009
©2009 editions didier millet pte ltd

Printed in Singapore.

All rights reserved. No part of this publication may be reproduced, stored in a retrieval system, or transmitted in any form or by any means, electronic, electrostatic, magnetic tape, mechanical, photocopying, recording or otherwise, without prior written permission from the publisher.

isbn: 978-981-4217-42-2

THIS PAGE: *The shirodhara oil treatment being administered at the spa in COMO Shambhala Estate in Bali.*
OPPOSITE: *A relaxing soak in one of the pools of Kayumanis Bali.*
PAGE 1: *A spa treatment in session at the Kamalaya Koh Samui.*
PAGE 2: *A luxurious bath experience awaits at Four Seasons Resort Bali at Jimbaran Bay.*
PAGE 28: *A guest enjoying a stretch-out at the Kamalaya Koh Samui.*
PAGE 110: *Guests are always given a warm welcome at the Shangri-la Hotel, Bangkok.*
PAGE 212: *The Mandara Spa is cocooned among the luxuriant tropical garden of Hua Hin Marriott Resort & Spa.*

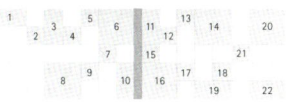

COVER CAPTIONS:

1: *A guest enjoying a foot massage outdoors at the Maya Ubud's spa.*
2: *A woman undergoing a laser treatment, Titan, for skin tightening and to treat facial wrinkles.*
3: *The traditional Indonesian massage beckons at the Kayumanis spas.*
4: *One of the ingredients—jasmine—found in the L'Occitane products.*
5: *Mineral-rich water channelled to a Japanese spa via bamboo pipes.*
6: *A relaxing spa treatment at Four Seasons Resort at Jimbaran Bay.*
7: *A variety of local spa ingredients used at the Maya Ubud's spa.*
8: *Women enjoying an outdoor spa in winter surrounded by scenic mountains in Japan.*
9: *Healthy and delicious spa cuisine prepared at the Cyberview Lodge Resort.*
10: *A guest enjoys a serene walk.*
11: *An expression of bliss after a spa session at the COMO Shambhala Estate in Bali.*
12: *A fruity treat from the menu of the Six Senses Destination Spa–Phuket.*
13: *Spa accessories found at the SHUI Urban Spa in Shanghai.*
14: *A female guest practises yoga at the Shangri-La's Rasa Sayang Resort & Spa.*
15: *A pair of soap ducks by SHUI Urban Spa.*
16: *A woman relaxing at the Four Seasons Resort Langkawi.*
17: *The signature CHI jade and silver tea cup from the Shangri-La Hotel, Bangkok.*
18: *The natural landscape surrounding the Four Seasons Resort Chiang Mai.*
19: *Special jade pieces for spa treatments at the Four Seasons Hotel Hong Kong.*
20: *The treatment pavilion at Island Spa at Four Seasons Maldives at Kuda Huraa.*
21: *Massage oils from the Maya Ubud's spa.*
22: *The clear waters in the Philippine islands are well worth a dive.*

contents

introduction 10

recent spa trends 16 • spa cuisine 18 • spa products 20 • destination spas + medispas 22 • healthy cuisine 26

therapies+treatments 28

traditional chinese medicine 30 • ayurveda 44 • jamu 60 • japanese healing rituals 72 • ramuan 82 • filipino traditions 92 • thai therapies 100

110 spas+retreats

china
pudong shangri-la, shanghai + shangri-la hotel, chengdu 112 • shangri-la hotel, beijing + shangri-la hotel, guangzhou 114 • shui urban spa (shanghai) 116 • zenspa (beijing) 118 • four seasons hotel hong kong 120 • plateau residential spa (hong kong) 122 • spa by mtm (hong kong) 126

maldives
anantara dhigu resort + spa, maldives 128 • conrad maldives rangali island 130 • four seasons resort maldives at kuda huraa 132 • four seasons resort maldives at landaa giraavaru 134 • soneva gili by six senses, maldives 136

bali, indonesia
como shambhala estate 138 • dala spa 140 • four seasons resort bali at jimbaran bay 142 • four seasons resort bali at sayan 144 • jimbaran puri bali 146 • kayumanis bali 148 • kupu kupu barong villas + mango tree spa by l'occitane 150 • maya ubud resort + spa 152 • nusa dua beach hotel + spa 154 • st regis bali 156 • ubud hanging gardens 158

tokyo, japan
four seasons hotel tokyo at chinzan-so 160 • the westin tokyo 162

malaysia + singapore
cyberview lodge resort + spa (malaysia) 164 • four seasons resort langkawi (malaysia) 166 • shangri-la's tanjung aru resort + rasa sayang resort (malaysia) 168 • st gregory spa (malaysia) 170 • the st regis singapore 172

the philippines
plantation bay resort + spa 174 (mactan island) • shangri-la's boracay resort + spa 176 • shangri-la's mactan resort + spa + edsa shangri-la, manila 178

thailand
absolute sanctuary (koh samui) 180 • anantara hua hin 182 • anantara phuket resort + spa 184 • anantara si kao resort + spa 186 • the barai (hua hin) 188 • chiva-som (hua hin) 190 • four seasons resort chiang mai 192 • i.sawan residential spa + club (bangkok) 194 • kamalaya koh samui 196 • pimalai resort + spa (koh lanta) 198 • pranali wellness spa (bangkok) 200 • salus per crystal® (nontaburi) 202 • shangri-la hotel, bangkok + shangri-la hotel, chiang mai 204 • six senses spa destination–phuket 206 • thann sanctuary gaysorn (bangkok) 208 • the racha (phuket) 210

index 214 • picture credits + acknowledgements 217 • directory 218 • spa glossary 220

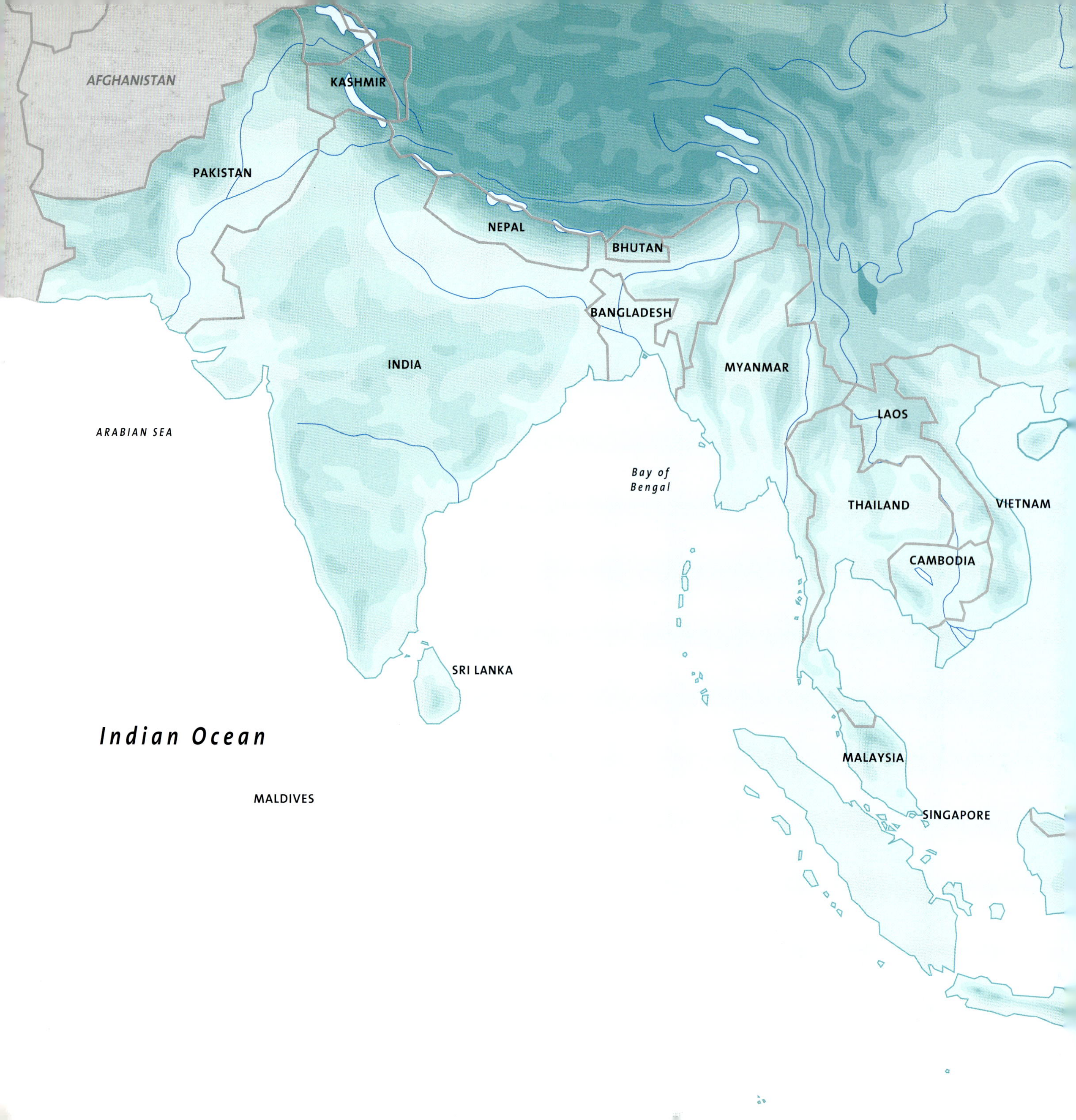

AFGHANISTAN
KASHMIR
PAKISTAN
NEPAL
BHUTAN
BANGLADESH
INDIA
MYANMAR
LAOS
ARABIAN SEA
Bay of
Bengal
THAILAND
VIETNAM
CAMBODIA
SRI LANKA
Indian Ocean
MALAYSIA
MALDIVES
SINGAPORE

asia

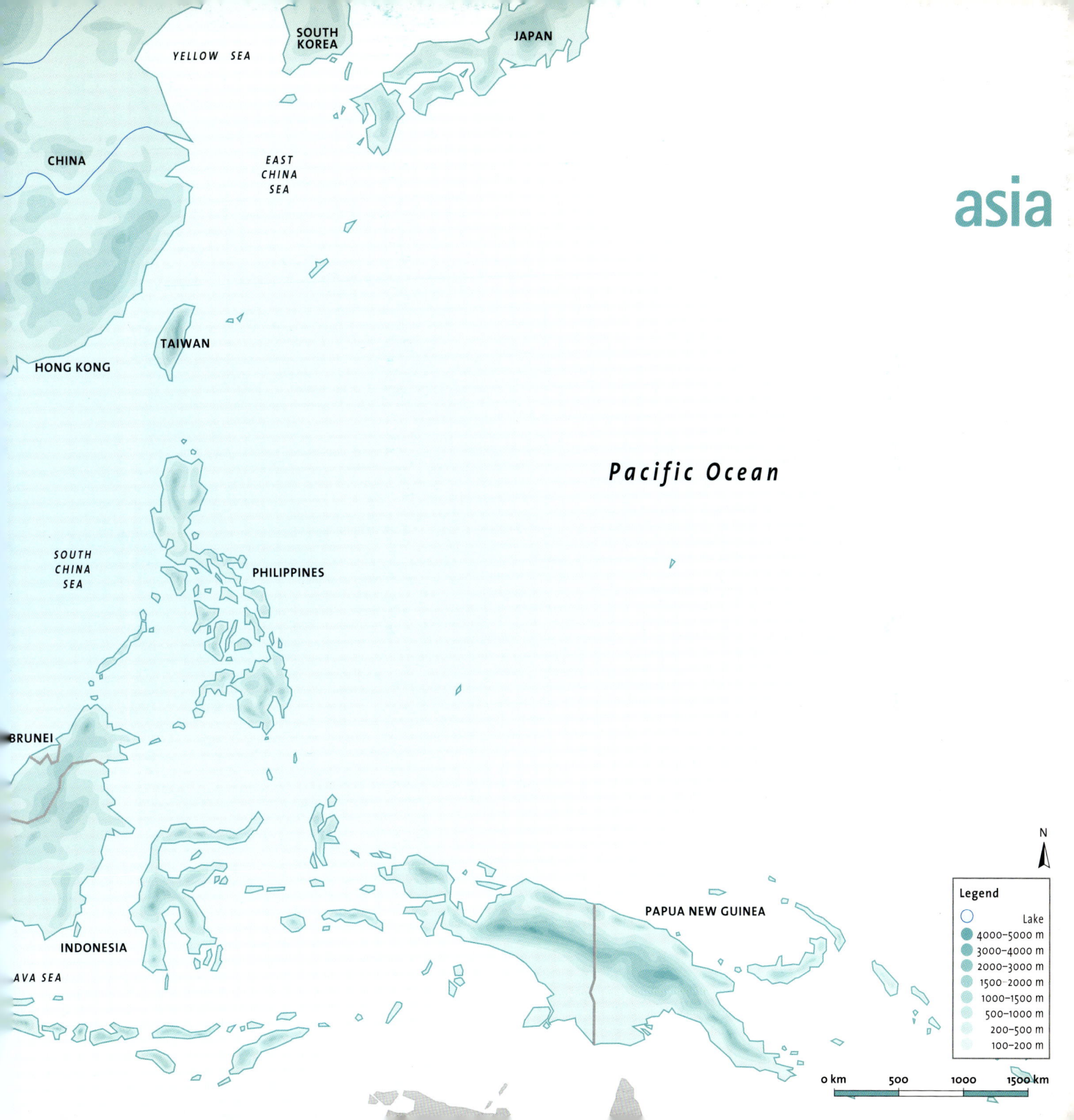

Pacific Ocean

Legend	
○	Lake
	4000–5000 m
	3000–4000 m
	2000–3000 m
	1500–2000 m
	1000–1500 m
	500–1000 m
	200–500 m
	100–200 m

0 km 500 1000 1500 km

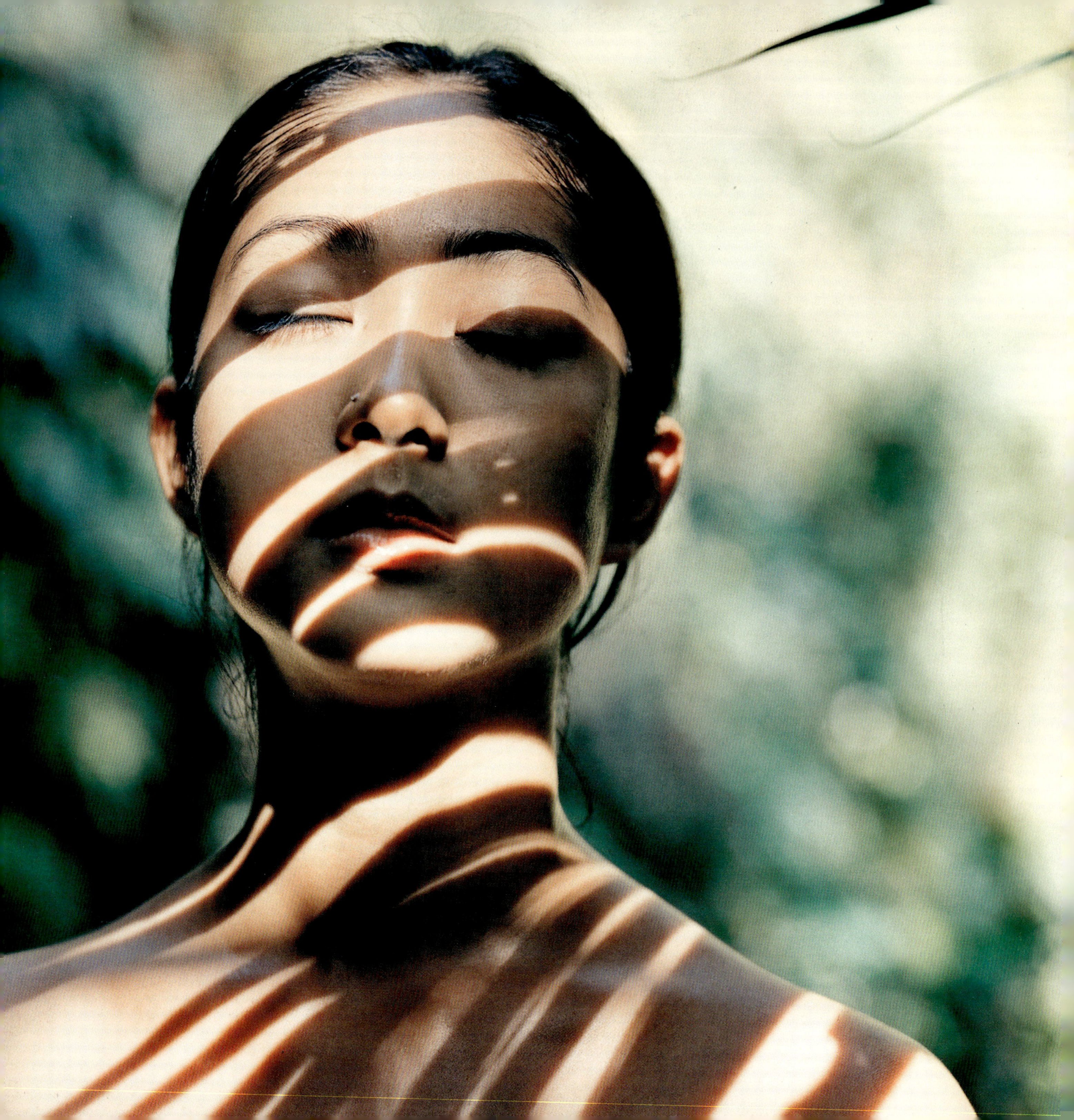

introduction

The word 'spa' is an internationally recognised term whose meaning is similar in almost every language. Derived from the Latin *Salus per aquam* or 'health through water', spa no longer only denotes a link with water. Its meaning has broadened to include a diverse combination of ancient philosophies and modern techniques, but the common thread—water—remains.

Healing through water is at the heart of the European spa experience. The name was adopted by the small spring-fed Belgian town called Spa that was founded in 1326, after a local ironworker was believed to have uncovered a hotspring that cured his rheumatism. From here the spa concept spread throughout Europe, and became a generic name for any place where the healing benefits of mineral springs were tapped to cure the ill, the over-indulgent and, as was referred to then, the mildly dyspeptic.

During this time, in the Far East, the Japanese took their daily plunge in the natural spring-fed communal bathhouse or *sênto*. The Japanese bathing ritual remains as sacred and vital today as it has been for thousands of years. In certain respects, the *onsen* regions in Japan mirror the European spa towns, but while Westerners tend to regard spas as cures for the excesses of daily life, to the Japanese spas are contemplative retreats, taken very seriously, to cleanse the spirit and ward off diseases.

Over the past two centuries, spas have become a global phenomenon that have matured through the years. Spas or health retreats were originally places where people went to rest and bathe in water believed to possess curative properties. Gradually, other treatments were introduced—osteopathy, nutritional guidance and manual physiotherapy techniques, among others—most of them performed within the strictest of medical guidelines and combined with harsh, unappetising dietary routines that were vigorously prescribed along with plenty of fresh air and rest. Regimented spas such as this still exist, especially in central Europe as well as in parts of Germany, France and Italy, but spas today have taken a different turn—more indulgent, cosseting and appetising, but no less therapeutic. The premise is the same—helping people look and feel better—but today's spa perpetrators have captured the time-tested secrets of health and wellness, and combined them with scientifically tested ingredients and techniques. From the opulence and luxury of Roman baths with their marble and mosaics, and the atmospheric

THIS PAGE: *The interior of a hammam dating back to the Ottoman empire.*
OPPOSITE: *A refreshed face after a luxurious spa experience at the COMO Shambhala Estate.*

...time-honoured rituals are usually complemented by lavish surroundings.

hammam of the Ottoman empire, to the traditions of some of the oldest medical philosophies on earth from ancient Persia, China and India, these time-honoured rituals are usually complemented by lavish surroundings. Add to this treatments originating from Indonesia, Malaysia, Thailand and the Philippines among others, combined with contemporary techniques, and the result is spa as we know it today.

Spas have something for everybody—those in need of serious exercise, detox, an energy boost or those searching for pure unadulterated pampering. As we begin to appreciate that listening to the voice within may be the answer to many health crises of the day, more and more spas now offer a spiritual dimension too—with yoga in its many guises, meditation, *tai chi* and a host of other spiritually grounded therapies and activities. This all-inclusive prescription that treats both body and mind is preventive medicine at its best and is at the core of enduring Traditional Chinese Medicine (TCM) and Ayurvedic philosophies.

So grounded in the spa experience is the healing touch of massage that many spas only offer a specialised menu of massages. No mystery surrounds the potential of massage, as the simple power of touch through kneading, stroking, pressing, rubbing and gliding hands has proven to unleash countless benefits—from easing stress and tension, to lowering blood pressure and helping to energise under-stimulated children. Besides this, the pure pleasure associated with the soothing effects of massage is therapy in itself, as touch calms and restores body, mind and spirit.

Spas can be fun too. Some are sexy, chic and a sybarite's paradise of soft lights, scented candles, sarongs and guilt-free cuisine overflowing with nature's vibrant goodness. Spa cuisine is a hot item in the spa scene now, with deliciously nourishing meals ready to be enjoyed in soothing environments. Some destination spas even have schools that provide lessons on how to recreate healthy dishes to guests who would like to continue this lifestyle in the home.

Today's spa-goers are more discerning, and their quest for quality spa products is becoming as important as the actual treatments available. A freshly blended body scrub of lime, pineapple, mango and coconut with a dash of cinnamon oil, hand-prepared in the spa's apothecary kitchen, is not uncommon, especially in many of the exotic spas dotting the Indian Ocean. Heightened knowledge and environmental awareness are influencing operators to create their own products using nature's

THIS PAGE (FROM TOP): *A relaxing and nourishing hand massage is a part of many treatments at the COMO Shambhala Estate; a guest meditating at a tranquil lily pond at Four Seasons Resort Bali at Sayan.*
OPPOSITE: *The Water Villa of the Conrad Rangali Island, Maldives, with the sun setting in the background.*

introduction 13

THIS PAGE (FROM TOP): A guest lounging at the pool villa of the Kayumanis Nusa Dua; a chic wooden 'Do Not Disturb' sign outside a villa of the Maya Ubud Resort & Spa.

OPPOSITE: Enjoy an exquisite bath overlooking the Indian Ocean in the Water Garden of the Soneva Gili by Six Senses.

rich bounty. Organic, bio-friendly, pure, natural, ethical—call them what you will—but it boils down to indisputable product integrity. And this mindset has become a growing trend among luxury hotels and resorts that are creating unique, evocative product blends which resonate with their spa philosophy and incorporate tangible wellness benefits.

Those seeking more medically based prescriptions can choose from the growing number of medispas that are popping up in both busy cities and on untouched islands. This model of 'medical tourism' where people travel to spas expressly for aesthetic or medical procedures is one of the latest trends in the development of the modern spa. From cutting-edge dermatological surgery and wellness diagnostics to dedicated destination dental clinics, the fusion of spa and all its luxurious trimmings with clinical medicine is big business and is destined for further growth.

In addition, the huge spa melting pot comprising the professionals—namely the masseurs, facialists, manicurists, crystal healers, yoga *guru*, naturopaths, doctors, acupuncturists and other specialists—as well as traditions, ingredients and therapies are united in their goal of helping people feel and live better. It is precisely this need for people to improve their lives and to escape the stresses of their everyday lives that accounts for the immense growth in spas.

Spas across the globe offer a panoply of trusted therapies. From tiny atolls in the Maldives to the foothills of the Himalayas, there are stylish chic retreats ready to indulge and pamper you. Savvy spa-goers can enjoy a *lomi lomi* massage in the United States or Australia, thousands of kilometres from its Polynesian origins; Thai poultices are available in London department stores, and traditional Seychellois *raspay* (or remedies using indigenous plants and herbs) can be experienced in Hong Kong.

Asia is the cradle of some of the world's oldest civilisations, a collection of deep and varied cultures with probably the richest spa knowledge on the planet. Deepen your appreciation of spas, learn about its roots in traditional healing systems and discover the rich offerings and truly unmatched therapies from China, the Indian Ocean, Indonesia, Japan, Malaysia, the Philippines, Singapore and Thailand. *Spa Chic* offers an insight into these ancient healing practices and showcases some of the most indulgent spas that can be found in Asia.

Spas... where people went to rest and bathe in water believed to possess curative properties.

recent spa trends

A trend that has recently emerged and is fast gaining popularity is medical tourism, where people travel abroad for medical as well as aesthetic treatments. Large hospitals in India and Thailand, for instance, can perform hip and knee replacements at a fraction of what it costs in the United States, the United Kingdom or in many other Western countries. What's more, many of these hospitals in Asia are fully integrated with spas, and we are witnessing today the advent of a chic new medispa concept where healthcare and hospitality are linked; where patients are now guests, and where patient-centred medicine and people-centred care are priorities. Medispas like these combine the most sophisticated medical diagnostic equipment and techniques with up-to-the-minute cosmetic procedures, luxurious spa facilities and services, all led by multi-disciplinary teams of medically qualified doctors, healthcare professionals, traditional practitioners and other wellness experts such as nutritionists and dieticians.

Destination spas are on the increase too. These well-being retreats are exclusively focused on helping individuals develop and maintain a healthy, balanced lifestyle through a combination of nutritious spa cuisine workshops, comprehensive programmes of fitness and stress reduction classes, therapeutic spa treatments and life-enhancing seminars. Many destination spas also conduct specialised therapy sessions on stress management, smoking cessation, visualisation, hypnosis, writing workshops and other healing and energising modalities. In an environment exclusively geared towards fitness, healthy eating, relaxation and renewal, these destination spas are delivering the results sophisticated clients demand. In fact, research has shown that people who routinely visit destination spas are fitter, happier, healthier, more alert and more agile than regular vacationers.

The rise of a more holistic and life-enhancing spa model is undoubtedly fuelled by the gross inadequacies of traditional Western healthcare systems, and our need to reduce the stress that is induced by the modern world. Instead of treating specific symptoms, this new paradigm embraces a preventive approach to healthcare by treating the body and mind as one. Whether people travel between countries or within their own countries for spa escapes, they are seeking cutting-edge medical and wellness treatments at competitive prices.

Whether the purpose of a visit to a medispa or a stylish destination retreat is for clinical medical procedures, cosmetic dentistry, dermatology or spiritual-oriented therapies, the ultimate goal of achieving a balanced, vibrant mind and body is the same, and this growing phenomenon is set to change the way healthcare is perceived across the world.

THIS PAGE: *The retreat villa sundeck surrounded by lush greenery is most suitable for quiet contemplation and relaxation.*

OPPOSITE: *Guests can enjoy the invigorating water jets of the Vitality Pool at the COMO Shambhala Estate.*

...food as nature intended it—with all the goodness intact... to nourish the body, mind and spirit.

spa cuisine

fresh + organic

The idea of spa cuisine is hardly new. Prior to the advent of spas as we know them today, people in search of rest and rejuvenation visited regimented health farms where daily exercise routines were complemented with bland, lacklustre, institutionalised meals that even the best-intentioned could not possibly want to whip up in the home. But as the spa scene has become more sophisticated, spa cuisine has risen to the challenge. Menus today are packed with fresh, seasonal ingredients, many of which are cultivated at the resorts' own organic gardens. Contemporary spa cuisine is much less about counting calories and fat content, but far more about diets known for helping to maximise brainpower and energy levels. In other words, food as nature intended it—with all the goodness intact, and textures and ingredients perfectly balanced to nourish the body, mind and spirit.

Whilst the basic ingredients of modern spa cuisine have been around for centuries, what is new is the science supporting the benefits of the eclectic mix of fresh, seasonal fruits, vegetables and wholegrains that are the mainstay of the deliciously vibrant menus offered at the world's top spa resorts and destination spas. It has been proven that these plant-derived nutrients offer the best natural protection against today's top killer diseases such as cancer and heart disease, while also protecting us against everyday pollution and toxic chemicals found in treated meats and vegetables. It is now widely accepted that the best supplements for maintaining sleek, shining hair, radiant skin and endless vitality are not pills but nature's 'superfoods' packed with health-promoting nutrients. 'Superfoods' is the term used to describe certain fruits, vegetables, nuts, seeds and wholegrains that are 'enzymatically alive' (ie wholesome foods that contain vitamins, minerals and antioxidants, such as vitamins A, C and E with trace elements of selenium and zinc). They also contain phytonutrients (or plant chemicals) that have favourable effects on our health. Terpenes, carotenoids, phenols, flavonoids and isoflavones are just a few of the scientific names that in essence translate into colourful and energy-giving foods such as blueberries, ginger, peppers, pineapples, pomegranates, grapes, spinach and tomatoes. These 'superfoods' are widely accepted as prerequisites for long, healthy and energetic lives. What research has also found is that the protective and beneficial effects of these foods are maximised when taken together as part of a mixed diet combining fruits, vegetables and wholegrains.

At the increasing number of cookery schools offered in top spas and resorts, guests can learn to combine a variety of beneficial foods to create healthy, vibrant wholesome meals in the home. Classes range from distinctively Asian to fusion-style cooking, combining the best of Asian and Mediterranean cuisine, and are the perfect partners to the fully integrative spa philosophy.

THIS PAGE (FROM TOP): *The chef prepares a deliciously healthy pizza; a trio of colourful desserts.*
OPPOSITE: *Staff picking fresh vegetables and herbs in the Six Senses Destination Spa-Phuket's own garden.*

spa products

THIS PAGE: *Bottles of house brand products at the Six Senses Destination Spa-Phuket.*

OPPOSITE (FROM TOP): *Lavender cultivated by L'Occitane in full bloom across the French countryside; enriching creams and oils for guests' use at the Four Seasons Hotel Hong Kong.*

Although the standards used to judge beauty vary across the world, what has remained consistent through the centuries is our collective pursuit and appreciation of nature in all its colourful diversity. Among today's most discerning spa clients, the authenticity and purity of spa product ingredients are becoming as important as the therapies available. Informed spa operators realise this and are moving towards the use of products made from fresh natural ingredients in their spas. Those who do not manufacture their own products increasingly choose to use natural skincare products, free from harsh and suspect chemicals, that nourish the skin as nature intended it. The market for these products is one of the biggest trends in spas today.

Much of this is possible because many of the most appealing spas are found in some of the world's most sought-after locations, where nature's freshest, purest ingredients coexist in harmony with the unspoilt beauty of the surroundings. In many of these regions, organic farming is the standard process of agriculture, and flowers, seeds and leaves are tenderly nurtured in the most fertile soils before being hand-gathered and concocted into nourishing skincare remedies.

Take the Indian Ocean, for example. Blessed with an abundant array of endemic healing plants and flowers, the Seychelles resembles an oversized apothecary. Many of the recondite Seychellois *raspay* (or traditional remedies) such as *pittosporum*, said to purify the blood, are being incorporated into masks, scrubs and skin tonics. Rose oil from the remote Himalayan region is among the purest and sweetest in the world. Local farmers gather the roses at dawn when they are at their most vibrant and fragrant. In Japan, Camellia oil is a centuries-old secret for radiant skin and hair. It continues to be incorporated into spa menus throughout the country, while virgin coconut oil remains the mainstay in many of the skin-nourishing products and therapies in the Philippines. In these and many other countries' traditions, a number of nature's tried-and-tested ingredients reign among indigenous skincare prescriptions.

Another new trend in the spa industry is found in the male-grooming market; in fact it is one of the primary drivers in global skincare today. Massages, facials, scrubs and wraps incorporating nature's most nourishing ingredients are the highlights of therapies for men.

With environmental issues at the top of the world's agenda and people striving for healthier and less toxic ways of living, it seems these natural products are the best way to beauty. Knowing that animals are not used in the testing and development of these products further enhances their appeal.

natural or organic

When it comes to defining skincare, there are no hard and fast rules. Natural or organic skincare does not necessarily mean chemical-free. Every ingredient is a chemical regardless of its origin. Water, for example, is a chemical component.

Cosmetics made from natural ingredients tend to market themselves as 'natural', containing primarily plant or mineral ingredients. The term 'organic' refers to ingredients that have been grown without artificial or chemical pesticides. By this practice, one creates harmony with nature, and healthy soil, nutritious crops and animal welfare is assured. Devotees attest to the superior feel and effectiveness of organic products in maintaining a radiant, youthful glow.

When purchasing skin and body products, always check the labels. If a product claims to be made from natural ingredients, read what it contains and most importantly what is left out (such as synthetic preservatives, fragrances, petrochemical products and other chemical derivatives). Always look for certification (natural or organic) from a credible certifying body, bearing in mind that while most ethical products bear the seals of authenticity, there are smaller and equally genuine manufacturers sharing this commitment who cannot afford to be certified. It might also help to check where the ingredients are produced and if the packaging is biodegradable or recyclable. In this way you can be assured that you are choosing products that are gentle, yet nourishing on the skin and are also kind to the environment.

destination spas + medispas

thailand: hua hin

For centuries, Hua Hin has been favoured by Thai royalty as the top choice for their royal retreats. This is where the renowned **Chiva-Som** (73/4 Petchkasem Road, Hua Hin, Prachuab Kirikhan 77110) has made its home. Set over 7 acres (2.8 hectares) of lush, tropical forests near the Gulf of Siam, Chiva-Som was Asia's first internationally acclaimed destination spa and remains a pioneer in combining an Eastern sensitivity to balance and wellness with contemporary results-driven Western therapies. A staff of 85 aestheticians, medical doctors, complementary health providers, nutritionists and personal fitness trainers guide the menu of over 150 beauty, medical and wellness therapies.

Through the years, Chiva-Som has kept to the original notion of spa—healing through water—with an impressive array of wet treatment areas including *watsu* pools, a bathing pavilion, exercise pool and plunge pool, a large hydro-jacuzzi, Kneipp therapy footbath, and a multi-level steam room. The spa also has separate male and female wet areas with a sauna, steam room, jacuzzi and relaxation room. The fitness facilities include a gymnasium, a dance studio and a pilates studio. An extensive yoga programme is available with celebrated *guru* offering their expertise in regular yoga retreats.

Guests can choose à la carte services from the holistic, medical or spa menus, or follow prescribed programmes designed by the spa's consultant. Special retreat programmes are available in areas such as fitness, weight management, stress management, detox and holistic health. The warmest Thai hospitality and mouthwatering spa cuisine menus complement the excellent spa menu.

thailand: phuket

The 7th Sense, a journey of rich innovative experiences, is good enough reason to visit the stylish **Six Senses Destination Spa-Phuket** (32 Moo 5, Tambol Paklok, Amphur Thalang, 83110 Phuket). Tucked away on the traditional Thai fishing island of Naka Yai, this destination spa represents a complete immersion into richer, more mindful living, surrounded by white sandy beaches, clear waters, coconut groves and sloping hills with breathtaking views across Phang Nga Bay.

The extensive 7th Sense spa facilities integrate four spa concepts (Indian, Chinese, Thai and Indonesian) with an all-inclusive menu reflecting the best of traditional wisdom from these diverse cultures. The Indian spa features traditional Indian-inspired therapy rooms and outdoor head massage and yoga pavilions; the Chinese spa is set in a bamboo garden with Oriental décor, a traditional tea bar and a comprehensive menu of Chinese therapies; the classic Balinese-style Indonesian spa features one of the world's largest *watsu* pools, sunken treatment rooms and three large caves; and the Thai spa is surrounded by native trees and offers the very best in traditional Thai healing that uses indigenous herbs and spices.

Its transforming Life Passages programme is a perfect reason for a longer stay. These three-day to three-week structured plans are designed to guide guests through life's challenges and transitions. All programmes include the best of Six Senses cuisine, be it the exclusively organic fishetarian menu or organic raw food cuisine, both packed with nutritious fresh seasonal foods.

thailand: koh samui

Kamalaya Koh Samui (102/9 Moo 3, Laem Set Road, Na-Muang, Koh Samui, Suratthani 84140) is a healing sanctuary centred around a cave temple that once served as a place of meditative retreat for Buddhist monks. The resort buildings are nestled amidst ancient granite boulders, gurgling streams and tropical vegetation.

The resort's integrated wellness approach is a synergy of its healing therapies (both East and West), inspired healthy cuisine and holistic fitness practices. Visitors have the option of taking part in group retreats or individual wellness programmes. The extensive menu of treatments features 70 multi-disciplinary mind-body therapies combining the very best in ancient and contemporary healing. It includes everything from massage, acupuncture, facial rejuvenation, cupping and colonic irrigation to naturopathy, yoga, *qi gong* and meditation. The Wellness routines include scientifically researched detox regimes that are matched with delicious and well-prepared detox meals which challenge the myth that getting rid of the body's toxins means depriving one's taste buds. Gifted healers-in-residence share their expertise while personalised life enhancement programmes invite guests on a journey that leads to sustained creativity and spiritual renewal.

Absolute Sanctuary (88 Moo 5, Tambol Bophut, Amphur Koh Samui, Suratthani 84320) is a boutique Moroccan-style destination spa resort specialising in detox programmes and yoga retreats. The sanctuary's Signature Detox Programme combines cutting-edge colon hydrotherapy equipment with customised detox drinks, herbal supplements, nutritious meals (where appropriate), yoga classes and detox massages to cleanse and revitalise from within. Other highlights of the resort's healing menu are medical-style massages specifically tailored to those suffering from chronic aches and the Healing Hands massage that combines *reiki* with sports massage to release pain and tension at both physical and emotional levels. The fully equipped yoga studio draws world-renowned teachers who come to share their various yoga disciplines (hot yoga, hatha, *pranayama* and meditation) in the spacious ambient surroundings.

indonesia: bali

COMO Shambhala Estate (Banjar Begawan, Desa Melinggih Kelod, Payangan, Gianyar, 80571 Bali) represents the pinnacle of the COMO Shambhala philosophy. Supported by specialist multi-disciplinary consultants, the specifically tailored holistic wellness programmes are

THIS PAGE (FROM TOP): Guests at the Six Senses Destination Spa–Phuket may want to tone their muscles at the resort's state-of-the-art gym; the capable hands of the therapist will soothe aching muscles.

OPPOSITE: The marble-adorned steam room at the Kamalaya Koh Samui is infused with cleansing essential oils that also help induce relaxation.

destination spas + medispas

designed to focus on better physical, mental and spiritual health for both the body and mind, all in the most stylish and comfortable environment. The selection of personal programmes covers detoxification, stress management, weight management, therapeutic nutrition and skin revitalisation packages, in addition to yoga and pilates retreats.

The extensive spa facilities feature nine treatment rooms, an outdoor hydrotherapy area, swimming pool, yoga pavilion, pilates studio, separate male and female steam rooms and saunas, a fully-equipped gym and consultation rooms. The Kadena (a water garden whose name translates to 'meadow of water') is set in a secluded area overlooking the river and is a peaceful place to enjoy the steam room, hot tub and outdoor baths and showers. Like the entire resort, the spa is supplied with water from The Source, a natural spring revered by locals for its spiritually healing properties.

china: macau

The **MALO CLINIC Spa Macau** at **The Venetian® Macao-Resort-Hotel** (Level 5, The Grand Canal Shoppes, Estrada da Baia de N Senhora da Esperança, s/n, Taipa, Macao SAR) is the world's largest integrative wellness centre of its kind and a good example of a medispa of the future.

Guided by a multi-disciplinary team comprising 50 medical doctors and licensed healthcare professionals as well as 100 wellness therapists, the clinic combines both cutting-edge medicine and spa therapy. The facilities boast the most sophisticated diagnostic technologies, six operating theatres, 58 spa treatment suites, hydro suites (with Vichy showers, dry floatation, hydro tubs and salt floatation), heat and wet installations (featuring steam showers, saunas, *hammam*, and vitality pools of different temperatures), a beauty salon, and complete leisure and fitness facilities.

On the medical front, the MALO CLINIC Spa Macau offers revolutionary dental medicine and cosmetic procedures, such as oral surgery and rehabilitation, dental implantology, periodontology, prosthodontics and orthodontics. It also offers routine internal medicine examinations and a complete surgical menu that includes general, digestive, cosmetic, plastic, reconstructive, urological, gynaecological, neurosurgical, paediatric and radiology procedures, among other services.

For the spa, its signature health and wellness packages include complete health screening, total body programmes combining clinical, traditional and healing therapies in one experience, and Life Long Wellness Programmes designed to address lifestyle diseases, common health concerns, and chronic illnesses through information, education and customised therapies. A line-up of hair loss, hair-strengthening and laser treatments are available too.

Complementing these medically precise procedures is a menu of traditional Chinese therapies to rebalance and reharmonise the body. In addition, a menu of massages, facials, scrubs, wraps and decadent beauty rituals awaits.

THIS PAGE (CLOCKWISE FROM TOP LEFT): Only at Chiva-Som resort may one experience the unique procedure known as Titan, which will tighten the skin and reduce facial wrinkles; the healing benefits of a traditional Indian head massage, available at Kamalaya Koh Samui, are many; the Chinese Spa Tea Room at the Six Senses Destination Spa-Phuket offers a variety of authentic teas.
OPPOSITE: Guests may wish to practise yoga in the cool early mornings at the COMO Shambhala Estate.

healthy cuisine

thailand: phuket
Clean, fresh, natural and raw is the mission in the kitchens of the **Six Senses Destination Spa-Phuket** (32 Moo 5, Tambol Paklok, Amphur Thalang, 83110 Phuket). The cuisine has a distinctively Asian orientation, reflecting the cultures from which the resort draws its healing inspiration—Thai, Indian, Chinese and Indonesian. The resort grows ingredients such as fruits and vegetables in its organic vegetable gardens, and lemongrass and basil in the private guest villa gardens.

An exclusive menu consisting of raw ingredients is also available to guests who prefer that no ingredient is subjected to heat over 42°C (107.6°F). Key ingredients include nut milks, soy, almonds, pulses and sauces based on *miso*, yoghurt, olive oil, vegetable purées and *tahini*. Only raw oils such as flaxseed, olive, grape and cold-pressed local oils are used.

thailand: hua hin
At Thailand's classy destination spa **Chiva-Som** (73/4 Petchkasem Road, Hua Hin, Prachuab Kirikhan 77110), spa cuisine is not just a highlight of your stay, it is an integral element of the Chiva-Som philosophy. Spa programmes emphasise the importance of balance in mind, body and spirit, a belief that carries through to the cuisine, which represents the very best of indigenous Thai, with light, tasty and immaculately presented meals. Regular cooking classes (for both groups and individuals) inspire guests to maintain this creative harmony in the home with easy-to-follow recipes, healthy cooking techniques and visits to the resort's organic garden.

thailand: sikao
A key feature of the **Anantara Spa Si Kao** at **Anantara Si Kao Resort & Spa** (198–199 Moo 5, Had Pak Meng, Changlang Road, Maifad, Sikao, 92150 Trang) is Wellness 360, a comprehensive programme designed to enhance health, beauty and overall wellbeing. Visitors may be interested to know that the resort's restaurants all offer deliciously healthy Wellness 360 menu choices.

While guests may opt for the weight-loss programme, food will not be restricted and healthy meals will be served regularly to optimise energy levels. Raw cuisine options are also available in all outlets, and most of the food is organic and free from monosodium glutamate (MSG), unnecessary colourings and additives. Cookery classes led by the resort's resident chef will guide guests through the principles of preparing low-fat, healthy dishes at home.

indonesia: bali
At the **COMO Shambhala Estate** at Begawan Giri (Banjar Begawan, Desa Melinggih Kelod, Payangan, Gianyar, 80571 Bali), guests can enjoy vibrantly nourishing meals packed with the best of nature's essentials. A daily menu featuring 20 targeted juices—created by the Estate's resident nutritionist and blended from local fresh fruits, vegetables and herbs—complement the spa programmes by boosting energy and radiance in the most natural way possible.

china: hong kong

Eating healthy doesn't come easier than at the **Plateau Residential Spa** at **Grand Hyatt Hong Kong** (1 Harbour Road, Wan Chai, Hong Kong). Following a night in the comfort of the Plateau's rooms, breakfast is an energising kick-start to the day, packed with juices and smoothies, wholegrain cereals, nuts and fruit platters to ensure guests can maximise their spa experience.

The emphasis at Plateau is light, healthy dishes that offer well-balanced portions of protein, wholegrains, fruits, vegetables and herbs. Food is served raw, steamed, poached or simmered without the addition of any saturated fats.

malaysia: langkawi

Four Seasons Resort Langkawi (Jalan Tanjung Rhu, 07000 Langkawi, Kedah Darul Aman) offers hands-on cookery experiences celebrating the rich history and fascinating traditions of eclectic Asian cuisine. With an emphasis on freshness, lightness and balance, the cookery classes feature locally grown produce. From the Sunday morning Chinese *yum-cha* tradition and the aroma of exotic Malay spices, to cross-cultural Nyonya food and fiery southern Thai delights, the cooking classes encourage guests to become more creative in the home. Guided by experienced Malaysian chefs, the essence of Asia is fully captured.

The other Four Seasons resorts including the **Four Seasons Resort at Jimbaran Bay**, the **Four Seasons Resort Bali at Sayan** and the **Four Seasons Resort Chiang Mai** also offer cookery school curricula.

THIS PAGE (CLOCKWISE FROM TOP): Only the freshest materials available are utilised in the cookery classes held at the Four Seasons Resort at Jimbaran Bay in Bali; a colourful array of body soaps made from natural ingredients by the famed l'Occitane, France; Malaysian fruit salad is one of the broad diversity of Asian specialities on offer at the Four Seasons Resort Langkawi's cookery school.

OPPOSITE: Freshly gathered herbs and fruits are used in many of the tasty dishes listed on the spa cuisine menus at the Four Seasons Resort Maldives at Landaa Giraavaru.

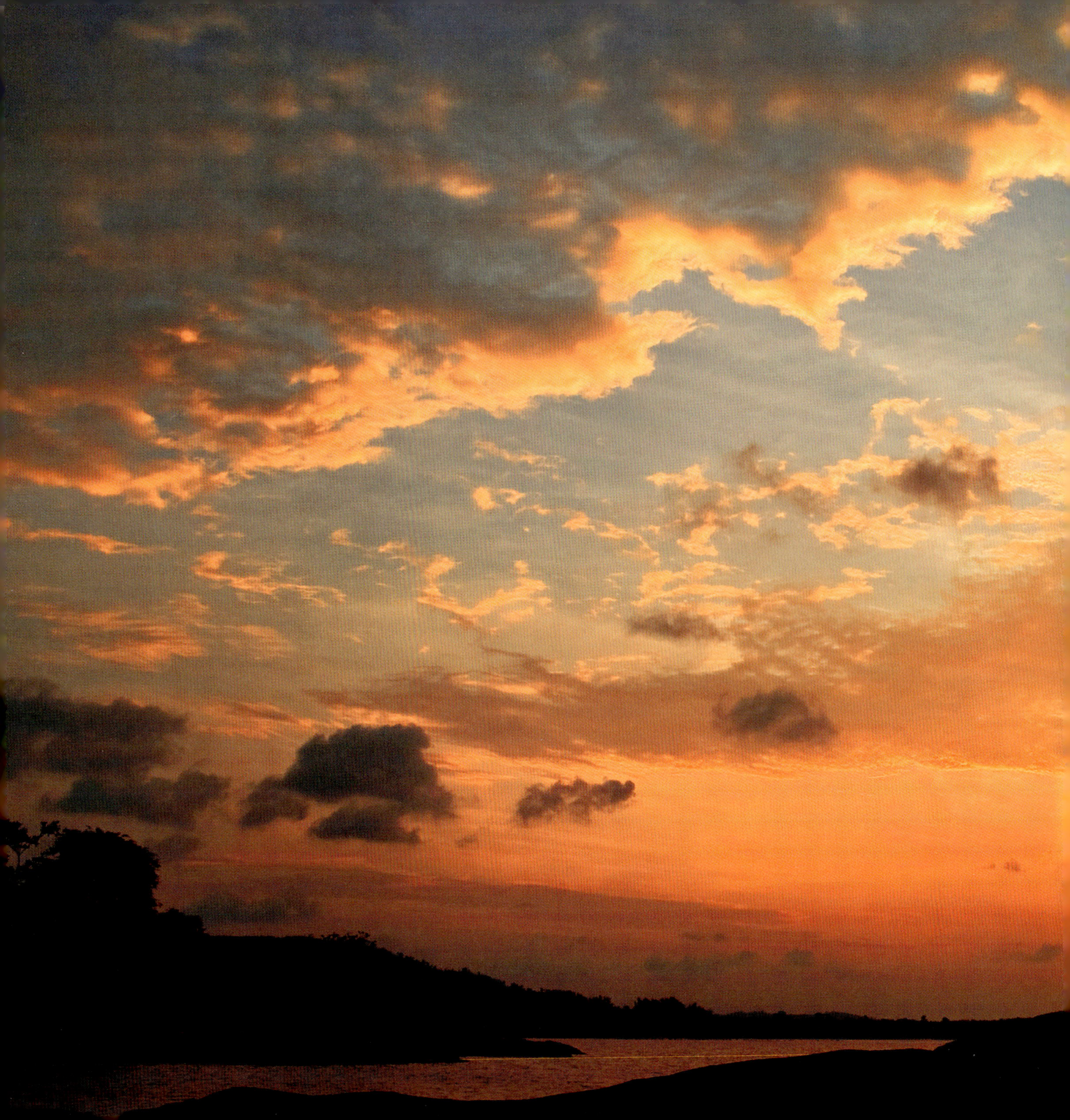

therapies+treatments

Asia's rich and time-honoured culture has been the perfect incubator for the birth of healing therapies and restorative treatments steeped in tradition and ritual. This section covers chapters on the ancient spa traditions of China, India, Indonesia, Malaysia, Japan, the Philippines and Thailand, along with features on contemporary spa trends, cuisine and products, all of which are re-defining the concept of the modern spa.

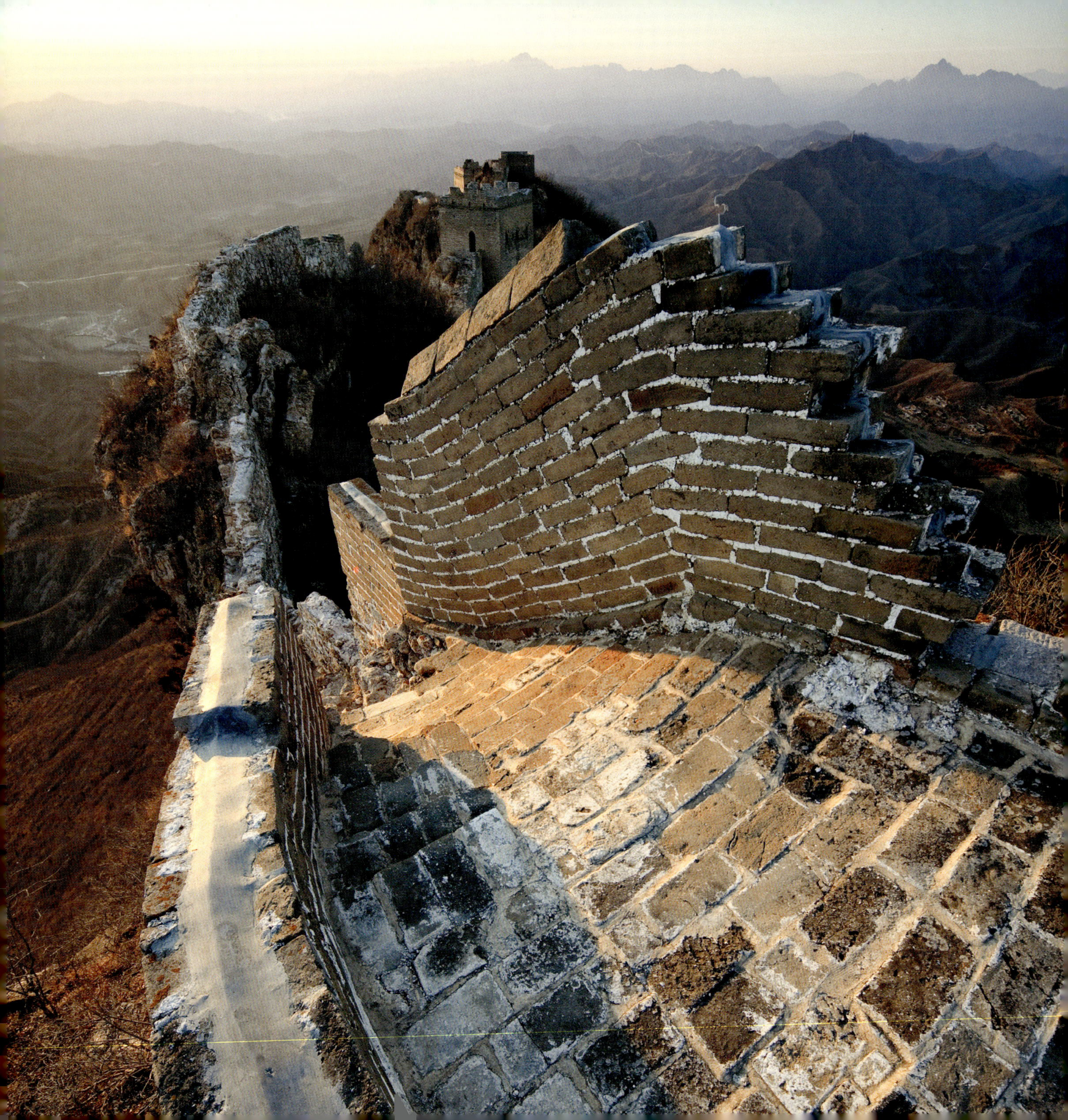

traditionalchinesemedicine

china

RUSSIA

MONGOLIA

HEILONGJIANG

JILIN

LIAONING

NEI MONGOL ZIZHIQU

Beijing › Shangri-La Hotel, Beijing
› Zenspa

HEBEI

NORTH KOREA

Japan Sea

SOUTH KOREA

NINGXIA

SHANXI

SHANDONG

Yellow Sea

GANSU

SHAANXI

HENAN

JIANGSU

Nanjing
Suzhou Shanghai

› Pudong Shangri-La, Shanghai
› SHUI Urban Spa

JAPAN

HUBEI

ANHUI

East China Ocean

Chengdu
SICHUAN

› Shangri-La Hotel, Chengdu

CHONGQING

ZHEJIANG

HUNAN

JIANGXI

FUJIAN

GUIZHOU

TAIWAN

YUNNAN

GUANGXI

GUANGDONG
Guangzhou

› Shangri-La Hotel, Guangzhou

MACAU   HONG KONG

› Four Seasons Hotel Hong Kong
› Plateau Residential Spa
› SPA by MTM

VIETNAM

LAOS

THAILAND

HAINAN

South China Ocean

Legend
- International Airport
- 6000–8848 m
- 5000–6000 m
- 3000–4000 m
- 2000–3000 m
- 1000–2000 m
- 500–1000 m
- 200–500 m
- 0–200 m

0 km   240   480   720 km

traditional chinese medicine

a holistic approach to health

When the World Health Organisation (WHO) first began to endorse indigenous healing systems, Traditional Chinese Medicine (TCM) was on the top of the list. This is hardly surprising as its influence has spread further and wider than any other form of alternative therapy. Many spa treatments around the world have their roots in the ancient Chinese healing traditions. While practices vary due to the availability of ingredients and the skills of individual therapists, the fundamental concepts are very much the same.

TCM embraces the classic Taoist belief of a holistic and preventive approach to health by focusing on diet, exercise, and spiritual and emotional wellbeing. Taoism is the fundamental healthcare philosophy that has been used by Chinese physicians, monks and meditators for more than 5,000 years, and with the present shift from Western thinking to a more integrative mind and body approach, it remains as relevant today as it was in classical China.

According to Taoism, the universe exists as a unified whole, comprising two opposing yet complementary forces known as *yin* and *yang*. It is the interplay between these forces that governs *qi*, the vital energy that flows along a network of channels or meridians to empower each and every organ in the body. Together with *jing* (essence) and *shen* (mind or spirit), they comprise the 'Three Treasures' that work in unison to maintain a person's physical, spiritual and emotional health. The real beauty and benefit of TCM is that it treats the body as a whole, and aims to prevent illness by maintaining overall health and balance.

From massage therapy to acupuncture, moxibustion, herbal remedies and *qigong*, the practice of these ancient traditions continues to be encouraged, not only as healing procedures, but as an essential component to preserve vitality, longevity and good health.

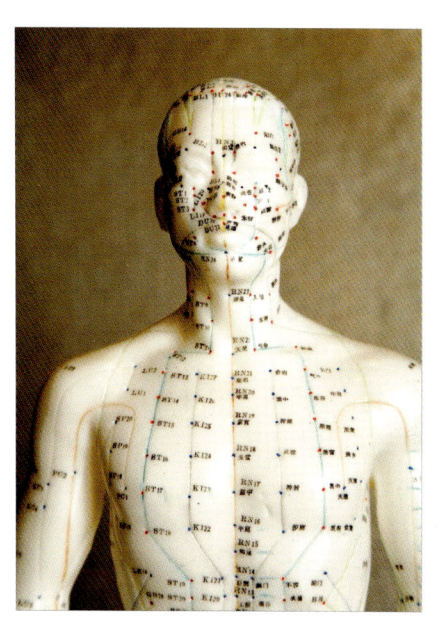

acupuncture

Acupuncture enjoys immense popularity all over the world. It is based on the premise of balancing the flow of *qi* by inserting needles at specific acupoints along the body's energy channels and meridians. To ensure that the skilled acupuncturist finds the exact position for the needle, he must first capture the *qi*, using a technique called *deqi*. This is done by twirling the needle a few times once in the skin, until the patient feels numbness, tightness and a dull pain as a gentle electric current is applied to the body to stimulate the *qi*. Needles are normally kept in place for up to 30 minutes, during which time various techniques can be used to either sedate, disperse or tone the *qi* for maximum effects.

Many diseases can be treated by acupuncture. Acupuncture is most suited to relieve the pain of specific conditions including digestive complaints, gynaecological and respiratory ailments,

THIS PAGE (FROM TOP): *The acupoints and meridian lines of a human body are clearly marked on this dummy, used by TCM practitioners; a woman undergoing an accupuncture treatment.*

PAGE 30: *The Great Wall is a reminder of China's rich, long history which influences many spa treatments today.*

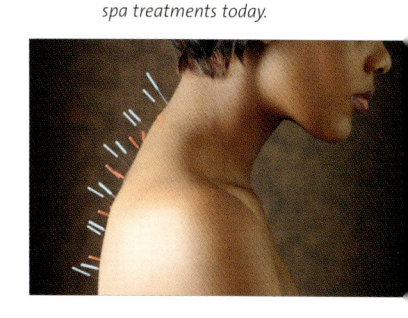

THIS PAGE: *Burning moxa on acupuncture needles are used to remove blockages and rebalance a woman's body.*

OPPOSITE (FROM TOP): *A Chinese physician places heated cups over acupressure points along the back to invigorate the body's qi; a reflexologist massaging the reflex zones in the feet during a treatment.*

headaches and migraines, tennis elbow, insomnia and muscular pain. Although Western medicine cannot explain in scientific terms exactly how acupuncture works, scientists know it does as its effects have been scientifically measured by monitoring changes in brain activity.

moxibustion

Moxa is the dried form of a herb commonly known as mugwort (*Artemisia vulgaris*). By applying it to specific acupoints, its warming and invigorating properties penetrate the skin and activate the body's internal energy. Moxibustion can be traced back to Chinese peasants who burnt herbs and placed them around specific parts of the body to relieve pain. The most common form of moxa used today is the moxa stick, a compressed moxa leaf resembling a mini cigar, which when lit is held or rotated above the skin of the affected area, causing heat to enter the body. This stimulates the circulation of blood and *qi*.

As both acupuncture and moxibustion help remove blockages along the meridian pathways, they can be combined for maximum effect. The end of the moxa stick can either be lit and held above the skin to warm the acupoint, or an acupuncture needle can be stuck directly into a moxa stick, which is then lit. When lit, the herb releases a curative effect that is released into the body.

chinese acupressure massage

Acupressure is a term encompassing any number of massage techniques that use manual pressure to stimulate energy points in the face and body. Targeting specific acupoints, firm hand and finger pressure is artfully applied to release energy obstructions and stimulate *qi*. The acupressure technique can be used in conjunction with other massage styles and is especially beneficial for relieving constipation, diarrhoea, insomnia, back pain and poor digestion.

reflexology

In TCM, the foot constitutes a full representation of the entire body with reflex points corresponding to every organ and gland. For example, the big toe is connected to the head, and manually stimulating it eases headaches and tension. A skilled reflexologist uses thumb pressure to press and deeply massage each of the tiny reflex zones in the feet to stimulate and activate the body's natural healing mechanisms and rebalance the *qi*. Reflexology is suitable for all ages and has been shown to help relax the body and treat a wide range of acute and chronic conditions from postnatal depression to constipation, diarrhoea, insomnia, back pain and muscle pain, as well as skin problems.

cupping

Cupping is an effective way of removing stagnant *qi* and realigning the body's internal energy balance naturally. Heated cups are strategically placed at various acupressure points on the skin. Using a pump to remove the air inside the cups, the vacuum cups help to increase the local circulation of *qi* and invigorate the body thoroughly.

gua sha

Loosely translated as 'to scrape for cholera' or 'scrape for fever', this ancient technique is still widely practised throughout China to reduce fever, headaches, muscular injuries and improve circulation, amongst other functions. The term '*gua*' means, 'to scrape' and '*sha*' refers to the

traditionalchinesemedicine 35

36 spachicasia

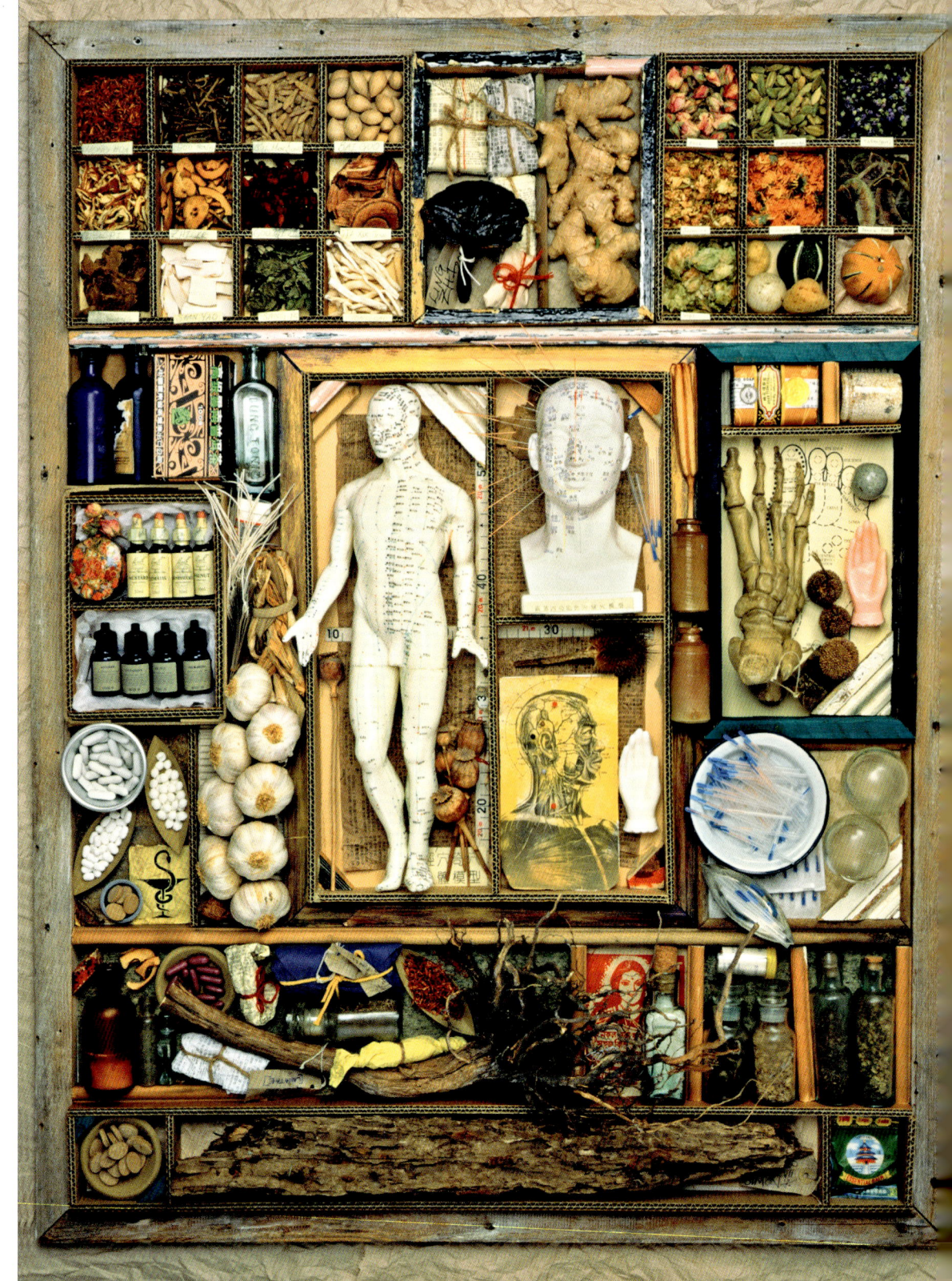

sudden attack of illness such as cholera or sunstroke during the summer and autumn seasons. 'Sha' also refers to rashes. Before the actual *gua sha* treatment begins, liquid medicine is rubbed on the painful area or acupoints to stimulate blood circulation in the body. The therapist then scrapes the skin using either a ceramic Chinese soup spoon, a simple metal cap or a jade or horn blade, with repeated strokes from top to bottom according to the direction of blood flow. Some blood capillaries will break, releasing blood which leads to the visible purple and black bruises that remain after treatment. Such stimulation can promote blood circulation and remove obstruction and toxins from the body, thereby relieving pain.

tui na

Literally translated as 'press and rub', *tui na* is the oldest form of Chinese acupressure massage that uses deep digital stimulation on vital points along the meridians to stimulate *qi* and relieve pain and fatigue. This rejuvenating therapy is especially beneficial for treating colds and headaches, insomnia, intestinal upsets, lower back pain, stiff neck and hormonal imbalances, although sensitive areas such as the face and neck may require gentler movements.

chi nei tsang

Chi nei tsang is a term loosely used to describe an internal organ massage of the abdominal area, believed to have been developed by Chinese Taoist monks as a method of detoxifying and strengthening the body. *Chi nei tsang* is based on the belief that the abdominal area (specifically the lower abdomen around the navel) is the centre of energy in the body. It is also the key location where metabolic processes such as digestion, detoxification and energy processing take place and the area where stress, tension and negative emotions can accumulate and congest. While other massage techniques work from the periphery inwards, *chi nei tsang* massage techniques target the internal organs, and work from the centre of the body outwards, cleansing and nourishing the organs. The procedure helps to improve circulation, stimulates the lymphatic system and eliminate toxins. This form of massage is also

THIS PAGE: *Drawers packed with traditional Chinese herbal ingredients at a Traditional Medicine Hospital in Beijing.*
OPPOSITE (FROM LEFT): *Ginseng is a herb that is believed to have many benefits, including revitalising the qi; an assemblage of traditional Chinese herbal ingredients and components in a wooden frame.*

THIS PAGE: *A combination of Chinese herbs prescribed to prepare a tonic soup.*
OPPOSITE: *People practising tai chi with red fans is a common sight in the mornings in Shanghai.*

thought to help correct misalignment of the feet, legs and pelvis and to relieve chronic pain in the back, neck and shoulders. One's emotional wellbeing becomes balanced too as negative emotion, stored in the digestive system, is cleared from the body.

herbal medicine

For thousands of years, Chinese medicinal plants have played an integral role in helping to prevent illness and promote health and longevity. Thus, herbalists in ancient China were paid to maintain their patients' health.

Through the centuries, the definition of 'Chinese herb' has expanded to include mineral elements as well as animal and animal parts—bones of tigers, deer antlers, dried gecko, seahorses, pig's bile, oyster shell, pearls and kaolin are some examples. Chinese dispensaries stock herbs in their raw form or as processed medicines in the form of extracts and tinctures, oils and potions, as well as preparations ground to create ointments or poultices.

Herbs are classified according to their nature (hot, warm, cool or cold), taste (sour, bitter, sweet, pungent, salty and bland), effectiveness and methods of preparation. Additionally, their basic biochemical composition and medicinal effects are considered, which together determine what herbalists call the 'natural affinities'. For instance, herbs used for liver ailments share an affinity with the liver meridian. When the herb is broken down in the body, its energy enters the liver meridian, and its therapeutic action directly targets the liver. Some spas may include herbal teas and tonics in their menus to complement physical treatments and re-establish the body's natural equilibrium. Some of the commonly used Chinese herbs today consist of ginseng (*Radix panax ginseng*), a powerful tonic that stimulates the nervous and endocrine systems and increases the body's vital energy; chamomile (*Matricaria chamomilla*), drunk as a 'tea' which soothes and calms the stomach and is especially beneficial for treating menstrual problems; and *dang gui* (*Radix angelica sinensis* or Chinese angelica), considered the queen of women's herbs. *Dang gui* is a tonic for the blood, helping to regulate the menstrual cycle and invigorate the entire system. It can be eaten raw or cooked, alone or combined with other herbs, in capsules or in liquid form.

TCM embraces the classic Taoist belief of a holistic and preventive approach to health...

traditionalchinesemedicine

spas in china

beijing

In **CHI, The Spa** at **Shangri-La Hotel, Beijing** (29 Zizhuyuan Road, Haidan District, 100089 Beijing), the double knot signifying eternity resonates throughout the premises: in the mahogany lattice-work, carpets, water features and lampshades. The effect creates an ambience of genuine time-honoured China that carries through to the spa treatments offered. The signature Empress Jade Journey is steeped in history, as this treatment was once reserved only for the Empress. Crafted jade is used to massage the meridian points on the face and body to revitalise stagnant *qi*. This is complemented by a lavish Imperial Jade Facial to cleanse and nourish the skin for an all-over radiant glow.

The **Aman at Summer Palace, Beijing** (1 Gongmenqian Street, Summer Palace, Beijing 100091) is housed in a series of palace dwellings once used by guests awaiting an audience with the Empress Dowager Cixi. Adjacent to the resort is the UNESCO-listed Summer Palace gardens, the archetypal Chinese garden ranked as one of the most beautiful in the world. Other breathtaking landmarks close by include the Forbidden City, Tiananmen Square and The Great Wall of China. With such a commanding setting, it is only fitting that the Aman spa subtly combines imperial Chinese medical ingredients with luxurious contemporary spa techniques to ensure a complete multi-sensory experience. For instance, the Black and White Sesame Scrub with Gold Leaf and

Honey or the Green Tea and Ginger Scrub are perfect for cleansing and nourishing the skin, while customised wraps such as the Lotus, Aloe Vera and Pearl Powder Wrap soothe and uplift the skin.

Raucous Beijing disappears as one enters **Zenspa** (House 1, 8A Xiaowuji Road, Chaoyang District, Beijing 100023), a restored Chinese courtyard filled with thought-provoking sculptures and splashed with vibrant colours commonly used by the Chinese. With a history dating back to the Han dynasty, the spa retains much of this rich past in its classic Chinese architecture, complemented by contemporary design features. The eclectic menu offers a range of multicultural treatments, but the pampering baths and unique form of acupressure that uses heat to stimulate the pressure points of the body are a must. As the spa is open till late in the evening, the silence and mellow lighting in the courtyard is a form of therapy in itself.

chengdu

One of the unifying design concepts of CHI spas is based on the traditional lattice design of the Himalayas, used on the teak sliding screens. This décor sets the mood and ambience of **CHI, The Spa** at **Shangri-La Hotel, Chengdu** (9 Binjiang Dong Road, 610021 Chengdu, Sichuan).

The comprehensive spa menu features a number of indigenous therapies, with the most popular being the Yin Yang Harmonising Massage. Using deep, rhythmical strokes along the back, the skilled therapist helps release the body's tension and rebalances the energy, thus instilling a deep sense of peace.

guangzhou

CHI, The Spa at **Shangri-La Hotel, Guangzhou** (1 Hui Zhan Dong Road, Hai Zhu District, Guangzhou 510308) draws its inspiration from the legend of Shangri-La, a place in the mystical mountains of the Himalayas.

Using many of the architectural principles of a Tibetan temple, the spa features Himalayan artefacts and design elements, whilst applying the Chinese principles of harmony and balance through its menu of authentic Chinese and Himalayan treatments and rituals. For instance, the Oriental Pearl Radiance Facial treatment capitalises on the renowned benefits of pearls, believed to be associated with clear, smooth skin. Using extremely fine-grained Nano Pearl Powder, the facial works from deep within to nourish and refine the skin for a radiant youthful glow. The ritual also includes a tension-relieving back massage and an antioxidant green tea face compress for maximum benefits.

shanghai

Envisioned as a sanctuary of tranquillity, the design concept of **CHI, The Spa** at **Pudong Shangri-La, Shanghai** (33 Fu Cheng Road, Pudong, Shanghai 200120) combines authentic Tibetan architectural principles and Himalayan design elements with time-honoured Chinese principles of harmony and balance. One of the most distinctive

THIS PAGE (FROM TOP): Traditional Chinese architecture dominates the restored courtyard of Zenspa in Beijing; the soothing ambience of a therapy room at CHI, The Spa at the Shangri-La Hotel, Guangzhou; the signature Empress Jade Journey uses customised jade to deeply massage meridian points on the face at CHI, The Spa at the Shangri-La Hotel, Beijing.
OPPOSITE: The lotus leaf decoration in the reception area of CHI, The Spa at the Shangri-La Hotel, Beijing.

spas in china

characteristics of the treatments at CHI is the use of exclusive blended oils, which evoke the mystical aspects of the Himalayas and complement the essence of CHI. These products are also designed to work on both the physical and emotional levels to reharmonise the body in accordance with Chinese philosophy. The oils are used on the body, and are incorporated in the incense and bath oils, as well as in oil burners.

The **SHUI Urban Spa** (5th floor, Ferguson Lane, 376 Wukang Road, Shanghai 200031) in Shanghai is a real respite for visitors and locals alike. Its clean contemporary design revolves around the interplay between white, shadows, cool textures and subtle mood lighting that, when combined, instantly induces a calm and peaceful mind. Plush amenities such as natural cotton robes and slippers, cosy blankets and personal DVD players are on hand to gently ease guests into the comfortable facilities.

The menu, consisting of competitively priced treatments, includes massages, body treatments, manicures, pedicures and facials based on the exclusive Dermalogica facial-mapping technique. High-performance facials and massages specifically designed for men are also available here.

hong kong

Immense windows that afford breathtaking harbour views and possibly one of the best spas in Hong Kong are just two of the reasons to visit **The Spa** at the **Four Seasons Hotel Hong Kong** (8 Finance Street, Central, Hong Kong). The spa remains a local favourite and a preferred destination for visitors to the island.

The emphasis of the treatments is on Chinese-inspired therapies using jade, as the Chinese believe this semi-precious stone increases the energy and prosperity of those who wear it. The indulgent Oriental Jade Ritual begins with a detoxifying bath, enjoyed while sipping a herbal elixir. An Oriental-style foot massage will then restore a balanced flow of energy. This is followed by a jade stone full-body massage—the cool stones elevate and purify thoughts while the warm stones boost the immune system. The ritual concludes with an Oriental-style head massage to stimulate the crown *chakra* and awaken both the body and mind.

An unforgettable experience awaits guests at the **Bliss Spa** at **W Hong Kong** (1 Austin Road West, Kowloon Station, Hong Kong). A varied menu of facials, massages, scrubs, manicures, pedicures and waxing is available to complement the trademark Bliss signature treatment—the Triple Oxygen Facial and Ginger Rub—and the legendary brownie buffet. At the nail bar, guests may also want to indulge in the Double Choc Pedicure treatment comprising a hot chocolate milk skin-smoothing soak and a shin-sloughing sugar scrub, accompanied by a cup of supremely creamy W Hong Kong cocoa served on the side.

SPA by MTM (Shop A, ground floor, 3 Yun Ping Road, Causeway Bay, Hong Kong) is a welcome escape from the city's frantic pace of life. Combining Oriental, Japanese and

Western techniques with MTM's customised skincare philosophy, all ingredients are specifically blended to meet individual guests' requirements. The spa's signature Sakura Revival Therapy, performed in the distinctively Japanese Wisdom Room, comprises a calming Sake Foot Soak, a revitalising Herbal Green Tea Body Wrap, Energizing Shiatsu Massage and nourishing Soy Bean Hot Spring.

Plateau Residential Spa at the **Grand Hyatt Hong Kong** (1 Harbour Road, Wan Chai, Hong Kong) is the only residential spa on the island. The luxurious overnight rooms offer the ultimate in privacy and comfort. With huge infinity bathtubs, terraces overlooking Victoria Harbour and *futon* beds topped with duck down mattresses, these are the perfect finale to an exemplary pampering experience. The menu focuses on skin-nourishing and wrinkle-defying facials, stress-relieving massages, scrubs and wraps, all performed by highly skilled therapists.

macau

With a mission to balance the senses, the **Six Senses Spa** at **MGM Grand Macau** (3rd floor, Avenida Dr Sun Yat Sen NAPE) is the perfect antidote to Macau's dazzling world of gaming and commerce. The spa offers an extensive spa menu combining Chinese-inspired rituals, Asian techniques and Six Senses' signature therapy. Complemented by amenities including *hammam*, saunas, herbal steam rooms, floatation and vitality pools, it is easy to quell excess heat and rebalance the body's energy in the utmost peace and comfort.

THIS PAGE (CLOCKWISE FROM TOP LEFT): The Plateau spa at the Grand Hyatt Hong Kong boast the magnificent view of Victoria Harbour; fragrance from oil burners fill the air in SPA by MTM with sweet scent; one of the lavish spa treatment rooms with complete amenities at Four Seasons Hotel Hong Kong; the therapists at the Four Seasons Hotel Hong Kong pay the finest attention to detail.
OPPOSITE: The contemporary décor of the SHUI Urban Spa in Shanghai is designed to put visitors at ease.

spasinchina 43

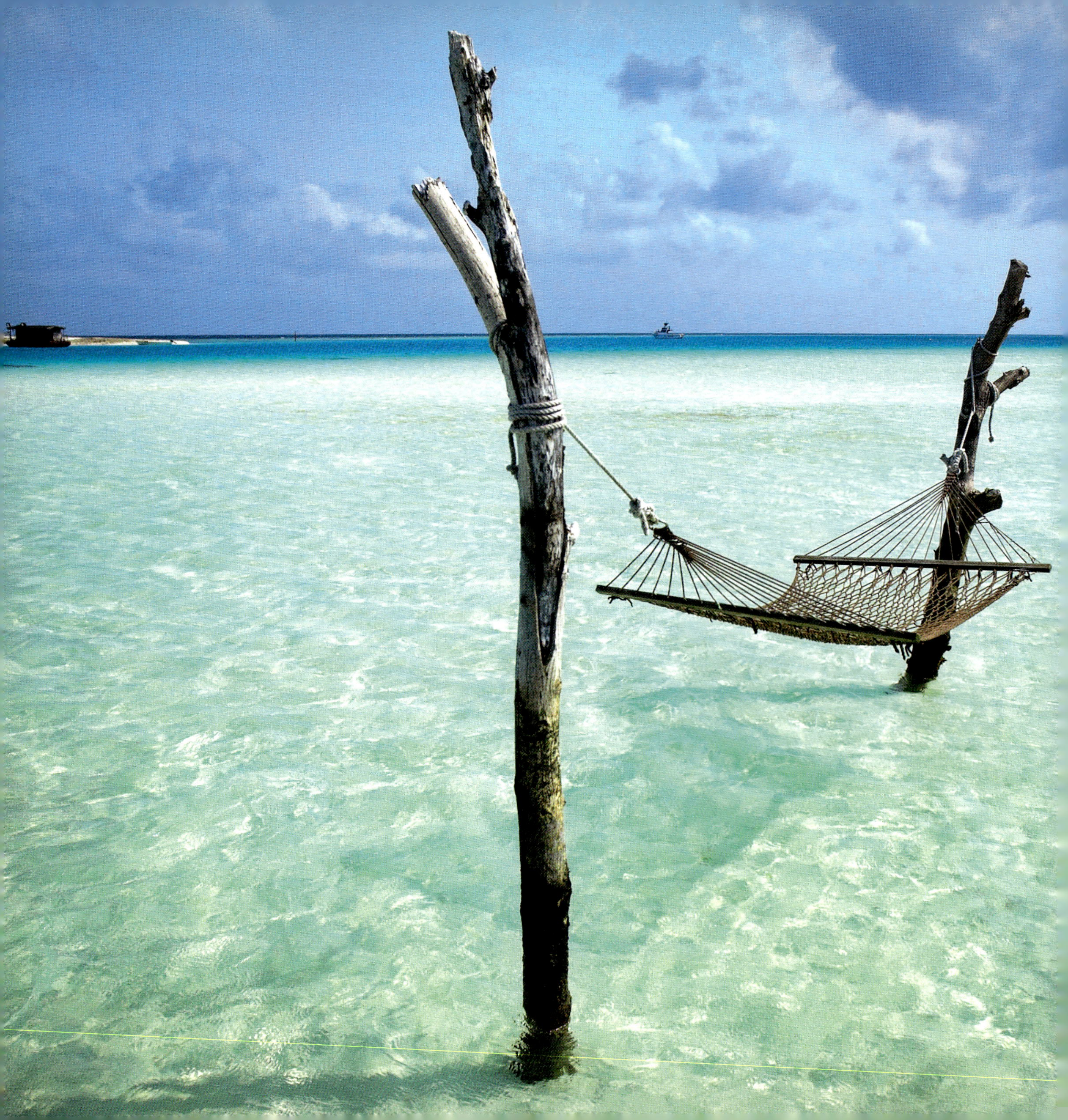

ayurveda

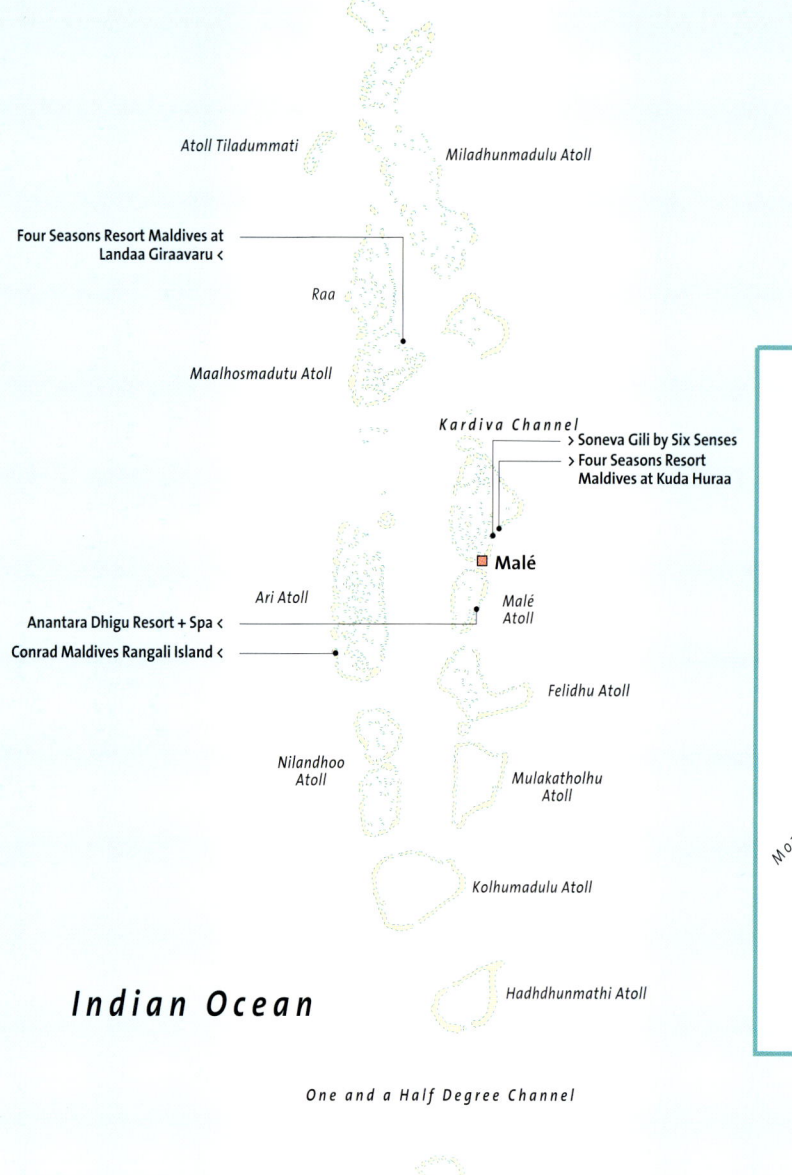

maldives

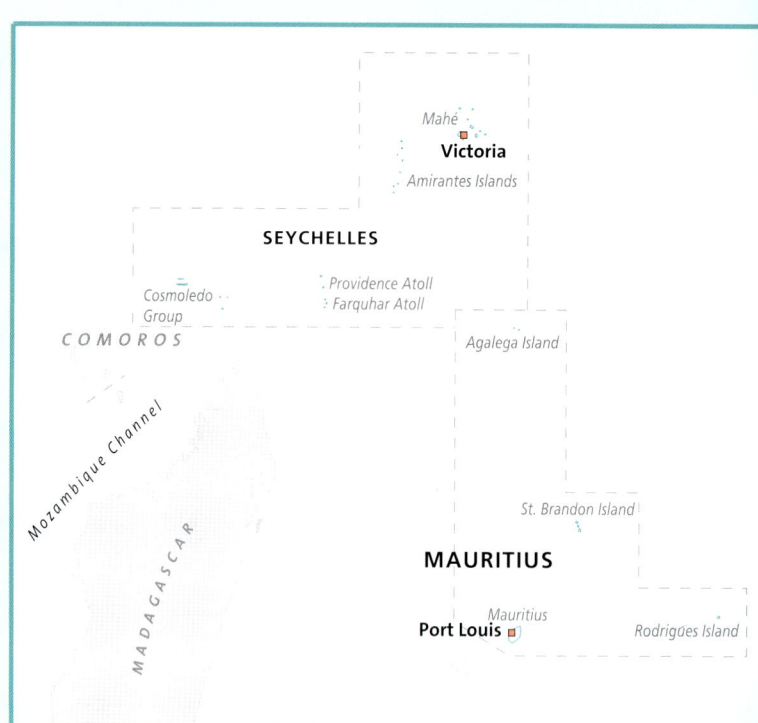

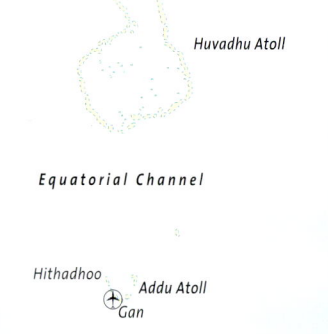

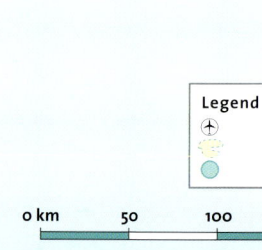

Atoll Tiladummati
Miladhunmadulu Atoll

Four Seasons Resort Maldives at Landaa Giraavaru

Raa

Maalhosmadutu Atoll

Kardiva Channel

> Soneva Gili by Six Senses
> Four Seasons Resort Maldives at Kuda Huraa

■ Malé

Ari Atoll

Malé Atoll

Anantara Dhigu Resort + Spa
Conrad Maldives Rangali Island

Felidhu Atoll

Nilandhoo Atoll

Mulakatholhu Atoll

Kolhumadulu Atoll

Indian Ocean

Hadhdhunmathi Atoll

One and a Half Degree Channel

Huvadhu Atoll

Equatorial Channel

Hithadhoo Addu Atoll
✈ Gan

Mahé
■ **Victoria**
Amirantes Islands

SEYCHELLES

Cosmoledo Group
Providence Atoll
Farquhar Atoll

COMOROS

Agalega Island

Mozambique Channel

MADAGASCAR

St. Brandon Island

MAURITIUS

Mauritius
Port Louis ■
Rodrigues Island

N ↑

Legend
✈ Airport
Atoll
0–153 m

0 km   50   100   150 km

ayurveda

the science of health

India's strikingly beautiful palaces and unique historical legacy are second to none. Well known for its deeply respected medical tradition, the country has a profound effect on all who visit.

Ayurveda is the time-tested Indian system of healing that is rapidly gaining the utmost respect in spas worldwide. Translated from the ancient Indian language of Sanskrit, Ayurveda is the 'science of life' (*ayur* meaning life, *veda* meaning knowledge). Its basic paradigm is derived from a series of revered Sanskrit texts that reveal a healing system steeped in Hindu philosophy. At the heart of Ayurveda is the concept that our bodies are a microcosm of the universe, with three governing forces or *dosha* at work: *vata* (air; related to movement), *pitta* (fire; digestion) and *kapha* (earth; body fluids). Each of us has a unique pattern of physical, mental and emotional energy that corresponds with these *dosha* and is part of our constitution. Although one *dosha* is generally dominant, all individuals possess the three *dosha* in varying degrees.

A person is said to be in good health when the *dosha* are balanced. The appropriate amount of *vata* promotes creativity and flexibility, while *pitta* generates understanding and analytical ability, and *kapha* engenders stability, affection and generosity. Imbalances of the *dosha* are thought to disrupt the flow of *prana*, the 'life force' that enters the body through food and the breath. The key to Ayurveda is treating the body, mind and spirit as a unified entity so as to maintain health, balance and harmony. Those who adopt this self-healing philosophy understand it to be a long-term lifestyle choice, with the full benefits reaped only when its core principles are adhered to in the strictest Ayurvedic tradition.

Unlike Western diagnoses that attempt to identify illness through common symptoms, Ayurvedic healing is highly personalised. Therapies are generally divided into curative or preventive depending on an individual's needs. A typical curative regime could include a series of therapeutic massages, oil therapy, a vegetarian diet, the consumption of healthy herbal tonics and a daily routine of yoga and meditation. For those in good health, preventive measures that keep the body working to the best of its ability can also be prescribed.

ayurvedic massage

Traditional Ayurvedic massage combines medicated herbal oils, specifically determined by the body's *dosha*, with manual techniques aimed at eliminating excess energy. It also enhances circulation and flexibility of the body. For best results, two therapists work in unison to administer the flowing rhythmic strokes of *abhyanga* massage. To relieve stubborn knots and aches, the therapist may use his feet in a specialised technique called *chavutti pizhichil*, in which the therapist suspends himself by a rope from the ceiling to apply extra pressure.

THIS PAGE: *A woman covered in an exfoliating and skin-nourishing mud mask.*
PAGE 44: *A stress-free afternoon can be spent on a hammock suspended over the pristine waters of the Indian Ocean.*

shirodhara

Often referred to as the 'massage of the third eye', *shirodhara* is an extremely powerful treatment designed to relieve mental tension by invoking a quiet and more centred mind. A steady stream of warmed medicated oil is slowly poured over the 'third eye', which is thought to be in the centre of the forehead, to calm and focus the mind. Although it is therapeutic in and of itself, *shirodhara* can also be performed together with other Ayurvedic therapies for a more fulfilling experience.

takradhara

Similar to *shirodhara*, *takradhara* is a calming therapy where medicated buttermilk is poured on the 'third eye' to bring relief to patients suffering from insomnia, depression and other stress-related problems.

panchakarma

One of Ayurveda's most effective regimes is full detoxification therapy or *panchakarma*. Several stages are involved, with the overall aim being the complete removal of toxins from deep within and the ultimate rebalancing of the body's *dosha*. *Panchakarma* is not for the faint-hearted as the full programme, beginning with the *purvakarma* phase (to cleanse the skin in preparation for detoxification) and comprising five separate stages, can be both time-consuming and difficult to adhere to. Depending on individual *dosha* and needs, *panchakarma* can be prescribed as individual treatments or as a complete programme that normally takes a minimum of two weeks. As the full regime is difficult to pursue in its entirety, it is not advised for those suffering from anaemia or weakness, pregnant women, the very young or the elderly.

marma point massage

Marma points are essentially vital energy points in the body, much like the acupoints in Traditional Chinese Medicine. In *marma* point massage, the therapist uses his thumb or index finger to work on releasing blocked energy from the *marma* points. Beginning with small clockwise circles, the therapist gradually increases both the motion and pressure applied. Traditionally, Ayurvedic medicated oils were used in the massage although essential oils such as lavender, eucalyptus or peppermint are as beneficial today.

mukh lepa

A proven beauty ritual for women, this traditional facial uses specific massage techniques and herbal ingredients to cleanse, tone, nourish and hydrate the face. A *dosha*-specific herbal *lepa* or plaster is applied to the face to completely cleanse and renew the skin from within.

THIS PAGE (FROM TOP): *Freshly ground spices are used in some traditional Indian therapies; another popular ayurvedic technique that utilises the masseur's feet to relieve aching muscles.*

OPPOSITE: *A shirodhara session in progress: warm oil drips over the 'third eye'.*

THIS PAGE (FROM TOP):
A cup of freshly brewed rose tea goes down well with a spa session; a woman is being given an Indian head massage.

OPPOSITE (FROM LEFT): A woman meditates on the boulders at the beach; a man practises yoga at dawn.

champissage

Known in the West as Indian head massage, *champissage* is an immensely popular therapy that has been used for centuries in India to treat headaches, muscle tension, eyestrain and a stiff neck. Traditional Indian head massage combines physical massage with the more subtle form of *chakra* or 'energy-centre' balancing. With its firm yet gentle rhythm, the massage helps unknot blockages, relieve tension and rebalance the body's energy with powerful effects. Advocates attest that a regular head massage with natural vegetable oils keeps their hair healthy, shiny and strong, and helps them to maintain an alert and more focused mind.

samana

Samana is the herbal medicine that is routinely prescribed in liquid, powder or tablet form to correct imbalances in the *dosha*. One of the more commonly used Ayurvedic medicines is *triphala*, a mixture of three indigenous fruits—*amalaki*, *haritaki* and *bibbitaki*—that is a powerful multi-functional rebalancer which can be eaten, used as a shampoo or body wash, taken as a laxative, emetic or snuff for the nose. Aloe vera is excellent for regulating the female monthly cycle as well as calming intestinal pain. It is also the perfect after-sun skin soother as it gently eases pain and swelling. *Brahmi* (*Centella asiatica*, and also known as *gotu kola*) is a powerful *dosha* balancer and revitaliser. Taken regularly as a tea, this herb strengthens memory, improves concentration, physical strength, digestion and brightens the complexion, making the skin more radiant.

yoga + meditation

Yoga is both a philosophy and a practice that enables its practitioners to reach a place of deep, lasting peace, harmony and happiness. Originally practised in ancient times by Hindus on their road to enlightenment, today yoga has become a mainstay for those seeking a more centred lifestyle. Practised regularly and correctly, ideally under the supervision of a skilled teacher, yoga is an effective exercise regime that also helps one to maintain a sense of calm amidst life's stressful moments.

Much of what is known of yoga today is derived from the *Yoga Sutra*, yoga's classical and seminal text, written in the 3rd century BC. Focusing primarily on matters of the spirit, the science of yoga consists of eight 'limbs': *yama* (laws of life), *niyama* (rules for living), *asana* (the physical postures), *pranayama* (breath control), *pratyahara* (the drawing of one's attention to silence), *dharana* (concentration), *dhyana* (meditation) and *samadhi* (spiritual union). Reaching bliss and peace in *samadhi* is the ultimate goal.

ayurveda 51

While all yoga styles seek to balance the body, mind and spirit, they are practised in a variety of ways. It's a matter of personal preference. Some of the more common styles of yoga widely practised today include *Hatha*, *Ashtanga*, *Kundalini*, *Lyengar* and *Bikram*. Regardless of the style chosen, regular practice makes for a strong and supple body.

Meditation is considered by many as the highest form of yoga practice as it calms and quietens the mind like no other routines. When pursued correctly, meditation slows the pulse rate and relaxes the brain, inducing a deep sense of peace and tranquillity. Meditation should take place in a warm and quiet atmosphere, where one is not likely to be interrupted. One should wear loose clothing during meditation. One should also not eat a heavy meal before meditating, or meditate when tired. Meditation should not be forced. In the rare instance that disturbing memories surface during meditation, its advisable to stop immediately.

indian ocean traditions

The Indian Ocean is home to the world's most beautiful and enchanting scenery that gives the region its enduring magic. A mesmerising melting pot of pristine sun-splashed beaches, vibrant underwater treasures and stunning landscapes, this archipelago of hundreds of iridescent islands is home to Mother Nature in her finest glory. The Indian Ocean embraces about 20 percent of the world's water surface and is, without doubt, a paradise for those craving pure unadulterated escape and timeless moments.

At many of the exquisitely chic retreats dotting unspoiled islands such as Maldives, Seychelles and Sri Lanka, an irresistible pharmacopeia of healing ingredients use in indigenous healing therapies—from the Ayurvedic-synchronised *abhyanga* massage and *shirodhara* to traditional Maldivian and Seychellois rituals—can be readily enjoyed.

THIS PAGE: *Partial view of a sun lounger on the jetty of Soneva Gili by Six Senses in the Maldives.*

OPPOSITE: *Jars of massage oil typically used during spa treatments in the Indian Ocean.*

THIS PAGE: *The calm turquoise water surrounding the over-water villas at the Four Seasons resort Maldives at Kuda Huraa provides guests the most relaxing break from the hustle and bustle of life.*
OPPOSITE: *A seaplane flying over the St Anne Marine Park, Seychelles.*

seychelles

Nature rules supreme in this effervescent group of islands off the coast of East Africa. Long before the advent of modern medicine, Seychellois-style healing was derived from the offerings of land and sea, and the wisdom of the ancient shamans or Madame Dibwa (a Creole title for healer). Even today, cutting-edge science continues to explore the last sanctuaries of this Garden of Eden for her hidden secrets. From the use of traditional *raspay* or medicinal plants such as yam weed (also known as *bwa torti* or *Morinda citrifolia*) for joint pain, tea bush (*Bazilik*) for intestinal issues and Madagascar periwinkle to strengthen immunity, to the time-tested benefits of the numerous other plants, bark, roots, fruits and flowers that thrive in the beautiful surroundings, nature's medicine chest is brimming over with healing gifts.

maldives

Cool and hip island resorts are the norm in the Maldives, with stylish retreats vying for their perfect slice of paradise. Spas are the norm here too, as healing traditions are woven into the fabric of the islands' culture. While each spa has its own customised offerings, all capitalise on the innate treasures of their heavenly environments to ensure perfect spa moments, be it a sumptuous water ritual or a traditional Maldivian sand massage accompanied by the soothing sounds of warm surf breaking on the whitest and purest of sands.

sri lanka

This pear-shaped paradise of the Indian Ocean has been known since ancient times as 'Serendib', and stumbling upon her eternal beauty that still remains little discovered by the rest of the world is truly serendipity. From the trade-capital Colombo to the cultural heritage of Sigiriya and Kandy, and the UNESCO-protected Galle Fort on the island's south, Sri Lanka is a mixed bag of contrasting treasures—golden beaches, emerald green highlands, thick rainforests and dusty plains—all sprinkled with charming and stylish resorts and spas. Wherever you stay, you are always welcomed into one of the most beautifully diverse and hospitable countries in the world. With its rich, deep Ayurvedic traditions, Sri Lankans have lived a holistic life for thousands of years. Now these timeless therapies combine with contemporary spa expertise to offer incomparable experiences that inspire guests to stay for weeks rather than days.

Nature rules supreme in this effervescent group of islands off the coast of East Africa.

spas in india + the indian ocean

india

In the heart of Delhi, just minutes from the grandeur of Rashtrapati Bhavan, the peaceful Lodhi gardens and other iconic sites, the **Spa at Aman New Delhi** (Lodhi Road, 110003 New Delhi, India) exudes an air of sophisticated calm from the moment you arrive. From the stylish décor to the timeless therapies, the spa offers a contemporary take on classic Indian rituals. The menu reads like a fairy tale romance offering indulgent baths, body wraps, scrubs, reflexology, face and body rituals as well as the *solah shringar*, the traditional pampering pre-wedding ritual for Indian brides-to-be. This innately Indian experience comprises a steam bath, body scrub, massage, facial, pedicure, manicure and a menu of 16 beautifying steps. These include the application of a *bindi* and *mahendi* on the hands and feet, putting on traditional fragrant essence or *ittar*, hair oil therapy, complete facial make-up and styling with a *sari* and customary wedding accessories.

Set in a 40.5-hectare (100-acre) estate of the Maharaja of Tehri Garhwal, surrounded by the majestic Himalayas and views of the Ganges meandering through the *ashram* town of Rishikesh, the hushed luxury of the spa at **Ananda-In The Himalayas** (The Palace Estate, Narendra Nagar, Tehri Garhwal, Uttaranchal 249175) instantly soothes one's spirit. A stylish yet authentic Ayurvedic spa awaits, featuring a full complement of healing therapies ranging from *abhyanga* massage and *shirodhara* treatment to more complex, medically-based and doctor-assisted programmes to cleanse and purify one's body and mind.

maldives

Many spas in the Maldives literally hang over the water, such as the **Spa Retreat** and the **Over-Water Spa** at the **Conrad Maldives Rangali Island** (Rangali Island, 2034 Maldives) which features treatment rooms with glass floors for gazing at the tropical fish below. Constructed above a coral reef, these spas are dedicated to providing holistic treatments with an emphasis on spiritual renewal. A dedicated menu of rituals created around the body's seven *chakra* (or energy centres) is available for those intent on achieving a spiritual awakening.

The **Four Seasons Resort Maldives at Kuda Huraa** (North Malé Atoll, Maldives) is located at the epicentre of one of the finest surf and diving spots in the Indian Ocean. The **Island Spa** is located on an island of its own, a two-minute *dhoni* (traditional Maldivian boat) ride from the resort.

Inspired by Moroccan oasis architecture, the tented reception is surrounded by thatched pavilions where a range of indulgent therapies is available, overlooking the seemingly endless blue sea. It goes without saying that nature's vibrant bounty is an integral part of the treatments offered. The signature Sea Escape Ritual, for example, celebrates the restorative powers of marine nutrients and comprises an Indian Oceanic bath, sea salt scrub, mineral body mask and the signature Kuda Huraa massage that, when combined, will leave both the body and mind renewed.

The architecture of **Four Seasons Resort Maldives at Landaa Giraavaru** (Baa Atoll, Maldives) is inspired by the Sri Lankan genius Geoffrey Bawa. As befits Bawa's distinctive style, the structure merges with light throughout, allowing the building to harmonise with the stunning beauty of its natural surroundings. At **The Spa and Ayurvedic Retreat** the options are varied—from traditional Maldivian massages and water rituals in the over-water pavilion and the nurturing Omkaara Tantric Ayurvedic ritual amidst the lush indigenous greenery of the spa's organic garden, to the village-style Ayurvedic Retreat with its spacious, open-air pavilions shrouded with natural vegetation.

Set within its own shimmering lagoon, the **Lime** spa at the **Huvafen Fushi Maldives** (PO Box 2017, North Malé Atoll, Maldives) is a wonderland of underwater and private island delights, where waterfalls trickle into indoor pools and therapy rooms open

THIS PAGE (CLOCKWISE FROM TOP): A face and décolleté mask made of mud can help nourish the skin; immerse the feet in a cleansing and invigorating floral foot bath; medicated Ayurvedic oil is an essential part of a rebalancing Ayurvedic back massage; breathe deeply of the heady scent of the blossoms as one enjoys the anti-ageing benefits of a rose bath.

OPPOSITE: Yoga enthusiasts in an early morning class in the music pavilion at Ananda-In The Himalayas.

spas in india + the indian ocean

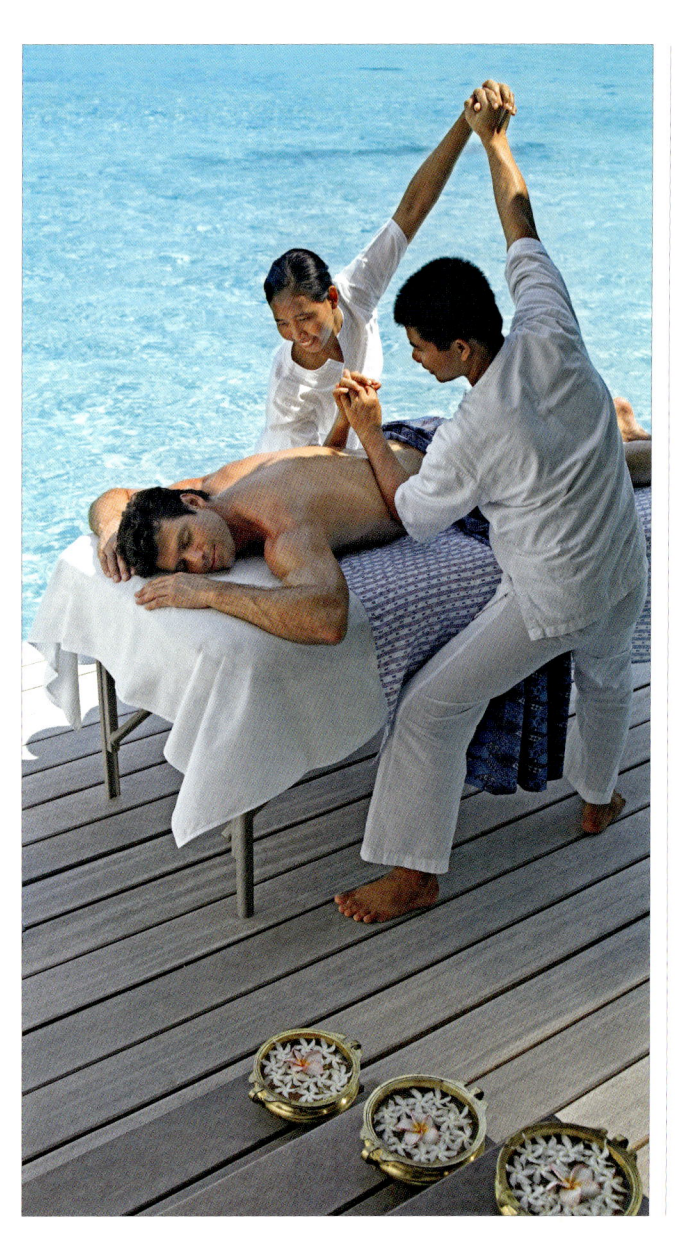

onto the lagoon as flying fish dart past. A refreshing menu of native and contemporary treatments awaits, along with natural spa products prepared primarily from local ingredients grown in the organic vegetable garden. In addition, regular retreats are coordinated by renowned visiting *yogi* and celebrated DJs. No wonder the resort remains at the top of the list of hip holiday destinations.

Six Senses is famous for their spas and healing therapies with the **Soneva Gili by Six Senses** (Lankanfushi Island, North Malé Atoll, Maldives) being no exception. The **Six Senses Spa** has an eclectic menu of healing rituals and programmes that work in harmony with delicious fresh foods, uninterrupted views and a peaceful ambience. One such treatment is the Maldivian Kurumbaa Kaashi Coconut Rub, which capitalises on the benefits of the island's harvest to leave the skin thoroughly refreshed and glowing.

The stylishly designed glass-floored over-water **Anantara Spa,** at **Anantara Resort Dhigu** (PO Box 2014, Dhigufinolhu, South Malé Atoll, Malé, Maldives) allows guests enjoying their customised therapies to observe the vibrant marine life within the azure waters below. A menu of exquisite holistic treatments, including Indian herbal therapies, Maldivian rituals, Moor mud therapy and exotic floral body wraps, will please even the most discerning guests.

seychelles

The Rock Spa at the renowned barefoot luxury hideaway of **Frégate Island Private** (PO Box 330, Victoria, Mahé, Seychelles) uses only the very best in fresh, seasonal organic ingredients harvested in Frégate's own hydroponics greenhouse. These are custom-blended into healthy scrubs, pastes and oils for truly revitalising therapies. The design is in tune with the spa's principal ethos of celebrating the earth's natural elements, with stone boulders interspersed by ponds and cascading waterfalls in a tropical setting. At night, flares illuminate the pathways and rock formations that surround the local Creole-style spa buildings. Every day at dawn, the spa's healer, Madame Dibwa, grinds the multitude of healing herbs and spices from the Rock Spa apothecary, which are then used in the concoctions necessary for the Papyion Body Scrubs, body wraps and facials.

The Creole-inspired spa pavilions of **The Spa** at the **Four Seasons Resort Seychelles** (Petite Anse, Baie-Lazare, Mahé, Seychelles) are located high on a hilltop to capture the stunning views over Petite Anse Bay. The open-air yoga pavilion is the perfect place to loosen tight muscles, steady one's breathing and enjoy some quiet meditative contemplation.

The Spa's therapy menu covers a colourful range of facials and body rituals, one of which is the sumptuous coco de mer couple's ritual, a must for all lovers. Celebrating the many tales of love of the famed coco de mer palm, the forbidden fruit of Eden's Tree of Knowledge, the journey includes a soothing sea kelp and coconut milk foot soak, passion fruit and coco de mer body cleanse, caviar body mask, coco de mer massage and coco d'amour bath. The programme is purported to unite body and mind in the most sensual way possible.

sri lanka

Ulpotha (near Embogama, Kurunegala District, Sri Lanka) is ecotourism at its purest and most refined. Ulpotha is a naturally spiritual and regenerative environment where massages and traditional Ayurvedic therapies are just a small part of the overall experience. Guests are encouraged to stay for a minimum of three weeks so that the Ayurvedic programme can have a chance to make a real difference. The money earned from these retreats is channelled to run Ulpotha's free clinic, where the resident doctor treats about 100 villagers each week. Ulpotha is the ideal place for visitors to spend quality time enjoying the natural gifts this place has to offer.

Hidden behind imposing walls on a golden slice of sand, the **Lime** spa at **The Fortress** (PO Box 126, Galle, Sri Lanka) is hip, chic and über-cool. From meditative yoga at dawn and cocktails by the pool at noon, to the stunning Sri Lankan sunset over twinkling waters when the day is done, relaxation couldn't be easier. The body is fully catered to by the spa's eclectic menu of healing therapies in addition to a variety of relaxation and fitness activities, while Ayurvedic programmes inspired by a pharmacopeia of local herbs and spices will restore the soul.

THIS PAGE (CLOCKWISE FROM TOP LEFT): Guests are welcomed to The Spa at the Four Seasons Resort Landaa Giraavaru with a pot of tea; sprawl on one of the daybeds at Soneva Gili by Six Senses and take a nap to the sound of lapping waves; cowrie shells and smooth stones are just some of the tools utilised by therapists during massages; Soneva Gili by Six Senses sprawls outward across turquoise waters.
OPPOSITE: A four-hand Ayurvedic massage is a treat not to be missed.

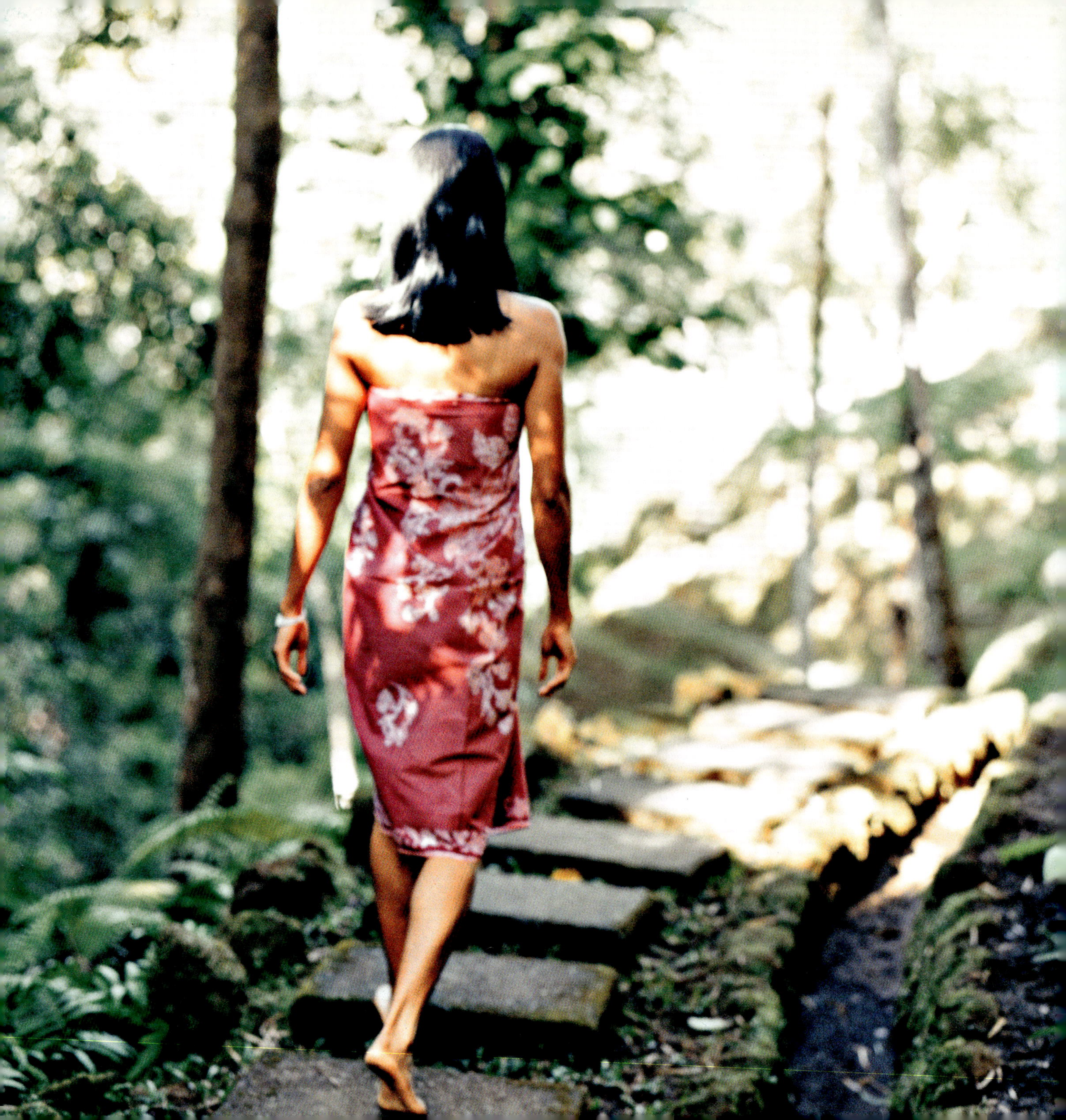

jamu

bali

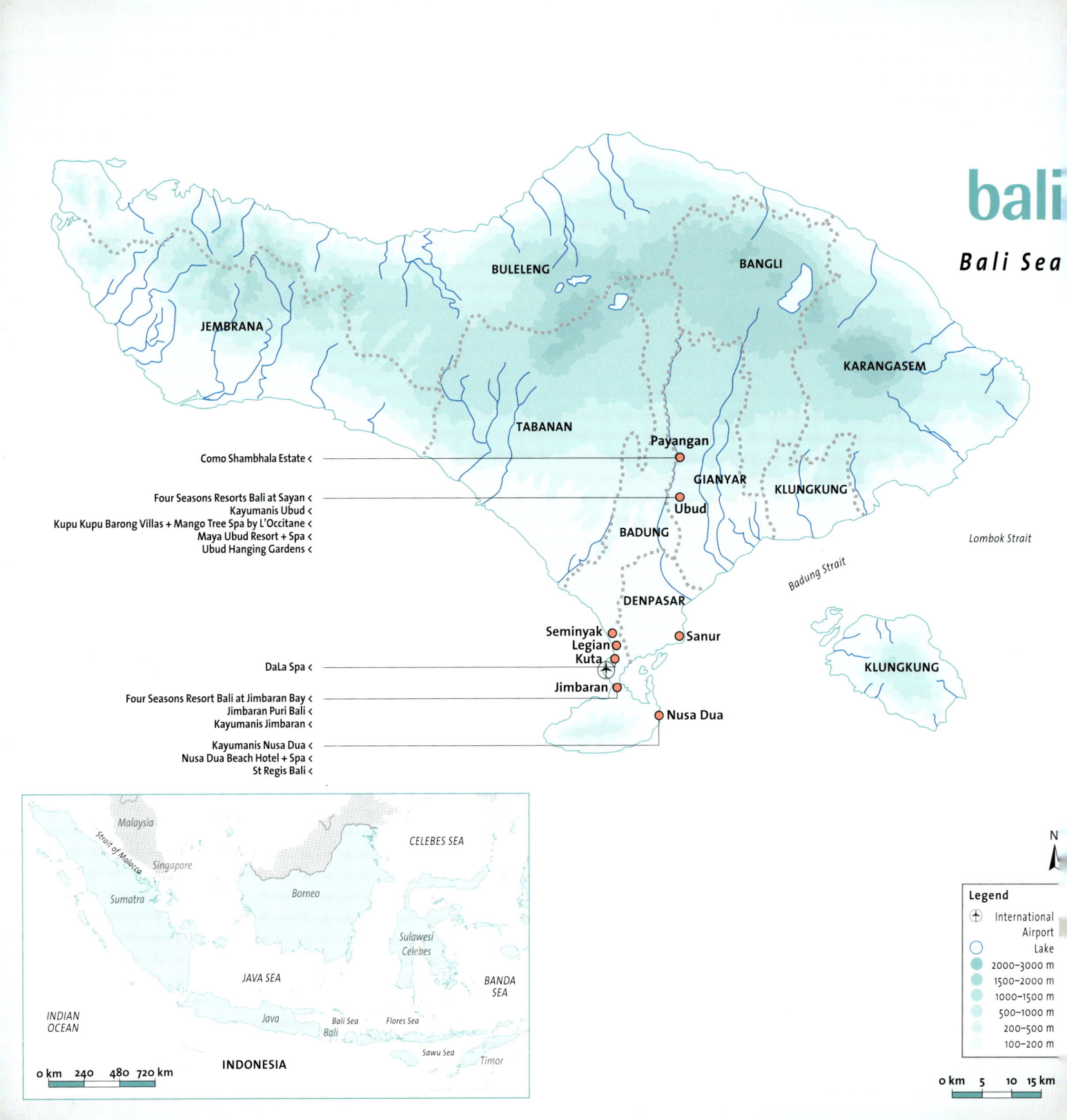

Bali Sea

JEMBRANA · **BULELENG** · **BANGLI** · **KARANGASEM** · **TABANAN** · **GIANYAR** · **KLUNGKUNG** · **BADUNG** · **DENPASAR**

- Como Shambhala Estate — Payangan
- Four Seasons Resorts Bali at Sayan — Ubud
- Kayumanis Ubud
- Kupu Kupu Barong Villas + Mango Tree Spa by L'Occitane
- Maya Ubud Resort + Spa
- Ubud Hanging Gardens
- Seminyak
- Legian
- DaLa Spa — Kuta
- Four Seasons Resort Bali at Jimbaran Bay — Jimbaran
- Jimbaran Puri Bali
- Kayumanis Jimbaran
- Kayumanis Nusa Dua — Nusa Dua
- Nusa Dua Beach Hotel + Spa
- St Regis Bali

Sanur

Lombok Strait · *Badung Strait*

KLUNGKUNG

Indonesia inset

Malaysia · Strait of Malacca · Singapore · Sumatra · Borneo · CELEBES SEA · Sulawesi / Celebes · JAVA SEA · Java · Bali · Bali Sea · Flores Sea · BANDA SEA · Sawu Sea · Timor · INDIAN OCEAN · **INDONESIA**

0 km — 240 — 480 — 720 km

Legend

- ✈ International Airport
- ○ Lake
- 2000–3000 m
- 1500–2000 m
- 1000–1500 m
- 500–1000 m
- 200–500 m
- 100–200 m

0 km — 5 — 10 — 15 km

N

jamu

spiritual diversity

The spiritually diverse archipelago of Indonesia is synonymous with spas in Asia. Its spa capital is undoubtedly Bali—home to the majestic Ayung River, abundant tropical vegetation and verdant rice fields. The Balinese carry compassion in their hands, and are therefore naturally skilled therapists. It is no wonder that massage is a fundamental aspect of daily life. They are fastidious about tradition and appearance, and every shrine, no matter how small, benefits from intense personal attention with offerings of food, colourful rituals and song.

The use of herbs in healing is as old as Javanese civilisation itself with evidence of their use etched on the walls of Borobudur, the famed Buddhist monument in central Java dating from 800–900 AD.

jamu

Although healing customs differ among the regions of Indonesia, one tradition that has remained constant is the use of *jamu*. Broadly speaking, *jamu* refers to any kind of traditional medicine. It is estimated that more than 350 *jamu* recipes have been passed down through generations and are in use today. Up to 150 ingredients are used to produce a single *jamu* potion, although only a few are used at any one time. Raw ingredients include the leaves, bark and roots of plants such as ginger, tamarind, turmeric and cinnamon, with natural sweeteners such as palm sugar often added for flavour. Today, *jamu gendong* (ladies selling *jamu*) can be seen throughout the villages carrying baskets slung over their shoulders, selling bottles of *jamu* and keeping the tradition alive. To the Indonesians, *jamu* is the elixir of life and despite a lack of scientific evidence to support its benefits, it is believed that a large percentage of the population drinks a glass of *jamu* every day.

Jamu is thought to have originated during the 17th century, when princesses in the central Javanese courts began to concoct beauty potions using plants, herbs and spices. Since then, its reputation has expanded considerably. An entire beauty regime, from facial masks to hair conditioners, scrubs and hand creams, can be created from *jamu* alone. It can be imbibed as a drink to prevent illnesses or used as treatment for chronic diseases. It is purported to relieve aches and pains, improve digestion and metabolism, and correct malfunctions such as infertility and menstrual irregularity. The use of *jamu* depends on the problem involved. *Jamu* can be taken as an infusion, distillation, brew or paste. Results are not instantaneous, and it is the job of the herbalist to ensure that the concoction is suitable for the specific ailment. Both males and females are introduced to *jamu* from birth, with recipes passed down from generation to generation.

THIS PAGE (FROM TOP): *A jamu gendong with all her health prescriptions in a basket; indigenous herbs and spices are mixed together in a traditional jamu recipe.*

PAGE 60: *A young woman walking along a jungle path surrounded by luxuriant greenery in a spa resort.*

The spiritually diverse archipelago of Indonesia is synonymous with spas in Asia.

indonesian massage

Massage is an integral element of health and beauty. While few Indonesian-trained therapists will have an in-depth knowledge of the anatomy, most will possess an in-built sensitivity to congested and tight areas in the body which they carefully relieve through the simple power of touch.

Traditional Indonesian massage can be classified into two main types: *urut* (Indonesian word for 'massage') and *pijat* (Javanese word for 'massage'). The *urut*-style massage works on the meridians and acupoints, as in Traditional Chinese Medicine. Applying oils obtained from native plants as lubricants, the skilled therapist uses his or her fingers, palms, knuckles and sometimes whole body to manipulate muscles and open energy pathways, thereby improving blood circulation and eliminating toxic build-up. This intense style of massage is most frequently used to treat specific medical complaints such as bone fractures and chronic backache. As firm pressure is applied throughout the procedure, there can be a lot of discomfort but to believers, it is a worthwhile exercise.

The *pijat*-style massage is the gentler option that continues to be practised in villages throughout the country. It comprises simple repetitive squeezing and kneading movements by the fingers and palms over the body to soothe and relax tired, tense muscles.

traditional lulur

To the Indonesian woman, a traditional *lulur* (Javanese word for 'coating the skin') is a fundamental step in the pursuit of beauty. This time-tested healing synergy of spice and yoghurt exfoliation, body polish and floral bath remains as popular today as it was in the palaces of Central Java during the 17th century. The treatment is most often associated with the pre-wedding ritual that traditionally lasts for over 40 days, during which the bride-to-be is kept in confinement. Modern brides tend to opt for a seven-day *lulur* without confinement. Today, in addition to *lulur* treatments in spas, people can opt for massages to moisturise, soften and hydrate the skin, while others choose to have an energising shower before the floral bath.

boreh

Body scrubs known as *boreh* work by removing the dead layers of skin, revealing the soft, supple skin beneath. They are a treatment in and of themselves as well as being part of the traditional *lulur* ritual. There are scrubs for all skin types, with most of the ingredients sourced from the rich native soil. Some of the more popular scrubs used today include volcanic clay-based ingredients for treating cellulite; *kemiri* or candlenut for rough, dry skin; coconut for sensitive skin and avocado-based scrubs to invigorate tired skin.

THIS PAGE (FROM TOP): *A woman receiving a traditional Indonesian massage; a rich concoction is being spread on the body for a lulur treatment.*

OPPOSITE: *The Bayugita villa pool at the COMO Shambhala Estate at Begawan Giri, Bali.*

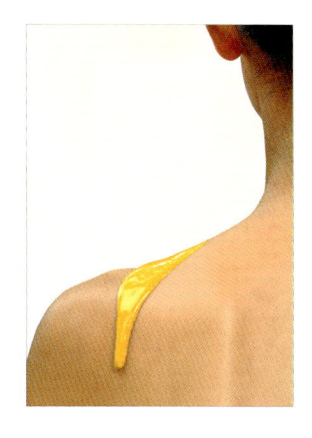

jamu 65

THIS PAGE: *A woman enjoying a shower of flowing water in the pool at Jimbaran Puri Bali.*

OPPOSITE: *The breathtaking volcanic landscape in Java at sunrise, comprising Mount Semeru, Bromo and Batok.*

The Balinese *boreh* scrub is a traditional village remedy that was handed down by rice farmers to relieve aching muscles and joints. A hand-crushed herb-and-spice mix comprising ginger, cinnamon, rice powder, turmeric and nutmeg, amongst other ingredients, is applied to the body for an all-over, deep heat experience. The *boreh* scrub can also be used to relieve fevers and headaches as well as to prevent colds.

indonesian wrap

The *bengkung* or Indonesian wrap is the local age-old answer to weight loss. This 40-day post-natal ritual has been passed down through the centuries and, to this day, is administered woman-to-woman in households throughout the country. It revives the lymphatic system, reawakens the organs, restores muscle tone and ultimately heals and strengthens the new mother's body.

The traditional treatment is normally performed by an *ibu pijat* (female masseur) who visits the new mother's home each morning. A herbal paste comprising betel leaves, lime juice, eucalyptus and crushed coral, among other ingredients, is applied all over the body. This paste is believed to cleanse the womb and firm and shrink the stomach. A long cotton sash measuring 8–15 m (9–16 yds) is then tightly wound around the abdomen and hips, and kept in place for as long as is deemed appropriate to ensure maximum effectiveness.

In the modern spa environment, the body wrap is far less complex. As with the traditional *bengkung*, a herbal paste is applied before the wrap. Once the wrap is removed (generally after 20 to 30 minutes), a luxurious floral bath completes the treatment.

mandi

Since the olden days when Javanese princesses soaked in milk as part of their beauty regime, *mandi susu* or milk baths have been associated with luxuriously soft and smooth skin. It is believed that the lactic acid in goat's, sheep's or cow's milk naturally dissolves the 'glue' that holds dead skin cells together. So in effect, a *mandi susu* removes dead skin to reveal soft, silky skin. Typically, women soaked in the bath for about 20 minutes before rinsing with water.

crème bath hair treatment

Before commercial shampoo was available, Indonesian women used the sticky gel from crushed hibiscus leaves and coconut milk to keep their hair healthy, strong and shiny. The heavier milk from the coconut was ideal for conditioning, washing and for use in massage, while the lighter milk was used to rinse the hair. The recipes used today are based on this rich, creamy gelatinous concoction, using ingredients chosen to suit each individual's hair type.

...the more popular scrubs used today include volcanic clay-based ingredients...

spas in bali, indonesia

jimbaran

The **Beach Spa** at the **Jimbaran Puri Bali** (Jalan Uluwatu, Jimbaran, 80361 Bali) is almost entirely shaded by towering palms, with only the gentle sound of the waves breaking on the beach to disrupt the silence. Native- and Ayurvedic-influenced therapies such as the *abhyanga* rhythmic oil massage and the *shirodhara* treatment are prescribed alongside meditation, a healthy diet and herbal medicines to induce a deep, lasting sense of inner peace and calm.

The Spa at the **Four Seasons Resort at Jimbaran Bay** (Jimbaran Bay, Denpasar 80361, Bali) is nestled on a limestone cliff overlooking Jimbaran Bay. The design style is based on authentic Balinese architecture, with thatched roofs, indoor and outdoor treatment facilities, wooden flooring and stone walls. The therapy menu incorporates various combinations of plant essences, aromas of healing flowers, ocean elements as well as Balinese and Indonesian herbs and spices, blended into modern-day healing and beauty rituals with the use of traditional recipes.

kuta

The warm-toned, cosy therapy rooms of the **DaLa Spa** at Villa de daun (Raya Legian, Kuta, Bali) are reminiscent of a vintage Parisian boudoir.

Formerly the exclusive privilege of royal brides, DaLa Spa's Royal Wedding Ritual is the perfect prescription for healthy, radiant skin. The rite combines a cleansing footbath, Balinese massage, Javanese *lulur* exfoliation, body polish and flower-filled milk bath to leave the skin beautifully soft and glowing.

nusa dua

The **Kriya Spa** at the **Grand Hyatt Bali** (PO Box 53, Nusa Dua, Bali) is inspired by the magnificent architecture of an ancient Balinese water palace. Reflecting its name, *kriya* (meaning 'ritual' in Sanskrit), the treatment menu boasts authentic Balinese rituals that guide guests through a transformation process geared towards attaining spiritual growth. There is a dedicated Ayurvedic menu consisting of specific rituals for complete cleansing, rejuvenation and inner radiance or harmony and calm.

The therapists of the **Nusa Dua Spa** at **Nusa Dua Beach Hotel & Spa** (PO Box 1028, Denpasar, Bali) work with the very best of time-tested healing herbs and spices to soothe, soften and calm even the weariest of bodies and minds. Plunge pools, aromatic saunas, steam rooms, Jacuzzis and lap pools are also available for those who enjoy the healing benefits of water.

Nestled near a koi pond by the beach, the **Remède Spa** at the **St Regis Bali** (Kawasan Pariwisata Nusa Dua Lot S6, PO Box 44, Nusa Dua 80363, Bali) is inspired by the poetry of Kabir (1398–1448). A moon-and-butterfly theme is evident—using subtle lighting effects, butterflies flutter around, creating an atmosphere conducive to relaxation. The spa's massage menu features an eclectic range of styles designed to soothe tired and tense bodies. Combined

THIS PAGE (CLOCKWISE FROM TOP): *For guests who prefer more privacy, therapy suites outfitted with a floral bath and relaxation area are a viable option in the Nusa Dua Spa; spa packages designed specially for males are becoming popular and more widely available; a cleansing foot soak is the prelude to treatments available at the COMO Shambala Estate.*

OPPOSITE: *Guests are encouraged to harness the cleansing benefits of the huge, elaborately tiled steam room of the Mango Tree Spa by l'Occitane. That a steamy session often incites relaxation is a bonus.*

spas in bali, indonesia

THIS PAGE (CLOCKWISE FROM TOP LEFT): *A cool, refreshing shower will slough off any cleansing body scrub applied, leaving soft, smooth skin; essential oils are vital to almost all the treatments offered in the spa at the COMO Shambhala Estate; enjoy a healing back massage in an outdoor therapy pavilion and be surrounded by nature as you relax.*
OPPOSITE: *A quick dip in the private pool of the stylish Ayung Spa at Ubud Hanging Gardens, overlooking the tropical forests in Bali, will invigorate and refresh the body.*

with a signature *lulur* exfoliation, a massage is certain to leave the skin recharged and glowing.

ubud + surroundings

The riverside **Spa at Maya** at the **Maya Ubud Resort & Spa** (Jalan Gunung Sari Peliatan, Ubud 80571, Bali) is a cluster of single- and double-storey treatment pavilions, dramatically suspended some 30 m (98 ft) down a gravity-defying cliffside. Fringed by lush jungle foliage, the canopied bathtub in each pavilion hangs over the waters of the Petanu River as it carves its way through the narrow valley below. With an emphasis on nature, the luxurious therapies offer native body scrubs, wraps, massages, baths and the signature Maya Facial, an invigorating blend of fresh natural ingredients that makes the skin glow.

Nestled among the groves of cinnamon trees and fragrant blooms, **Kayumanis Ubud** (Sayan Village, Ubud 80571, Bali) overlooks the Ayung River and the tropical forests nearby. The resort's **Kayumanis Spa** features four open-air treatment pavilions, a restaurant, an infinity-edged pool and a series of inspiration decks from which the serene beauty of Bali's tropical foothills can be enjoyed. The signature Sensory Surrender retreat is a six-hour ritual comprising yoga practice, a cleansing tea tree bath and body scrub, a frangipani-and-coconut body wrap, a stone massage and a facial.

The lush and beautiful Balinese jungle is the spotlight from all corners of Bali's stylish **Ubud Hanging Gardens** (Desa Buahan, Ubud 80571, Bali) retreat. The treatment pavilions at the

Ayung Spa open onto the verdant surroundings. In the signature Ayung massage, the therapist's long soothing strokes help release blockages in the energy channels along the back so as to rebalance the body completely.

Embracing 3 hectares (7 acres) of tropical woodland on the outskirts of Ubud, the **Kupu Kupu Barong Villas** (PO Box 7, Kedewatan, Ubud 80571, Bali) merges effortlessly into the greenery, with thatched roofs, red-wood walls, teak panelling and rich local textiles. Here at the **Mango Tree Spa by L'Occitane**, treatments are performed in quaint tree houses perched on the top branches of mango trees overlooking the tropical countryside. The specially formulated products using mangoes will cleanse and nourish even the most sensitive skin.

At **The Spa** of **Four Seasons Resort Bali at Sayan** (Sayan, Ubud Gianyar 80571, Bali), therapies are performed in the Spa Villa cradled in the rice fields. The best of nature's offerings—clays, spices, herbs, leaves and native flowers—feature in the menu of soul-restoring and revitalising rituals. The massage menu comprises Balinese-style therapy using long kneading strokes, aromatherapy, herbal oil massage, Indian head massage and a four-hand synchronised massage, during which two therapists work in harmony to eliminate tension.

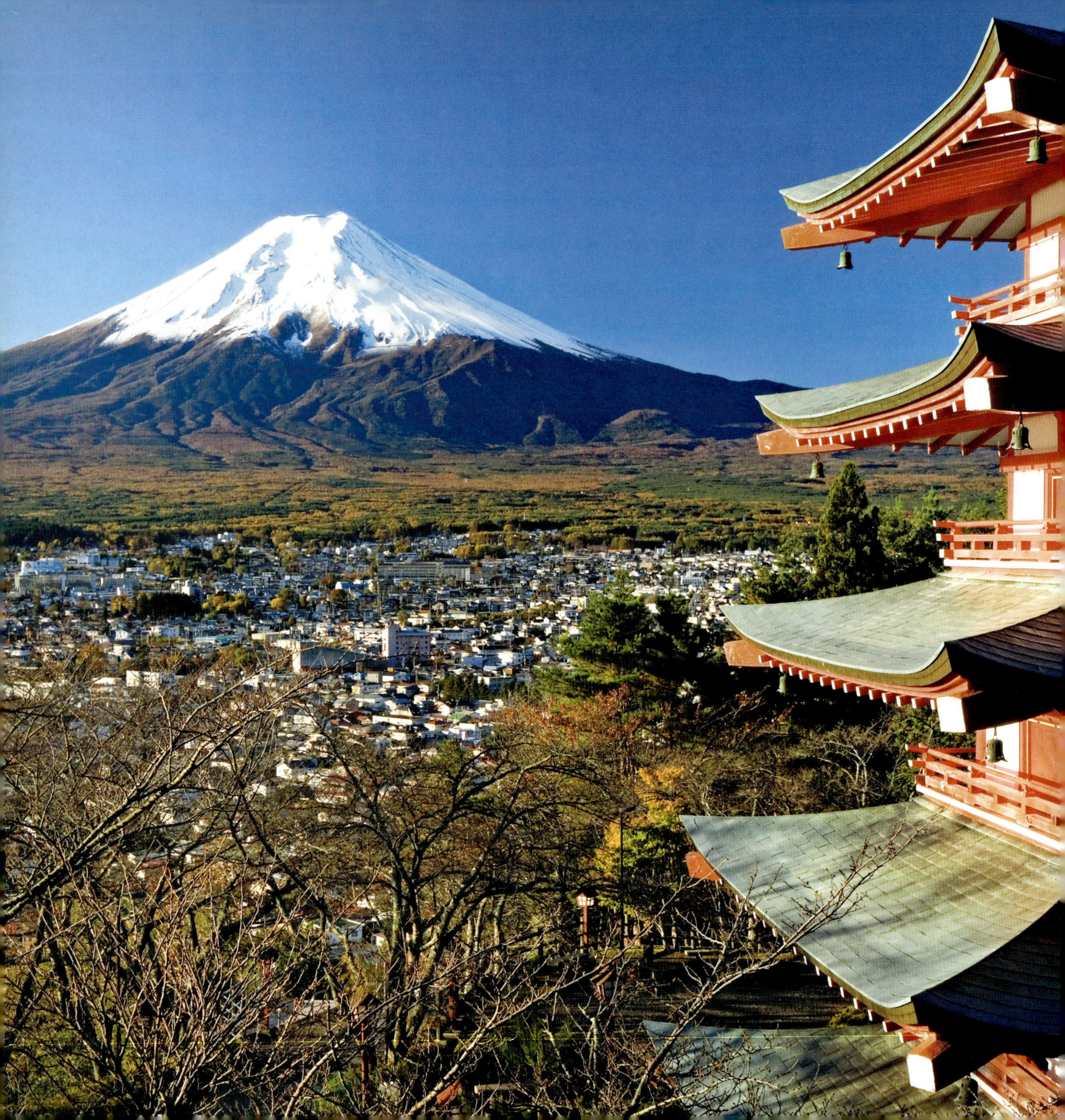

japanesehealingrituals

japan

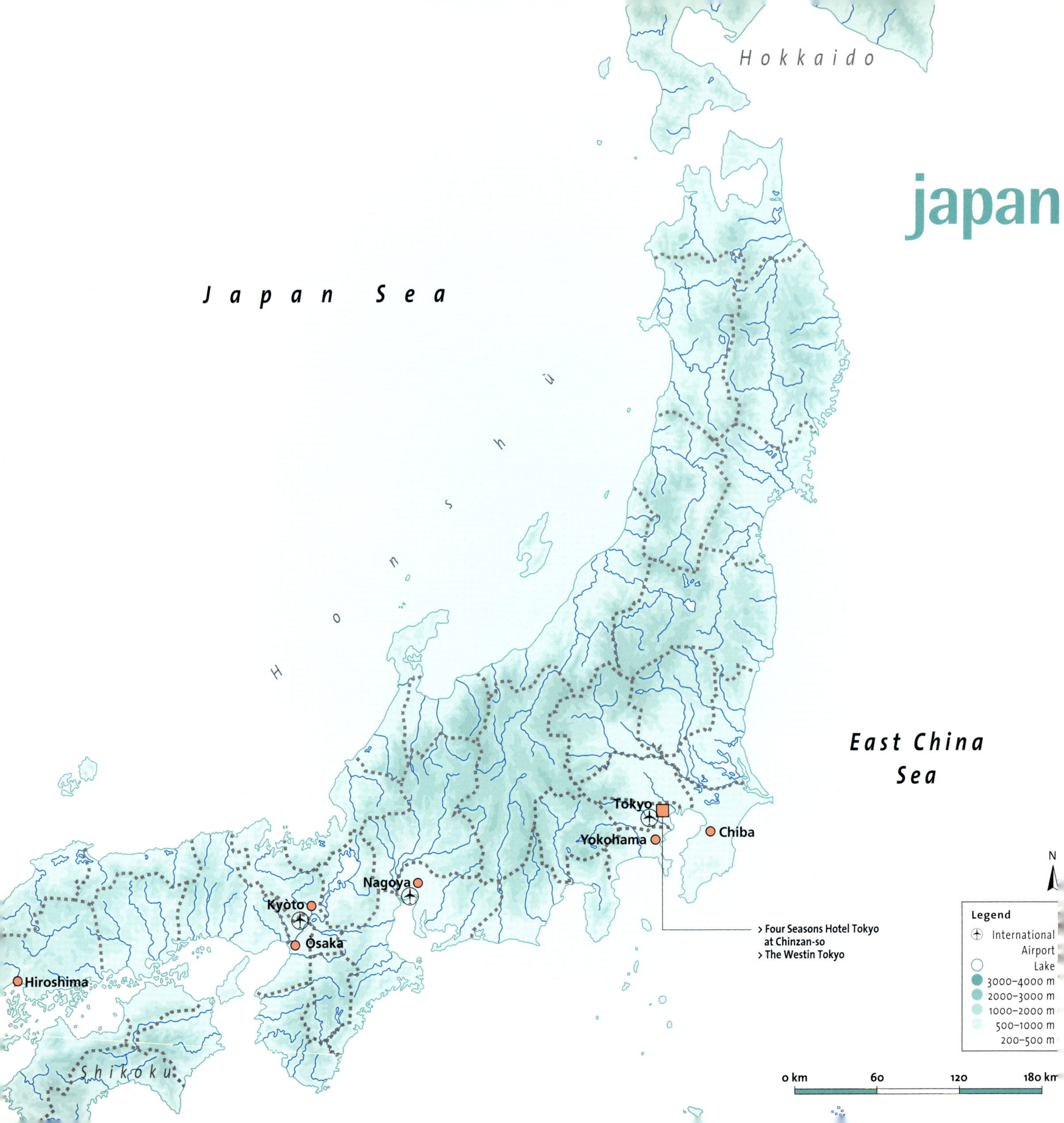
Hokkaido
Japan Sea
Honshū
East China Sea
Tokyo
Chiba
Yokohama
Nagoya
Kyòto
Ōsaka
Hiroshima
Shikoku
> Four Seasons Hotel Tokyo at Chinzan-so
> The Westin Tokyo
N
Legend
International Airport
Lake
3000–4000 m
2000–3000 m
1000–2000 m
500–1000 m
200–500 m
0 km
60
120
180 km

japanese healing rituals

a culture steep in deep tradition

The pure, clean and orderly society depicted in countless movies still exists in modern Japan and is taken extremely seriously. These traditions have survived the test of time—from the meticulous preparation and presentation of Japanese foods such as *sushi* and *sashimi* and the intricate perfection of the traditional *kimono*, to the near absence of English being spoken on the streets, the straw *tatami* mats omnipresent in homes throughout the country and the importance of bathing in daily life.

Traditional Japanese belief holds that illness is the result of possession by vengeful spirits (*kami*) and the cure requires purification rites (*harai*) or exorcism by shamans. Purification is therefore fundamental, more as a preventive rather than curative measure. Even today, bathing rituals to clean and purify the body and careful attention to personal hygiene are an intrinsic part of Japanese etiquette and society as a whole.

Ki is the vital life force that sustains the body. The principal aim of any of the range of time-tested Japanese therapies is *kyo-jitsu-ho-sha* or the manipulation of *ki*, which is achieved by either replenishing a *ki* deficiency or dispersing excess *ki* to regain overall balance and harmony in the body and the mind.

shiatsu

Literally translated as finger (*shi*) pressure (*atsu*), *shiatsu* is a relatively modern therapy, popularised only a century ago by Japanese physician Tokujiro Namikoshi. Often described as 'acupuncture without needles', *shiatsu* uses the fingers, palms and especially the thumbs to apply pressure to manipulate the body's acupoints and improve the flow of *ki*. It helps correct imbalances and realigns the body naturally. Therapy is tailored to individual concerns—be it back pain, migraine, neck and shoulder discomfort, menstrual issues, sports injuries or rheumatic pains. Regular sessions can help to boost stamina, improve digestion and concentration, relieve stress and calm both the mind and body.

reiki

Reiki is a trusted method of healing for body, mind and spirit. It rates as one of the most widely taught and practised therapies in the West today. This technique is believed to have been discovered in ancient Tibetan Sanskrit *sutra* (Buddhist teachings) during the late 1880s by Dr Mikao Usui, who went on to teach *reiki* in Japan.

THIS PAGE (FROM TOP): *A Japanese garden requires the same meticulous attention to detail as a Japanese spa experience; a therapist performing reiki treatment on a woman's stomach.*
PAGE 72: *Volcanoes such as Mount Fuji are sources of mineral-rich hotsprings.*

76 spachicasia

Reiki is an extremely calming form of touch therapy during which the attuned practitioner harnesses his ability to control his ki to heal others. During a typical session, the reiki healer transmits energy to the client by placing his hands over or on the specific body parts requiring attention. When the energy is channelled through his hands, it activates the recipient's innate healing ability to rebalance their ki. For example, placing the hand of an experienced reiki practitioner over or on a woman's abdomen helps rebalance her ki and is believed to cure certain digestive problems and ease menstrual cramps, while hands placed over the head can relieve upper body tension and headaches. Reiki is reputed to be effective in relieving many illnesses including arthritis, insomnia and migraine, and apart from treating others, it can also be used for self-healing.

kanpo

The Japanese system of kanpo (herbal medicine) is adapted directly from Chinese herbal medicine. It is formulated to rebalance and strengthen the body through specific herbal recipes, primarily based on plant and animal ingredients. The remedies concocted are tailored specifically to the individual, not to the disease, and are prepared as teas, decoctions, pills and granules to be taken daily. The prescriptions are carefully combined to ensure that each ingredient acts in synergy.

hotspring baths

The Japanese bathing ritual remains as sacred today as it has been for thousands of years, since the time when animists worshipped nature in all its forms. It is well known that long before the advent of indoor plumbing, most Japanese cleansed themselves daily in communal bathhouses or sênto, which were usually fed by natural springs.

Cleansing the spirit and warding off disease are the reputed benefits claimed by some 3,000 onsen or hotspring baths dotted throughout the mountainous islands of Japan. The term onsen can refer both to a single bathing facility or an entire town or hotspring area. Onsen range in size, from small tubs for one person to enormous pools that can accommodate over 100 bathers at one time. The baths are measured in tatami mats, a traditional Japanese unit of measurement based on the size of the straw mats used in the home. A variety of hotsprings can be found throughout the country, comprising uchi-buro (indoor baths), rotenburo (outdoor

THIS PAGE (FROM TOP): *Mineral-rich water piped into an onsen; some onsen provide guests with eggs while they enjoy the spa experience.*

OPPOSITE (FROM LEFT): *A young woman in a hotspring bath; a Japanese common bath in Gifu prefecture.*

baths) and *mushi-yu* (steam baths). In addition, baths can be designed for use lying down or standing up, and can be divided into those only for men or exclusively for women.

To the Japanese, bathing in an *onsen* is as serious a ritual as sipping tea. Before going into an *onsen*, the body is washed first as the tub at the *onsen* is used exclusively for soaking. Devotees attest that a long soak at the end of the day not only divests the body of dirt but also nourishes the spirit. Unlike most other spas where the healing experience is essentially a private ritual involving only the therapist and the recipient, going to an *onsen* is a communal affair. Most people spend about half an hour in the bath every night and parents will generally bathe together with their young children.

When bathing, the extra-deep tub is filled to the brim with very hot water, in which the person sits submerged to the neck. The body is washed and scrubbed clean before entering the bath as soap should not get into the tub. Sitting on one of the small stools provided, soap is rubbed into the *tenugui* (small towelling cloth) before the towel is used to rub over the entire body. Once the old skin cells are removed and circulation stimulated, a quick rinse leaves the skin soft and smooth. Then the real *onsen* experience begins.

Many *onsen* are found close to areas with volcanic activity, as bathing in mineral-rich waters is believed to cure numerous illnesses. People suffering from ailments as diverse as rheumatism and nervous disorders to circulation problems, skin irritations, aches and fatigue travel to bathe expressly to *onsen*-rich areas to bathe in these therapeutic waters. The seasons are important too, as bathing washes sweat off during the hot summer months and warms the body during winter. These days, aromatic baths are gaining popularity, with fruits, herbs and spices used to complement the seasons. For example, mandarin orange peel is used during autumn, *yuzu*, an aromatic citrus fruit, is traditionally used during the winter solstice in December, and ginger helps to warm the body during the colder winter months.

In order to provide accommodation to visitors from afar, many *ryokan* (traditional Japanese inns) are strategically located near *onsen*. At these inns, Japanese customs such as sitting cross-legged on the wooden floor to eat and sleeping on *futon* (cotton mattress) prevail. With the proximity of the *ryoken* to the mineral-rich hotspring waters, guests can both complete their rejuvenating experience and enjoy the surrounding natural environment.

THIS PAGE: Women enjoying a hotspring outdoors, accompanied by a scenic mountain landscape.

OPPOSITE: An onsen town in winter, a welcome haven from the snow and frost.

...bathing in mineral-rich waters is believed to cure numerous illnesses.

spas in japan

THIS PAGE: *A soak in a geothermal spa will serve to relax the body.*

OPPOSITE (CLOCKWISE FROM TOP): *The sight of the leaves changing colours in autumn is amazing when viewed from the luxurious comfort of a hotspring resort in Tochigi-ken; the interior of a traditional ryokan; bathing accessories used during an onsen ritual include a small towelling cloth known as a tenugui.*

tokyo

YU, THE SPA at the **Four Seasons Hotel Tokyo** at Chinzan-so (10-8, Sekiguchi 2-chome, Bunkyo-ku, Tokyo 112-8667) is an urban sanctuary in the heart of Tokyo. The premises house traditional indoor Japanese cedar baths, a heated pool with a retractable roof and an intimate couples' therapy suite, which showcases a traditional Japanese garden installed with a granite onsen-style bath. The customised products are centred around the seasonal herbs and flowers found in the hotel's gardens. One of the spa's signature treatments is the Sake Clay Cocoon, a nourishing body wrap. The highlights of the Red Plum Blossom Mindfulness Ritual—another signature—are a plum-and-orange blossom foot wash, a bamboo body polish and a plum blossom-and-chrysanthemum cream mask.

A respite in the middle of one of the world's most exciting cities, **Le Spa Parisien** at **The Westin Tokyo** (1-4-1 Mita, Meguro-ku, Tokyo 153-8580) is modelled around classical Parisian opulence with Aubusson tapestries, epoch-style furniture, French-influenced antiques, standing chandeliers and authentic handmade copper bathtubs. The spa's aqua area includes an aromatherapy steam room, therapeutic jet baths and

Tokyo's first Aqua Sound Bath for an underwater music experience. The comprehensive menu of European-style body therapies, refining skin polishes, replenishing wraps and restorative facials is certain to cleanse and beautify the skin of even the most stressed client.

Specially designed spa programmes booked in blocks of time called Time Rituals™ are available at the **The Spa** at **Mandarin Oriental, Tokyo** (2-1-1 Nihonbashi Muromachi, Chuo-ku, Tokyo 103-8328). Located on the top two floors of this stylish hotel, with state-of-the-art facilities including a vitality pool, water lounge, sauna, fitness centre and cosy relaxation lounge, guests can enjoy remarkable experiences enveloped by breathtaking city views. For a taste of authentic Japanese therapies, Kiatsu, a *shiatsu*-inspired treatment in which pressure is applied to various points on the body using thumbs, fingers and palms, and the Azuki Ritual, a deep-cleansing body scrub using *azuki* beans and sea salt, are a must.

outside tokyo

Tobira Onsen is a hotspring village in the mountains on the outskirts of Matsumoto in Nagano prefecture. The therapeutic waters of the hotspring baths at **Tobira Onsen Myojinkan** (8967 Iriyamabe, Matsumoto-shi, Nagano-ken 390-0222 Nagoya), about three hours from Tokyo, calm and nurture the skin. Combined with fresh wild mountain vegetables, seafood and organically grown ingredients, the overall experience at this *ryokan* is perfect for complete rejuvenation.

spasinjapan 81

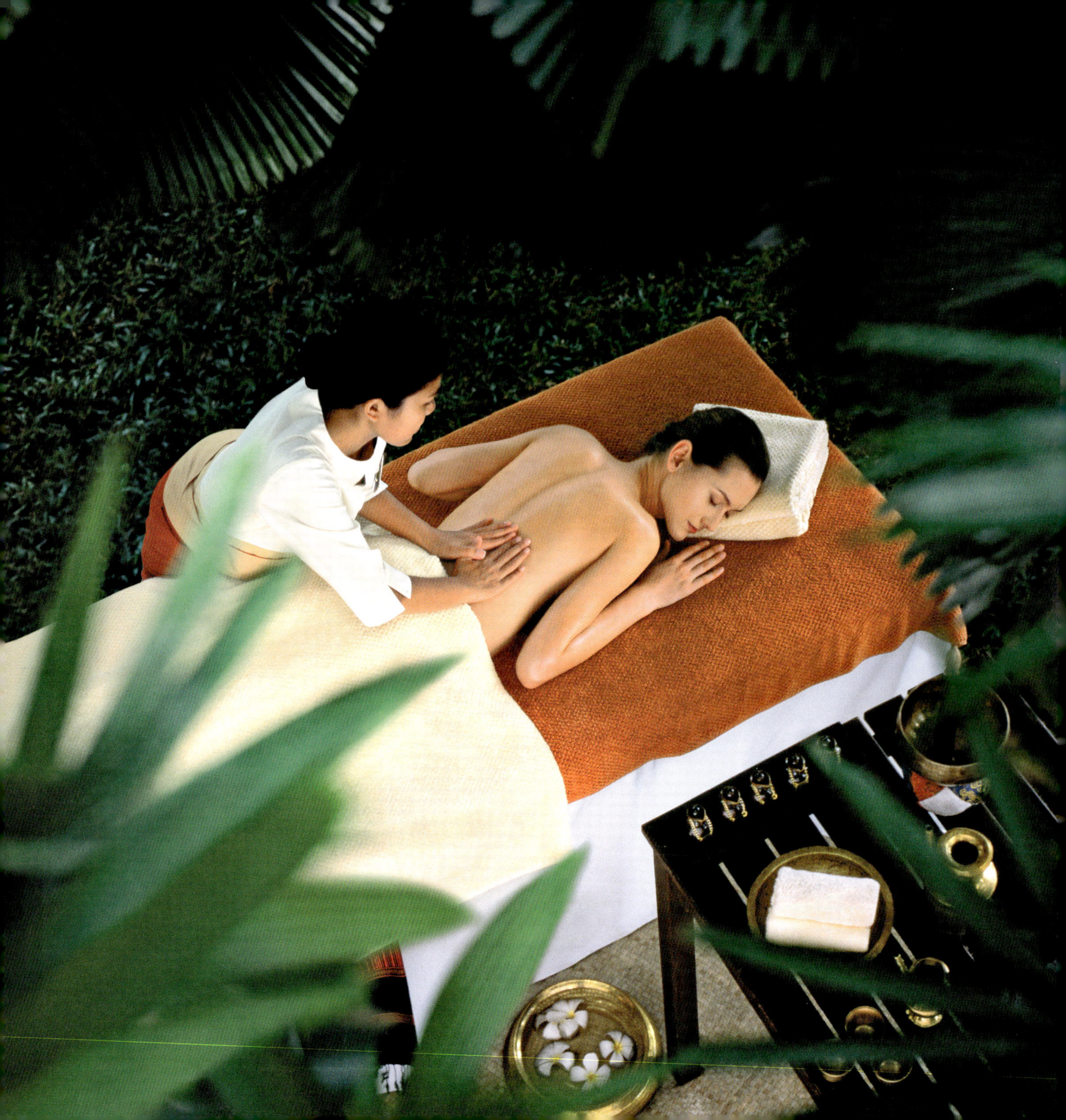

ramuan

malaysia + singapore

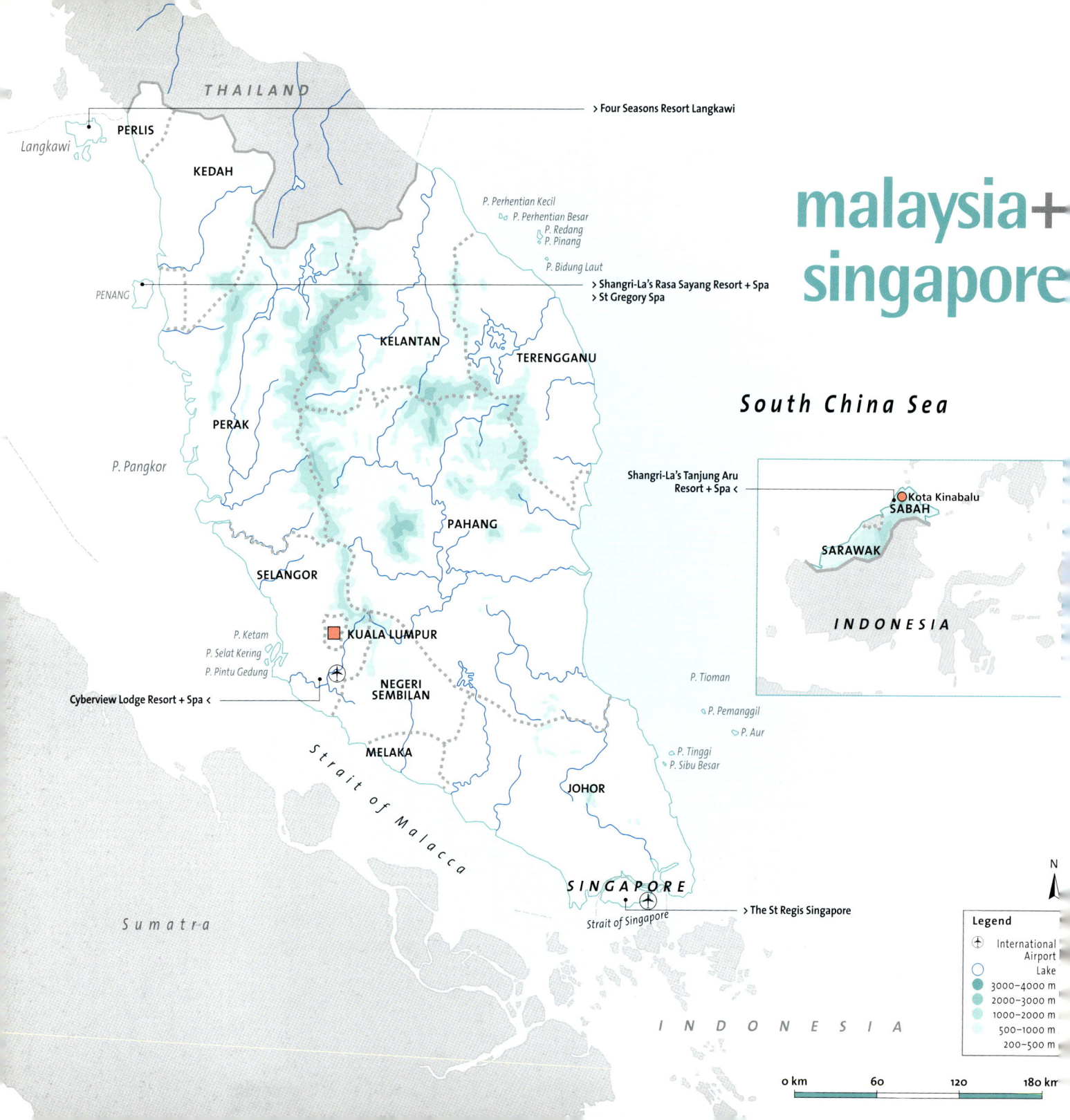

> Four Seasons Resort Langkawi

> Shangri-La's Rasa Sayang Resort + Spa
> St Gregory Spa

Shangri-La's Tanjung Aru Resort + Spa <

Cyberview Lodge Resort + Spa <

> The St Regis Singapore

South China Sea

Strait of Malacca

Strait of Singapore

Legend
- ✈ International Airport
- ○ Lake
- 3000–4000 m
- 2000–3000 m
- 1000–2000 m
- 500–1000 m
- 200–500 m

0 km 60 120 180 km

N

Peninsular Malaysia labels: THAILAND, PERLIS, Langkawi, KEDAH, PENANG, P. Perhentian Kecil, P. Perhentian Besar, P. Redang, P. Pinang, P. Bidung Laut, KELANTAN, TERENGGANU, PERAK, P. Pangkor, PAHANG, SELANGOR, P. Ketam, P. Selat Kering, P. Pintu Gedung, KUALA LUMPUR, NEGERI SEMBILAN, MELAKA, P. Tioman, P. Pemanggil, P. Aur, P. Tinggi, P. Sibu Besar, JOHOR, SINGAPORE, Sumatra, INDONESIA

East Malaysia inset: Kota Kinabalu, SABAH, SARAWAK, INDONESIA

ramuan

malaysian healing traditions

Malaysia is home to a myriad of ethnic groups that live cohesively in this lush tropical land. The Malays, Chinese, Indians and Arabs who live here impart a diverse richness of healing cultures that are employed in spas throughout the country. It is common for one to find age-old Ayurvedic beauty regimens working in synergy with Chinese reflexology, acupuncture, Middle Eastern *hammam*, Malay baths and *ramuan* (indigenous medicinal plants and herbs).

As with other ancient Eastern healing philosophies, traditional Malay medicine believes that balance within the universe and the body is the foundation of health and wellbeing. Malays believe that outer beauty is a reflection of inner health, and to this end traditional healers advocate a varied, primarily plant-based diet comprising vegetables, fruits, grains and the best of nature's healing roots, bark, stems, seeds and flowers from the region's tropical forests. These plant-based healthcare remedies are handed down from mother to daughter in the Malay household.

Traditional Malay medicine combines the wisdom and practices of early Orang Asli (indigenous people) with those of the culturally more advanced Malay traders and voyagers who first settled in the region from as early as 1000 BC. Malaya, being on the Spice Trade Route, had the advantage of attracting congregations of traders from India, China and the Arab world who added their own medical philosophies to the Malay traditions. The biologically rich and diverse tropical rainforests, moreover, were and will continue to be an amazing source of ingredients.

tungku batu

The *tungku batu* or heated stone therapy has been used by the locals to help increase strength and vitality, as well as provide other benefits. This therapy is now one of the most popular among the traditional Malay therapies offered in spas throughout the country. River or clay stones are first wrapped with selected spices and herbs, which include fenugreek, black seed and leaves of betel and morinda. These are then tied together, using a cotton cloth to create a pouch. Medicated ointment is applied on the affected areas before the hot pouch is used as part of a deep-pressure massage to loosen muscles completely, alleviate pain, reduce inflammation and thoroughly relax the body. The technique is still widely practised by women after childbirth, as it helps to improve blood circulation and the functioning of the uterus; it also helps to

THIS PAGE: *Dawn is breaking on a misty morning over the hilly Malaysian highlands, home to an array of nature's rich harvest.*
PAGE 82: *A traditional body massage helps to ease the aches of a tired body.*

restore a firmer body after birth. In addition, the *tungku batu* is used to enhance agility in men. This treatment is recommended to relieve pressure on the spinal cord, and has proven effective in helping to correct and overcome chronic backache.

urut melayu

The *urut Melayu* is a traditional Malaysian massage that uses oil along with long kneading strokes to stimulate the flow of blood and energy through the *urat* (veins and arteries). The therapy is meant to invigorate the body.

muka berseri-seri

The *muka berseri-seri* is a traditional Malaysian facial treatment that makes use of a mini herbal pouch packed with commonly used local herbs, such as turmeric and wild ginger, to cleanse and recharge the skin. During the facial, the warmed pouch is pressed against the skin together with specific massage techniques, leaving the skin fresh and revitalised.

THIS PAGE (FROM TOP): *Vials of oil used in the urut Melayu massage; local ingredients such as spices and banana leaves are used in some spa rituals.*

OPPOSITE: *A woman relaxes in a mandi that can be enjoyed on its own or as part of a spa regime.*

lapis-lapis

The *lapis-lapis* or Malay herbal wrap was traditionally performed prior to a Malay massage as it draws out impurities from within the body. The wrap comprises a mixture of fresh warming herbs such as betel, ginger, lemongrass and galangal that is applied to the body. The body is then cosseted in warm sheets to induce sweating and detoxification, and to promote lymphatic drainage. Cooling aloe vera, turnip and cucumber wraps can also be used to cool down a build-up of excess heat.

ikal mayang

The *ikal mayang* or hair cream bath is just one of a range of hair care treatments traditionally used by women to keep their hair healthy, shiny and strong. Originally practised by Malay princesses, this treatment makes use of a combination of coconut oil, rice stalks and pandan leaves to deeply condition and strengthen hair from the roots to the tips.

mandi

A wide variety of Malay baths (*mandi*), often taken as a prelude or finale to a treatment, is offered in Malaysian spas. An eclectic mix of fruits, roots, leaves and flowers is added to the water to relax and heal the body. For example, in the *mandi bunga* or floral bath, exotic flowers such as roses, jasmine, *cempaka* and *kenanga* in addition to medicinal-aromatic woods such as sandalwood and *gaharu* combine to cleanse and thoroughly refresh the body.

ukup

The *ukup*, also known as body steaming, is the traditional method of internal cleansing. In the past, during this procedure, a person would sit over an earthenware pot (or *buyung*) filled with an aromatic concoction of roots, flowers and rose water heated to boiling point; this mixture was specially formulated

THIS PAGE (FROM TOP): *A platter of Indian spices that are routinely used in spas throughout Malaysia; a selection of indigenous Malaysian herbs including yellow nasturtium, variegated oregano, bay, Moroccan mint, fennel and curry grown in an organic garden.*

OPPOSITE: *A heated stone therapy session enjoyed on a beach.*

to provoke intense sweating and toxin elimination in the person undergoing treatment. *Ukup* was believed to be one of the quickest ways to bring the body back to equilibrium.

Unlike the traditional *ukup*, a variety of steam infusions is used in spas today, including *ukup wangi* or scented body steaming, which uses infusions from pandan leaves, tropical blooms such as jasmine and splashes of fresh kaffir lime leaves or rose water to penetrate the skin and leave the body refreshed and radiant; *ukup rempah* or spicy steam has a powerful detoxification effect, while *ukup kering* is a dry herbal steam that rejuvenates body and mind.

ramuan

Ramuan describes a carefully selected blend of medicinal plants and plant parts that Malaysians regularly consume to promote health, beauty and a balance in their daily lives. The variety of plants used in traditional *ramuan* depends on a combination of their medicinal properties. Several distinct plant parts including roots, rhizomes, bark, stems, fruits, flowers and seeds can be consumed as both medicine and food to optimise general wellbeing and health. For example, *ubat periuk* is a detoxifying herbal drink comprising senna leaves, betel leaves, galangal, ginger, and ingredients like *temu lawak*, *sepang*, *jemuju*, *cekur* and *lempoyang* that purge the body of excess heat and excess waste.

ulam

A significant number of edible plants double up as beauty aids and are widely consumed as *ulam* or herbal cocktails. The most common culinary herbs employed are mint, pandan leaves, lemongrass, kaffir lime leaves, torch ginger flowers and curry leaves, all of which are believed to have anti-ageing and skin-enhancing benefits. These herbs are combined with local health-promoting vegetables to make the freshest, most delicate *ulam*. Today, these herbal ingredients are available in markets throughout the country.

With its roots firmly grounded in Traditional Chinese Medicine, typical Malay therapies also incorporate Chinese techniques such as *tui na*, reflexology, moxibustion and acupuncture. These are all designed to rebalance, revitalise and harmonise the mind, body and spirit.

...balance within the universe and the body is the foundation of health and wellbeing.

spas in malaysia + singapore

west malaysia
The Spa at **Four Seasons Resort Langkawi** (Jalan Tanjung Rhu, 07000 Langkawi, Kedah Darul Aman) is quietly framed within stunning Moorish-inspired architecture that brilliantly captures the romance of this tranquil oasis. The *beras berseri* ritual at The Spa was created around a traditional skin-softening rite that begins with a rice-and-tamarind body polish to exfoliate and soften the skin. A warm rice flour-and-milk steam wrap follows, before the *urut Melayu* massage soothes the body.

Surrounded by century-old trees and lush vegetation, the spa villas at **CHI, The Spa** of **Shangri-La's Rasa Sayang Resort & Spa** (Batu Feringgi Beach, 11100 Penang) open onto thriving greenery, with outdoor bathtubs for soaking up beautiful views of the surroundings. The spa menu is heavily influenced by the ancient trade routes that brought spices through the region, incorporating the best of Thai, Ayurvedic and Chinese therapies using native herbs, spices and ointments. The signature Rasa Asmaradana is a gentle yet deeply penetrating massage that employs long firm strokes along with a heated herbal pouch to soothe the muscles.

Flanked by magnificent beaches and swaying palms, the **St Gregory Spa** at **Parkroyal Penang** (Batu Ferringi Beach, 11100 Penang) incorporates distinct Persian elements that blend subtly with native Malay artefacts to lend a warm ambience. A holistic menu of body therapies and rituals is available. Children are catered for too, with a mini menu of relaxing baths, body masks, manicures and pedicures that are the ideal introduction to the world of spas and wellness.

Located at the heart of the Multimedia Super Corridor in Cyberjaya, the **Sembunyi Spa** at **Cyberview Lodge Resort & Spa** (Persiaran Multimedia, 63000 Cyberjaya, Selangor) is a welcome respite from the dizzy world of technology. This Asian-themed spa comprises four thatch-roofed pavilions with stone façades, joined by a series of walkways and gardens. With an extensive menu of facials, body scrubs, wraps and bathing rituals, tension is eased in the most luxurious way possible. The massage menu features the *tungku batu* warm stone technique as well as herbal, vitality, serenity and tranquillity-styled therapies to de-stress and rejuvenate the body.

For a taste of authentic traditional Malay healing, the **Spa Village Tanjong Jara** (Batu 8, off Jalan Dungun, 23000 Dungun, Terengganu) is the place. Built to reflect the elegance and grandeur of the 17th-century palaces of Malay sultans, the spa focuses solely on traditional Malay healing practices. Every treatment begins with a *mandi bunga* (floral bath), the customary pre-wedding ritual for both genders to rid the body of negative energies. The overall philosophy of the resort is the Malay concept of *sucimurni*, which roughly translates as wellness through purity of mind, body and spirit. All the treatments offered use spa products made from indigenous herbs and plants.

east malaysia

One of the most stunning features of **CHI, The Spa** at **Shangri-La's Tanjung Aru Resort & Spa** (20 Jalan Aru, Tanjung Aru, 88100 Kota Kinabalu, Sabah) is the dramatic Yoga Pavilion. Strategically situated on the western side of the island, with a timber deck partly suspended over the water, it offers breathtaking views of the ocean and sunsets to yoga enthusiasts.

The all-inclusive menu features a range of Chinese, Himalayan and Malaysian-inspired therapies, among which the exotic Borneo Therapy is a highlight. Inspired by the traditions of the island's healers (*bobohizan*), this treatment begins with a foot ritual using seven types of herbs that, when combined, are believed to remove negative energy. It is followed by a massage that awakens sluggish energy and revitalises the body.

singapore

Stylish sophistication is easily within reach at Asia's first **Remède Spa** in **The St Regis Singapore** (29 Tanglin Road, Singapore 247911), with customised skincare being just one of the reasons to experience the enticing range of decadent spa therapies. Based on the origins of spa, the finest bathing rituals are reinterpreted in an innovative and contemporary manner. From genuine cedarwood Finnish saunas, eucalyptus-scented steam chambers, ice fountains, traditional Middle Eastern *hammam* and Rasul experiences, the healing benefits of water promise to flush out toxins completely and leave the skin cleansed and hydrated.

THIS PAGE (FROM TOP): Warm jade is used in some therapies offered at the well-furnished Remède Spa; guests may wish to relax in the wet lounge area of the Remède Spa.
OPPOSITE: The CHI, The Spa therapy suites in Shangri-La's Rasa Sayang Resort & Spa are appointed to soothe guests, readying them for their chosen treatment programme.

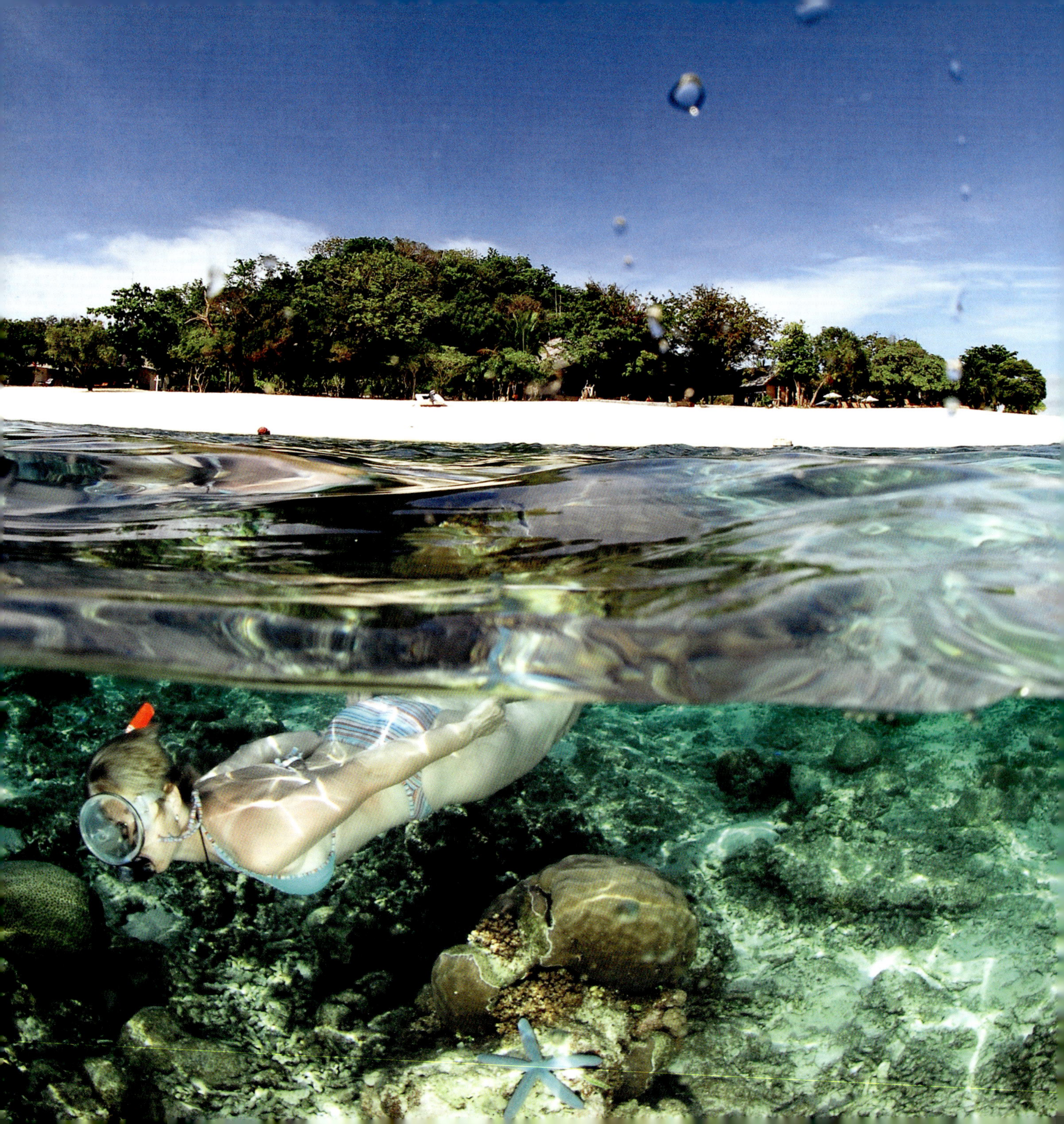

filipinotraditions

the philippines

filipino traditions

indigenous island healers

The Philippines consists of myriad islands separated by vast stretches of sea. As the Philippines was colonised by both Spain and America, and has been influenced through trade by the great medical traditions of China, India and Greek-Persia, the country is culturally unique. Traditional healers whose wisdom has been passed down through generations remain at the forefront of healing practices throughout the 42,000 villages countrywide.

As with other Asian indigenous therapies, Filipino healers believe that the universe (macrocosm or *kalawakan*) and humankind (microcosm or *sangkatauhan*) are intricately connected. Healers tend to hold the utmost respect for their environment and hold the view that nature and humankind should live together in harmony and peace. As such, they believe that any fluctuations occurring within the body are a direct consequence of environmental change.

hilot

Hilot is the oldest and one of the most popular traditional healing therapies in the Philippines, still practised daily, even in the most remote villages. Its reputation has spread well beyond the Philippines and can be found on spa menus throughout the world. Technically, *hilot* is a massage therapy in which the *hilot* therapist harnesses the energies from the surrounding world—the environment, the oils and herbal poultices being used during therapy—and transfers them to the client through specialised indigenous massage techniques geared to rebalance the body and restore harmony.

paligo

Paligo is a bathing ritual using decoctions of tropical medicinal leaves and flowers. When combined in a warm bath, the mixture helps relieve symptoms ranging from lethargy to coughs and colds, as well as remedying fertility issues.

oslob

Oslob is a therapy in which the patient inhales the steam from infusions of a mixture of medicinal herbs. The herbs used are normally 'hot' in nature and include *yerba buena* (mint leaves), *sambong* (Blumea camphor) and *balanoy* (sweet basil), among others. The patient lies under a small cotton tent while the steam infused with this herbal cocktail induces a state of deep calm and relaxation. *Oslob* is used primarily to treat those suffering from excessive 'cold' or 'wind' energy.

THIS PAGE (FROM TOP): A massage pavilion at dusk at Mandala Spa Borocay; a hilot therapist traces the acupoints in a patient's hand to relieve pain.

PAGE 92: A woman swimming in the pristine waters surrounding the Philippine islands.

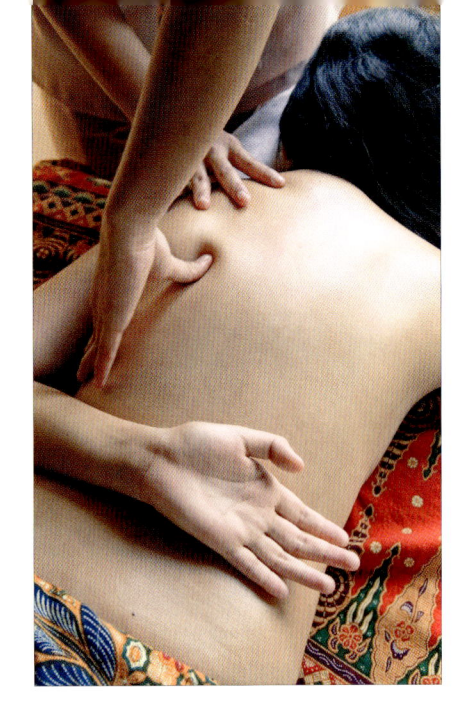

dinalisay

Dinalisay are decoctions of indigenous medicinal foods and herbs grown in certified organic farms in the Philippines. The decoctions can be classified as Hot, Cold, Earth, Wind, Fire and Water and, when taken according to the prescription, will help restore overall balance to the body. For example, a hot *dinalisay* may contain 'hot' foods and herbs such as ginger, tamarind, capsicum, mango and jackfruit which will help rebalance the body's energy. In contrast, a cold *dinalisay* may utilise 'cold' foods and herbs such as avocado, guavaand banana to cool and realign the system.

kisig galing

Kisig galing is a form of biomagnetic energy healing performed exclusively by gifted traditional healers, who use their hands as a medium for the transfer of positive energy (*kisig*) to the patient with the aim of healing (*galing*) and rebalancing the body.

tapik kawayan

The *tapik kawayan* or bamboo tap is a massage technique that is routinely used to clear blocked energy so as to stimulate and reharmonise the body. Using a special long bamboo stick (*kawayan*), the therapist focuses on the specific parts of the body believed to house energy blocks. By gently tapping with the stick, the blocked energy is released, tension is eased and the body is revitalised. This technique is generally applied on the back and gluteal muscles, the upper and lower arms and the thighs and legs.

moxa ventoza

Derived from the ancient Chinese therapy called moxibustion, *moxa ventoza* is a time-tested method for clearing toxins and excessive 'cold' energy from the body. Heat-resistant glass vacuum cups are warmed and applied to key energy points, primarily along the back, to create a vacuum that draws out toxins and cold energy from within the body. Following that, a soothing massage using native virgin coconut oil will nourish and calm the skin.

dagdagay

This authentic tribal foot massage commences with a warm footbath infused with native flowers. The footbath helps to draw out impurities from the skin. A herbal clay mask is then applied on the feet to cleanse and exfoliate the skin. After removing the clay, bamboo sticks are gently tapped against the soles of each foot to stimulate blood and energy flow in the feet, before a soothing leg and foot massage is administered to invigorate the body.

THIS PAGE (FROM TOP): A woman enjoying a full-body massage; the therapist uses a herbal clay mask to exfoliate the skin of the feet as part of the traditional dagdagay tribal foot massage.

OPPOSITE: A guest relaxes beside a private bath surrounded by greenery at the Edsa Shangri-La, Manila.

...Filipino healers believe that the universe... and humankind... are intricately connected.

filipinotraditions 97

spas in the philippines

boracay island

Yoga devotees will love practising yoga in the floating studio built over a tranquil pond at **CHI, The Spa at Shangri-La** in Shangri-La's **Boracay Resort & Spa** (Barangay Yapak, Boracay Island, Malay, Aklan 5608). In the signature Boracay Sand and Sea therapy, a blend of fine white silica, natural sea salts and virgin coconut oil combines to deeply exfoliate and purify the skin, before a stimulating lymphatic massage further cleanses from within, leaving the skin radiant.

cebu

The exquisite Water Shiatsu pavilion in **CHI, The Spa** at **Shangri-La's Mactan Resort & Spa** (Punta Engaño Road, Lapu-Lapu, Cebu 6015) is the setting for experiencing *watsu* (water *shiatsu*), a specialised body therapy that eases your muscles and improves flexibility while you float weightlessly in a pool of warm water. The CHI Water Garden Pavilion, complete with infinity-edged vitality pool, aroma-infused beds and body scrub *sala*, is the perfect prelude to every spa treatment.

Also in Cebu, the luxurious **Mogambo Springs** spa at **Plantation Bay Resort & Spa** (Marigondon,

Mactan Island, Cebu 6015) is designed to resemble an 18th-century Tokugawa-period village, complete with waterfalls, a creek and ambience that is filled with a fog-like mist.

A tempting range of therapies is available—from facials, mineral baths, hydro-massage and saunas, to the German Dorn Method of spinal alignment. This is purported to relieve a range of back and neck disorders. For those wanting to indulge further, the Ultimate Mogambo Springs experience combines many therapies into one extravagant spa ritual.

manila

For a taste of authentic Philippine healing, a visit to **CHI, The Spa** at **Edsa Shangri-La, Manila** (1 Garden Way, Ortigas Centre, Mandaluyong City 1650) is a must. With a menu of treatments packed with native herbs, flowers and virgin coconut oil—which is renowned for its benefits when applied to the skin and hair—the spa is a place where peace and serenity can be restored. The private library lounge and cosy comforts of CHI soothe both body and mind.

pamalican island

The island of Pamalican is home to **Amanpulo** (Pamalican Island, Philippines), a tropical hideaway surrounded by the brilliant blue Sulu Sea. The rich healing traditions of the Cuyonin islanders feature in the spa's menu of scrubs, wraps, soaks, massages and facials. These luxurious spa treats are available in the privacy of your own spa *casita* or in the resort's open-air Garden Sala.

THIS PAGE (CLOCKWISE FROM TOP): Opulent furnishings come together in the therapy suites of CHI, The Spa to create cosy nooks where guests can relax before or after treatment; the signature CHI cashmere robes enfold guests in warmth; indigenous herbs are often used to create compresses that play a part in therapeutic massages.

OPPOSITE (FROM TOP): *Himalayan stones are an intrinsic element of the exotic Himalayan-inspired rituals on offer at CHI, The Spa in Shangri-La's Mactan Resort & Spa; a traditional floral bath is involved in several of the programmes available at Mogambo Springs.*

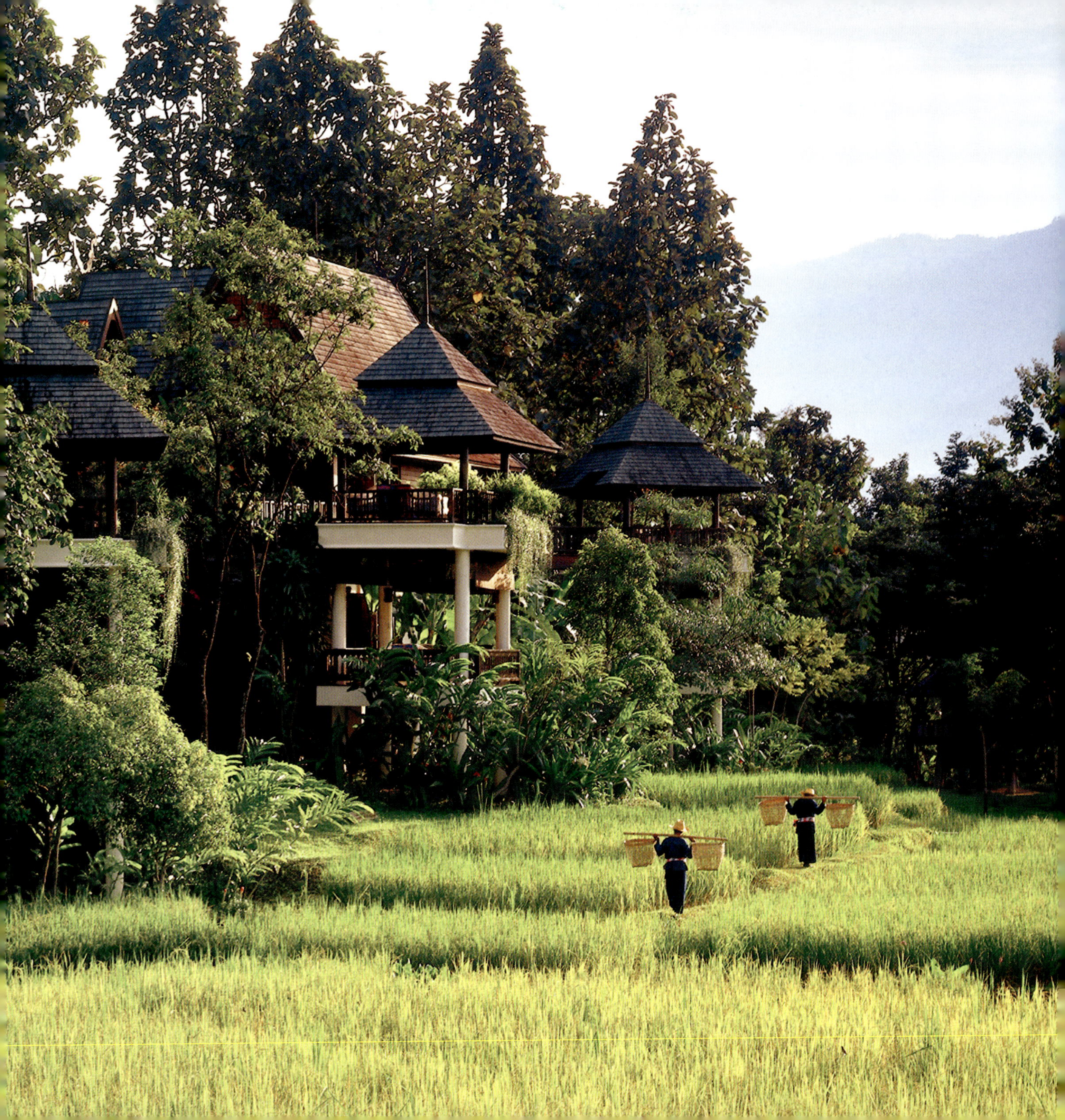

thaitherapies

thailand

North Thailand
- Four Seasons Resort Chiang Mai
- Shangri-La Hotel, Chiang Mai

Bangkok
- Salus Per Crystal®
- Grand Hyatt Erawan, Bangkok
- i.sawan Residential Spa + Club
- Pranali Wellness Spa
- Shangri-La Hotel, Bangkok
- THANN Sanctuary Gaysorn

Hua Hin
- Anantara Hua Hin
- Chiva-Som
- THE BARAI

Koh Samui
- Absolute Sanctuary
- Kamalaya Koh Samui

Phuket / South
- Anantara Phuket Resort + Spa
- Six Senses Destination Spa - Phuket
- The Racha
- Pimalai Resort + Spa
- Anantara Si Kao Resort + Spa

Legend
- International Airport
- Lake
- Dry Salt Lake
- 2000–3000 m
- 1000–2000 m
- 500–1000 m
- 200–500 m
- 0–200 m

0 km 50 100 150 km

thai therapies

buddhist origin

With its rich cultural heritage, history of indigenous medicine and appetising cuisine, Thailand is a popular spa destination for discerning travellers. From the effervescent city of Bangkok to the hilly northern region of Chiang Mai and the tropical beaches on the islands of Phuket, Krabi and Koh Samui, numerous exotic spas are available for experiencing the very best in Thai healing and pampering.

Buddhism is the dominant religion in Thailand, with temples on almost every street bearing testimony to the Thais' religious devotion. In the past, Buddhist temples were centres of learning, both of religion and worldly matters such as astrology, medicine and healing.

It is a Thai belief that most diseases flow from a troubled heart or mind, so Thai-style healing is enveloped in a rich and intricate tradition of prayer, meditation and mantras. In Thai medicine, the key to overall health lies in maintaining the balance between body and nature.

Thai medicine is split into three disciplines: religious or spiritual healing, manipulative (Thai) massage, and diet or herbal medicine. As herbs and food have a profound effect on the healing process, they are considered fundamental therapies in themselves.

thai massage

Thai massage or *nuat bo'rarn* is one of the oldest and most popular forms of Thai treatment offered in spas throughout Thailand and around the world. It is a traditional healing art developed by Jivaka Kumar Bhaccha or the revered 'Father Doctor' of Thai medicine. Thai massage is based on the stretching techniques of Indian Ayurveda and Chinese acupressure.

To the uninitiated, Thai massage is associated with pain and discomfort, involving contortions of all sorts of unimaginable body positions while being kneaded deeply by a therapist. To the devoted, Thai massage is a healing, physically energising and spiritual experience that aids relaxation and helps to prevent disease.

A typical massage is performed on a floor mat with both the therapist and recipient wearing loose comfortable clothing. In accordance with Buddhist philosophy, the session begins with a meditative prayer or *puja* (in the original Pali language), designed to help the therapist reach a meditative state that is in turn imparted to the recipient during the session. After gently squeezing the limbs to warm the body, the therapist uses his or her hands, forearms, knees and feet to apply pressure to the body's *sên* or acupoints to encourage a smoother flow of energy.

THIS PAGE (FROM TOP): Thai healing traditions originate from the country's Buddhist temples; a young woman experiencing authentic Thai massage.

PAGE 100: The Four Seasons Resort Chiang Mai is surrounded by acres of flourishing greenery.

THIS PAGE (FROM TOP): *Herbs and spices are wrapped in a herbal compress, ready to be used in herbal bolus treatment; body masks are one of the range of decadent therapies offered at the Pimalai Spa.*

OPPOSITE: *Everyone should stay in a luxurious pool villa at the Anantara Phuket Resort & Spa at least once in a lifetime.*

While Thai massage does not necessarily seek to relax the body, it is a dynamic physical experience that integrates body, mind and spirit. When performed in a quiet, meditative atmosphere, the technique loosens the body completely, releasing tension and thoroughly invigorating the system. Relaxation is an incidental bonus of successful massage session.

herbal healing

Thais fervently believe that herbal medicine is an essential part of health and wellness. They use it primarily to maintain good health rather than to treat specific diseases. Using time-tested recipes, the toxic effects of pollution and pesticides can be reduced while energy, immunity and sexuality are enhanced; the result is overall happiness and longevity.

Most of the plant-based ingredients are taken from the local fields and kitchens, and are chosen specifically for their effects on the body. For instance, turmeric is a natural antioxidant and helps to cleanse the system; ginger nourishes, moisturises and warms the body; garlic, galangal and chilli help protect the body from illness.

The ingredients can either be blended according to time-honoured recipes and consumed as a tonic, or used directly on the body as a compress or paste. The paste is spread over the body, paying extra attention to drier areas such as the elbows, knees and feet, after which the body is massaged.

In the Thai herbal *bolus* treatment, herbs and spices are tightly wrapped in muslin or cotton fabric, and the *bolus* is infused in steam. The infusion is inhaled by the patient and absorbed through the pores to calm and rebalance the system. This therapeutic hot *bolus* can also be used as an aid in body massage to relieve tension and stimulate circulation. It is especially popular with women who have recently given birth as the hot *bolus* soothes and calms the muscles while the herbal steam eases the mind.

Other Thai beauty rituals that are very popular in spas throughout the country include face and body masks made of specific herbs, flowers and fresh foods. The ingredients are blended into a paste which is then applied to the skin. Classic examples include the traditional honey-and-cucumber facial and the papaya body polish.

...numerous exotic spa abodes are available for experiencing the very best in authentic Thai healing.

spas in thailand

bangkok + surroundings

A sense of space pervades the sprawling **CHI, The Spa** at **Shangri-La Hotel, Bangkok** (89 Soi Wat Suan Plu, New Road, Bangrak, Bangkok 10500). The Garden Suite is the largest spa suite in Bangkok and features a private tropical garden with an infinity bath set in a lotus pond. The signature Himalayan Tsangpo Ritual is inspired by the pure waters of the Himalayan plateau and combines a gentle salt exfoliation with a cleanser made from indigenous salt, mud and *silagit* (a rare, rejuvenating mineral extract). After being wrapped with mud in the warmth of a heated plinth, the treatment session ends with a soothing Himalayan Head and Shoulder massage.

In Thai mythology i.sawan is the fifth level of heaven. On the fifth floor of the **Grand Hyatt Erawan** in Bangkok (494 Rajdamri Road, Bangkok 10330) and surrounded by frangipani gardens, the attractively designed spa cottages of **i.sawan spa** are the ideal haven; one can sleep, eat, enjoy a spa treatment and simply relax within this secluded retreat. Of note, the Man Space menu is a series of high-performance face and massage therapies specifically tailored to cater to the needs of busy executives.

Bangkok's stylish **Pranali Wellness Spa** (989 Siam Paragon Tower, Rama 1 Road, Pathumwan, Bangkok) is dedicated to complete wellness. It combines contemporary aesthetics with ancient healing practices, sophisticated technology and custom-created products to recharge stressed-out city types. The spa's eclectic menu features slimming, fitness, anti-ageing,

THIS PAGE (FROM TOP): *The view over the water from the infinity pool at Anumba Spa is breathtaking; guests may wish to enjoy a Thai massage in one of the outdoor pavilions at CHI, The Spa at Shangri-La Hotel Bangkok.*

OPPOSITE: *Practising yoga at dawn overlooking the lush tropical vegetation at the Four Seasons Resort Chiang Mai helps release the stresses of everyday life.*

skin management and detox treatments in addition to yoga, pilates and other trusted practices deliberately chosen to rejuvenate and harmonise both body and soul.

At **THANN Sanctuary**, the ambience of the day spa (3rd floor, Gaysorn, 999 Ploenchit Road, Lumpini, Patumwan, Bangkok 10330) instantly invokes a feeling of peace and calm. Using the famed THANN organic product range that is now available in stores from Tokyo to Paris, THANN Sanctuary spa is the perfect place to experience the natural healing benefits of these products.

Detached from the stresses of the busy Bangkok streets, **Sareerarom Tropical Spa** (117 Thonglor Soi 10, Sukhumvit 55, Wattana, Bangkok 10110) is an institution for holistic wellness. A typical journey to health incorporates a doctor or dermatologist's consultation before a regime of massages, scrubs, wraps, baths and facial therapies is prescribed and customised to individual needs.

Crystal Day Spa by **Salus per Crystal®** (189/5–6 Moo 7, Liangmuang Road, Bangtarad, Pakkret, Nontaburi) is an extraordinary charcoal-grey structure in the Bangkok suburbs that has been hailed as an architectural masterpiece. The spa's comprehensive menu includes facial treatments, scrubs, wraps, a variety of massages (using stones, hot chocolate, aromatherapy and Royal Thai techniques) and crystal therapy. In the latter, skilled therapists use a combination of colour and crystal therapy to gently manipulate the body's energy and release pain and stress.

spas in thailand

THIS PAGE (FROM TOP): Therapists hold their hands over a guest's forehead to calm the mind before treatment begins at Absolute Sanctuary; some time spent soaking in a floral bath at The Spa at Four Seasons Resort Chiang Mai may help relax the body and restore the soul.

OPPOSITE (CLOCKWISE FROM TOP): The highly trained staff cater to guests' every whim at Absolute Sanctuary; the Emotional Freedom Technique at Chiva-Som is effective in helping one release negative feelings; sit on the balcony and sip a cool drink after your treatment at the Anantara Si Kao Resort & Spa.

hua hin

The award-winning design of **The Barai** at **Hyatt Regency Hua Hin** (91 Hua Hin–Khao Takiap Road, Hua Hin 77110) is inspired by the grandeur of the Khmer culture. Throughout the deep corridors and fortress-like walls of the 1.8-hectare (4.5-acre) site, art merges with design and sunlight dances with shadows to lead guests on a journey to inner peace. The signature custom Thai Herbal Compress is as authentic as it gets. Combining the healing power of touch with specific herbal recipes, it eases emotional tension and realigns the body's energy in the gentlest way.

Anantara Hua Hin Resort & Spa (43/1 Phetkasem Beach Road, Hua Hin 77110) is nestled in 5.7 hectares (14 acres) of magnificently manicured tropical gardens overlooking the Gulf of Thailand. The resort is surrounded by royal palaces, world-class golf courses and fishing villages—all in the heart of historic Hua Hin.

At the **Anantara Spa**, each of the spa's seven suites is set in its own individual garden courtyard. The menu reads like a gourmet meal, with a mouthwatering selection of tempting exotic treatments to choose from. The signature Culture of Anantara ritual begins with a *shirodhara* head massage, which is considered one of the most powerful Ayurvedic treatments available. This is followed by a stress-relieving back massage that utilises firm pressure to relieve tension in the body. The treatment then culminates in a luxuriously rich honey-and-milk bath that will leave the skin silky soft and radiantly glowing.

phuket

The Anantara Phuket Resort & Spa (888 Moo 3, Tumbon Mai Khao, Thalang, Phuket) is set in Sirinath Marine National Park, a natural playground consisting of sea caves, mangrove forests and coral reefs. The Signature Massage at **Anantara Spa Phuket** allows guests to experience the benefits of traditional Thai healing in chic surroundings. Working with the body's meridian lines, the therapist uses a unique blend of oils and specific massage techniques to stimulate blood circulation and rebalance the body.

Anumba Spa at **The Racha** resort (42/12–13 Moo 5, Rawai, Muang, 83130 Phuket).on Racha Yai island, the Southern tip of Phuket, seamlessly fuses cutting-edge design and facilities with the stunning island landscape. Each of the nine therapy suites features a terrazzo plunge tub, steam shower and outdoor rainshower scattered among coconut and frangipani trees—the perfect respite for soul therapy.

sikao

The over-water therapy rooms at **Anantara Si Kao Resort & Spa** (198–199 Moo 5, Had Pak Meng, Changlang Road, Maifad, Si Kao, Trang 92150) are elegantly designed in traditional Thai style. A key feature of the therapy menu at the **Anantara Spa** is Wellness 360, a programme designed to enhance health, beauty and overall wellbeing. Treatments are tailor-made by the resident naturopathic doctor and performed by highly trained therapists using massage, yoga, meditation and detox techniques customised to individuals' needs and desires.

chiang mai

CHI, The Spa at **Shangri-La Hotel**, Chiang Mai (89/8 Chang Klan Road, Muang, Chiang Mai 50100) is fashioned around a northern Thai fishing village. The stylish design combines endemic Thai Lanna bamboo and flowering plumeria with signature water features. The spa's Lanna Blend Massage incorporates Thai massage movements with rhythmic strokes. The added application of warm healing stones ensures relief from muscle tension and encourages the smooth flow of energy through the body.

Waterfalls, elephants and cicadas create a symphony of sound that resonates through the rice paddy, lakes and gardens that encircle **The Spa** at **Four Seasons Resort Chiang Mai** (Mae Rim–Samoeng Old Road, Mae Rim, Chiang Mai 50180). The therapies capitalise on the plentiful supply of indigenous herbs, spices and aromatic oils (many from the resort's organic garden) which, once applied using intense massage techniques, soothe and restore the body.

koh lanta

Set in 40.4 hectares (100 acres) of tropical vegetation overlooking the Andaman Sea in southern Koh Lanta, the straw-roofed *sala* of **Pimalai Spa** at **Pimalai Resort & Spa** (99 Moo 5, Ba Kan Tiang Beach, Koh Lanta, Krabi) blends with the jungle. Here, the Royal Siam Massage with Luk Pra Kob combines aromatic Thai herbs prepared as steaming poultices with manual pressure on the body's energy lines and stretching manipulation to relieve tension and restore the body's energy.

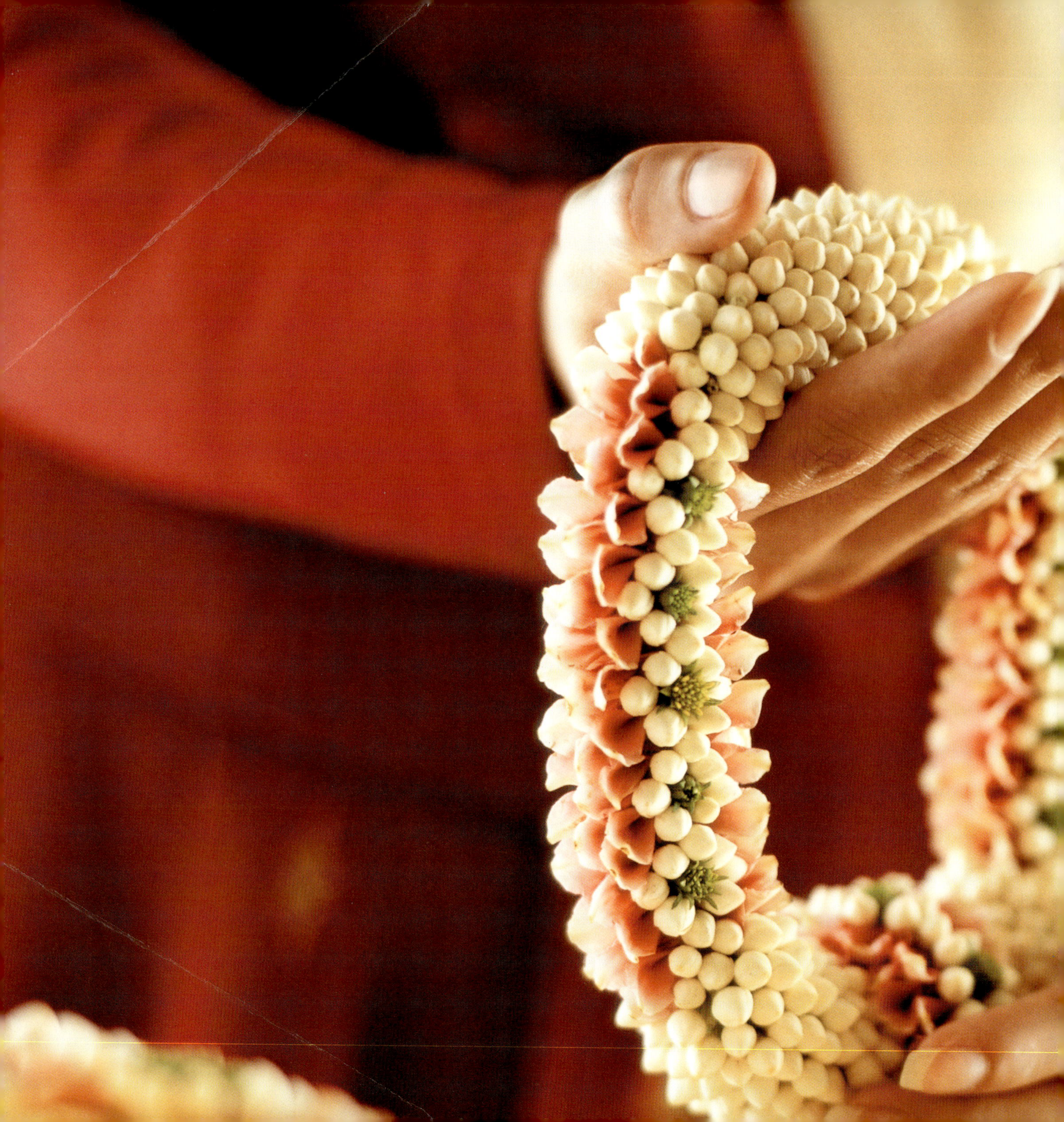

spa+retreats

From spas set in tranquil beach resorts to chic urban city spas, from destination spas nestled against stunning mountain backdrops offering alternative medicine to state-of-the-art medispas featuring cutting-edge treatments, these are our recommendations of the very best that the exciting Asian spa scene has to offer.

pudong shangri-la, shanghai + shangri-la hotel, chengdu

Traditional Chinese medicine and healing techniques form the basis for countless remedies used worldwide. From an intimate understanding of herbal ingredients, to an advanced alternative map of human physiology, the Chinese civilisation holds answers to many of our newest health concerns.

Built upon these foundations is CHI, The Spa, an imprint of the Shangri-La luxury hotel group devoted to creating unique sanctuaries where such ancient principles may be honoured. Designed to combine the wisdom of China and the Himalayan region with contemporary service and amenities, each property offers its menu of exclusive Eastern treatments in stunning surroundings inspired by Himalayan temples and architecture.

After the concept was first unveiled in Bangkok in 2004, mainland China became a natural choice for the brand's future expansion.

Over 20 spas are to open in the near future, proving the mainstream appeal of traditional Chinese techniques. As in all things valued for their natural and healthy traits, however, it is always better to head straight for the source.

Pudong Shangri-La, Shanghai

The prestigious Pudong Shangri-La in Shanghai became the site of China's first CHI, an 800-sq-m (8,611-sq-ft) collection of nine spacious spa suites in the heart of the Lujiazui commercial district, overlooking the activity on the Huangpu River and the Bund. Readily accommodating both single guests as well as couples, each suite is designed to be a 'spa within a spa' with private infinity baths, steam rooms, showers, changing areas and lounges where guests can relax after treatments.

Every visit is informed by the theory of the Five Elements central to Chinese philosophy and the concept of inner life-force. Upon arrival,

THIS PAGE (FROM LEFT): *The Crystal Facial is a signature treatment at Pudong Shangri-La; a spa suite complete with a resting lounge, ideal for couples, is a fabulous treat for guests to Pudong Shangri-La, Shanghai's CHI, The Spa.*
OPPOSITE: *Be spoilt by the spacious pool at the Shangri-La Hotel, Chengdu.*

china **shanghai + chengdu**

guests are treated to a personal consultation which determines their unique 'element signs', allowing for customised treatments aimed at restoring the balance between the fire, wood, metal, water and earth elements within the body. A menu of more than 40 signature therapies, body massages, facials and skincare treatments are available, put together by a team of experts and delivered by CHI's highly trained spa professionals.

Shangri-La Hotel, Chengdu

Over at the Shangri-La Hotel, Chengdu, in a city on the old Silk Road, ringed with mountains and home of China's much-loved pandas, all of CHI's superb services are available. With its Shanghai counterpart, this is one of the first to introduce a new Crystal Energising Facial treatment from Futuresse, a German luxury cosmetics line made from Asian ingredients. The facials use gemstones blended into rich creams to spark skin regeneration at the cellular level.

Himalayan Water Therapies are a great way to start off a visit by putting the entire body at ease with relaxing music, aroma oils and a soak in a bath of natural salts or even a soothing Lotus Milk blend from Myanmar by Futuresse. Choose a Yin Yang Harmonising Massage or the one-of-a-kind Himalayan Healing Stone Massage, inspired by the ancient rituals of Lake Kokonar, where a combination of hot stones are treated in aromatic essential oils in order to induce a complete release of tension.

rooms
Shanghai: 948 rooms and suites •
9 spa villas
Chengdu: 593 rooms and suites •
11 spa villas

food
Shanghai: Yi Café • Jade on 36 • Nadaman • Sushi Bar by Nadaman • Gui Hua Lou • Fook Lam Moon
Chengdu: Café Z • Shang Palace

drink
Shanghai: Gourmet • Jade on 36 bar • Lobby Lounge • The Lounge
Chengdu: Businessman Lounge • Lobby Lounge • Mooney's Irish Pub

features
traditional Chinese and Himalayan treatments • hydrotherapy suites • steam rooms and showers • gyms and health club

nearby
Shanghai: The Bund • Huangpu River • shopping • nightlife • Oriental Pearl TV Tower
Chengdu: Panda Research Base • China Lane • Jinli Street

contact
Shanghai:
33 Fu Cheng Road
Pudong, 200120 Shanghai, China •
telephone: +86.21.6882 8888 •
facsimile: +86.21.6882 6688 •
email: slpu@shangri-la.com •
website: www.shangri-la.com

Chengdu:
9 Binjiang Dong Road
610021 Chengdu, Sichuan, China •
telephone: +86.28.8888 9999 •
facsimile: +86.28.8888 6666 •
email: slcd@shangri-la.com •
website: www.shangri-la.com

shangri-la hotel, beijing + shangri-la hotel, guangzhou

The concept of *chi*, or inner energy, is well understood in Chinese society; it forms a common point between major philosophies that concern health and the body, from acupuncture to traditional herbal medicine. The ability to unblock areas where the flow of inner energy has stopped is intrinsically linked to recovery and wellbeing. That belief forms the foundation of CHI, The Spa, a one-of-a-kind spa concept from the Shangri-La group that has found an ideal home in the cities of Beijing and Guangzhou.

Inspired by the healing traditions of ancient Chinese, Himalayan and other Asian cultures, CHI, The Spa seeks to restore harmony in accordance with the Five Elements Theory. This concept is based on the interrelationship between metal, water, wood, fire and earth. According to the theory, all substances fall into one of these categories, and the elements need to be balanced within the body. All staff are highly trained in this ancient philosophy, which guides CHI, The Spa's menu, with many graduating from additional training at Shangri-La's highly regarded spa academy.

CHI, The Spa in the Shangri-La Hotel, Beijing and Guangzhou were both designed in line with the Himalayan and Chinese origins of many of the treatments. The interiors are furnished like Himalayan temples, with symbols such as the eternity double knot appearing in every detail. The teak sliding doors, Himalayan drums, carved sandalwood and other artefacts on display also help to shape a wholly authentic Eastern spa experience. However, since each spa offers its own exclusive advantages, lovers of luxury will do well to visit both.

THIS PAGE (FROM LEFT): *Savour a steaming cup of herbal tea in the beautiful garden at Shangri-La Hotel, Beijing; upon stepping into the Reception Sanctum at Shangri-La Hotel, Guangzhou, one immediately appreciates the refined design touches and the serene atmosphere.*

OPPOSITE: *Suites at the Shangri-La Hotel, Guangzhou have cosy places to relax, outfitted with plush armchairs, soothing lighting and aromatic scents.*

china beijing + guangzhou

Shangri-La Hotel, Beijing

The Shangri-La Hotel, Beijing debuted its CHI, The Spa in March 2007, in conjunction with the opening of a Valley Wing extension. A full 1,000 sq m (10,764 sq ft) is devoted to the spa's 11 treatment suites, which adopt CHI, The Spa's signature 'spa within a spa' concept. Creating a self-contained sanctuary in every suite for the ultimate in luxury and privacy, this design approach equips each spacious room with its own colour-therapy bath, herbal steam shower, relaxation lounge, bathroom and changing area.

A fine example of how Chinese traditions are woven into the experience is the Empress Imperial Jade Journey, which was inspired by a beauty treatment once reserved for royalty. First, guests will experience the Luxurious Lotus Milk Bath and the Milk and Honey Wrap, followed by a back massage and the Luxurious and Pampering Imperial Jade Facial. The latter is a massage performed with a piece of rare jade and 'golden caviar', an opulent caviar extract with anti-ageing and anti-wrinkle properties.

Shangri-La Hotel, Guangzhou

At the Shangri-La Hotel, Guangzhou, CHI, The Spa offers a similarly extravagant facial treatment. The Oriental Pearl Radiance Facial utilises the finest Nano Pearl Powder for greater absorption into the skin, where the substance's amino acids and minerals can go to work on improving clarity and elasticity. The procedure also includes a back massage, pressure-point face massage and a green tea compress to complete what is known in Chinese medicine as a 'cooling' procedure to combat the effects of stress and toxins.

rooms
Beijing: 670 rooms and suites • 11 spa suites
Guangzhou: 704 rooms and suites •
11 spa suites

food
Beijing: Blu Lobster • Café Cha • Nishimura •
Shang Palace • The Delicatessen
Guangzhou: coolThai • il Forno • Nadaman •
Summer Palace • WOK TOO Café

drink
Beijing: Cloud Nine Bar • Lobby Lounge •
The Garden Bar and Terrace
Guangzhou: Lift Bar • Lobby Lounge •
Poolside Bar and Grill

features
traditional Chinese and Himalayan treatments •
private steam rooms and showers •
health clubs • pools • hydrotherapy suites

nearby
Beijing: Beijing Exhibition Hall • Beijing Zoo •
Hou Hai Hutong and Bar Street • Financial Street • Zhongguancun Technology Area •
Summer Palace
Guangzhou: International Convention and Exhibition Centre

contact
Beijing:
29 Zizhuyuan Road
Haidian District, 100089 Beijing, China •
telephone: +86.10.6841 2211 •
facsimile: +86.10.6841 8002 •
email: slb@shangri-la.com •
website: www.shangri-la.com

Guangzhou:
1 Hui Zhan Dong Road, Hai Zhu District
510308 Guangzhou, Guangdong, China •
telephone: +86.20.8917 8888 •
facsimile: +86.20.8917 8899 •
email: slpg@shangri-la.com •
website: www.shangri-la.com

shui urban spa

THIS PAGE: Sprawl on plush daybeds on the terrace, and watch the clouds go by before one's therapy session begins.

OPPOSITE (FROM LEFT): The striking 'wave light' wall behind the reception desk immediately welcomes guests to the signature white-on-white design and makes a stylish allusion to the spa's name, which is Mandarin for water; when guests leave, they take home with them cute white rubber ducks as souvenirs.

Shanghai's recent explosive growth and the changes that it has wrought on the social landscape have been widely discussed, but the steady attraction of the general populace to such new luxuries as day spas can also be attributed to the dedicated efforts of a few talented entrepreneurs. The SHUI Urban Spa, located in downtown Shanghai, is the product of two such people, an investment banker from New York and a corporate lawyer from Boston. They embarked on this newest joint venture only after achieving international success with three other spas.

Every facet of SHUI Urban Spa's design seems geared towards creating a brand new standard for spas in China and introducing the joys of regular spa visits to new visitors. For one, its location is superbly convenient. Housed in a restored Art Deco building on Ferguson Lane, the spa has a coffee house, wine gallery, homeware store and a couple of designer boutiques for neighbours, making the already central address an all-in-one lifestyle destination. The spa also eschews the common tropical paradise aesthetic favoured by many local establishments, instead setting itself apart with a clean, contemporary décor scheme that is predominantly white but is tempered with soft lights and shadows—in step with the city's fashionable character.

That is not to say that SHUI Urban Spa is unapproachable; in fact it's the very opposite. A sense of playfulness pervades the 350-sq-m (3,767-sq-ft) space. References to its brand name—Mandarin for 'water'—are hidden everywhere. Some are subtle while others are adorable, such as the little white rubber ducks that adorn the reception area; these are later presented as mementoes to visitors as they leave. Thoughtful details in every one of the six treatment rooms ensure comfort at every step. Temperature and ambient music are individually controlled in each one, and underfloor heating is present throughout the premises. Clever planning allows the rooms to be reconfigured to form larger spaces that can accommodate couples, or even groups.

In aspiring to give modern Shanghainese a reason to fall in love with day spas, SHUI Urban Spa offers in its repertory a blend of

china **shanghai**

Eastern and Western techniques, as well as a variety of massages, facials, manicures, pedicures, waxes, prenatal treatments and even a range specifically tailored to male clients. The treatments exclusively utilise Dermalogica products, and SHUI has the distinction of being the only independent spa in the city to have them. Best of all, prices fall comfortably below what one would expect to pay at a comparable five-star hotel spa. Thus, regular indulgence is encouraged and even rewarded—every 10 massages grants two complimentary ones in return

A visit typically begins with a warm reception in the front lounge, where clients are invited to fill in a short questionnaire that helps tailor the experience to their individual needs, while enjoying a complimentary cup of calamansi or cinnamon ginger tea. After that, guests change into plush cotton robes and are offered the option of retreating to the separate men's and women's relaxation lounges, where they can browse a library of DVDs and magazines. Or they may wish to head straight to such incredible pleasures as a four-handed massage. Alternatively, there's an outdoor terrace with Moroccan-style daybeds and lovely views of the district.

It seems almost cliché to say that one spa can make a difference, but with its unusual approach, SHUI Urban Spa has a good shot at breaking the Shanghainese spa market wide open, putting world-class quality on the map for many more people.

rooms
6 treatment rooms •
2 manicure/pedicure stations

drink
complimentary welcome teas

features
body treatments • facials • relaxation lounges • terrace with daybeds • personal DVD players • separate facilities for men and women

nearby
cafés • boutiques • shopping

contact
5th floor, Ferguson Lane
376 Wukang Road, Shanghai 200031, China •
telephone: +86.21.6126 7800 •
facsimile: +86.21.6126 7801 •
email: info@shuiurbanspa.com.cn •
website: www.shuiurbanspa.com.cn

zenspa

Located in a *siheyuan* (a traditional Chinese courtyard house), Zenspa provides a tranquil, luxurious retreat that contrasts sharply with the fast-paced lifestyle of Beijing, China's bustling capital. With an array of full-day treatments which guests may enjoy in the open courtyard or in one of the spa's private treatment suites, Zenspa invites visitors to relax under the ministrations of well-trained hands. Visitors should also allow themselves some time to properly admire the building's lovely, centuries-old architecture.

While the exterior retains all the original features—such as roofs finished with curved tiles, intricate motifs, carefully restored lattice screens and bright red wooden columns—the interior displays a strikingly minimalist style. Outfitted by David Ng, the acclaimed founder and designer of Matchit furniture, Zenspa's layout incorporates elements of antique furniture, stones and wooden planks to create an atmosphere that is simultaneously modern and natural. The Hong Kong-based designer makes use of his signature lacquer boxes in a rainbow of vivid colours to complement the rustic tones of the surrounding bare wood. With a contemporary tension pool, precise stone cladding and customised furniture, the overall visual effect is simply stunning.

Adopting a holistic approach to the physical and spiritual wellbeing of its guests, Zenspa provides a sanctuary for its visitors. With its top-notch facilities and services, it should come as no surprise that Zenspa was the only spa featured in the official promotion documentary for the Beijing 2008 Olympic Games, or that it was invited to participate in the Olympic Village. Zenspa also received *SpaAsia*'s 'Best Spa National Category (China) Reader's Choice Award' in 2007.

Zenspa has one of the widest selections of treatments available in Beijing. Guests are spoilt for choice with naturopathy, clinical aromatherapy, Ayurvedic *shirodhara* therapies and Thai as well as Indonesian massages. In addition, two saunas and a relaxation area are open for visitors to unwind in, and services such as body scrubs, body wraps, massages and facial care are also available.

A popular therapy among patrons is the Ultimate Indulgence, which lasts four and a half hours. Guests are pampered with a body scrub that utilises gold leaves, imported Thai herbs and rose petals, followed by a honey wrap and either a Royal Thai Floral Bath or a Cleopatra Milk Bath. The finishing touch is Zenspa's signature Burmese Thanaka facial, which nourishes the skin and protects against ultraviolet rays, among other effects.

THIS PAGE (FROM LEFT): The spa's relaxation rooms are ideal for a post-treatment nap; a variety of spa ingredients are used in the therapies.
OPPOSITE (FROM LEFT): The spa boasts an air of serenity that helps guests forget their troubles; some of the treatments involve flowers imported directly from Thailand.

china **beijing**

Guests who wish to immerse themselves completely in luxury may consider the four-handed massage, which has been likened to a choreographed dance. The masseurs work in perfect unison to ease stress and tension.

Visitors may also choose to indulge in any of the spa's range of body wraps, such as the Green Tea Body Masque. This involves an antioxidant-rich blend that boosts immune system function, enhances the metabolism and eliminates toxins. Japanese green tea is also supposed to protect one's skin from the effects of stress and pollution, leaving the complexion healthier and better oxygenated.

Also available are some specially designed spa packages which usually begin with a body scrub and wrap that will invigorate a fatigued body and mind. A thorough massage and a rejuvenating facial treatment—such as the spa's signature Burmese Thanaka facial—soon follow, adding a glow to the body. Guests will surely feel refreshed and pampered upon completion of their treatments.

To maintain their peaceful state of mind, guests are encouraged to fully enjoy Zenspa's soothing ambience. A lounge area and a bar which serve healthy snacks and juices provide refreshment while guests relax.

rooms
1 reflexology treatment room • 5 rooms • 4 suites

features
facials • lounge • massages • reflexology • snack bar • spa treatments

nearby
Temple of Heaven Park • Ancient Observatory • Beijing Amusement Park

contact
House 1, 8A Xiaowuji Road
Chaoyang District, Beijing 100023, China •
telephone: +86.10.8731 2530 •
facsimile: +86.10.8731 2539 •
email: info@zenspa.com.cn •
website: www.zenspa.com.cn

four seasons hotel hong kong

Four Seasons Hotel Hong Kong is located on the lifeline of local business, commerce and transportation, putting its services where they are needed the most. The International Finance Centre and IFC Mall are right beside this Victoria Harbour-facing hotel, adding a wealth of shopping and entertainment to the already exceptional pleasures of the infinity pools, expansive spa complex, 399 luxurious rooms and five bars and restaurants.

The sixth-floor rooftop also offers an infinity pool, lap pool, whirlpool and plunge pool for guests' use. The infinity pool and lap pool both feature underwater music systems, while the former is temperature-controlled so that guests can keep in shape or enjoy a relaxing dip even during the winter.

Occupying three levels of the hotel, The Spa is possibly the city's finest urban retreat. Following a warm reception, guests get dressed in plush robes and slippers to partake in Chinese herbal tonics and teas. Male and female guests are then led to their separate Vitality Lounges, each with a specific focus on aquatherapy: for the men, a Eucalyptus-scented Finnish sauna and steam room, and for the women, a soft sauna and Amethyst Crystal Steam Room.

THIS PAGE (FROM LEFT): *Sweeping harbour views add yet another touch of luxury to the spa, complementing the elegant interior design and the top-of-the-line treatments; water is involved in many of the therapeutic regimes on the spa's extensive menu.*
OPPOSITE (FROM LEFT): *Each of the spa's airy rooms is a serene environment where guests may fully appreciate their chosen treatment; the Oriental Jade Ritual, a full-body massage that employs both warm and cool jade stones, aims to induce a state of contemplation and boost the immune system.*

china **hong kong**

rooms
hotel: 345 rooms, 54 suites •
spa: 14 treatment rooms, 2 suites

food
Caprice: French • Lung King Heen: Cantonese •
The Lounge: international • Pool Terrace:
light meals

drink
Blue Bar: cocktails, fine wines

features
pools • gym • Pilates • Vitality Lounges •
oxygenated yoga studio

nearby
Victoria Harbour • IFC Mall •
Macau Ferry Terminal • Star Ferry • airport

contact
8 Finance Street, Central, Hong Kong, China •
telephone: +852.3196 8900 •
facsimile: +852.3196 8909 •
email: spa.hkg@fourseasons.com •
website: www.fourseasons.com/hongkong

A total of 14 treatment rooms and two suites are available, all elegantly designed with contemporary, clean lines. Flooded with natural light, the rooms and suites feature spectacular harbour views. Embodying the elements of a luxury hotel room and a self-contained spa, the suites are furnished with all the modern conveniences and luxurious features that a guest could want, such as vitality pools, steam showers, daybeds, vanity areas, LCD televisions and minibars.

Some of the recommended treatments include the following experiences: the Pure Indulgence, a two-hour body and scalp treatment that utilises a soothing concoction of organic buttermilk, honey, orange oil, jojoba pearls and mango butter; the Aromatic Caress, an aromatherapy massage and facial treatment; and the Oriental Infusion, during which a medley of Chinese herbs with either *yin* or *yang* properties are employed along with acupressure to release muscle tension in the back, feet, neck and head.

Open until the late hour of 11 pm every night, The Spa is nothing if not a welcome and convenient timeout for many of Central's busy inhabitants and visitors. When coupled with the five-star service and the magnificent views at Four Seasons Hotel Hong Kong, it becomes an indispensable pleasure.

plateau residential spa

Overlooking the lights of the famed Victoria Harbour, Grand Hyatt Hong Kong represents the peak of refinement in this cosmopolitan city. However, those in the know will attest to the existence of another dimension beyond the rarefied halls and lofty suites of the property, one that promises to take luxury to a whole other level.

Built at the cost of more than US$10 million with the involvement of some of the world's foremost artistic talents, the Plateau Residential Spa, on the Grand Hyatt's 11th floor is an urban sanctuary like none other.

Integrating five-star accommodation directly into the spa facility, Plateau effectively creates a standalone resort with all the comforts, services and conveniences one can expect from a premier metropolitan hotel.

Occupying over 7,400 sq m (79,653 sq ft), this audacious development contains 23 rooms and suites, with more than half of them facing the harbour. The sleek facility bears the hallmark style of esteemed architect John Edward Morford, celebrated for his work in hotel and spa design. In this particular spa, his signature humanistic

THIS PAGE: *Lush greenery coaxes guests to relax and enjoy the fresh air in the courtyard.*
OPPOSITE: *The decadent Plateau Deluxe Room will surely result in an unforgettable stay.*

...an urban sanctuary like none other.

design approach has yielded environments of remarkable calm and grace, singularly dedicated to easing the senses into a state where they might be most receptive to the pleasures to follow. External noise is almost non-existent—a rarity in a city such as Hong Kong—and the ebb and flow of natural light through the blinds contributes an uplifting phototherapeutic effect.

Meticulous indoor landscaping makes it almost possible to believe that all of this takes place somewhere else; what other way is there to explain the presence of a waterfall, numerous fountains and reflecting pools? Playful ceramic animal sculptures by artist Emma Chan show up in the most unexpected places, while original prints by the renowned German photographer Vera Mercer decorate the sumptuous spaces.

In each of Plateau's harbour-facing rooms and suites, lavish details are everywhere to be found. For instance, to ensure comfort while receiving in-room treatments, these lodgings feature king-sized *futon* beds covered with Egyptian-cotton duvets. The Plateau Deluxe Room measures an incredible 50 sq m (538 sq ft), which encompasses many extras such as a spacious balcony, a bathroom equipped with huge spa tubs and rainshower stalls and floor-to-ceiling glass walls for views of the city skyline. Minibars, large 30-inch flat-screen televisions with DVD players, and in-room safes are some of the additional amenities to expect in the rooms.

The 114-sq-m (1,227-sq-ft) Plateau Deluxe Suite, which boasts three rooms, has almost everything it needs to be called a spa on its own. Separate sleeping and living areas make for two rooms, with the third forming a private treatment room complete with a 2.8-sq-m (30-sq-ft) hydrotherapy tub, soaking bath, steam room and rainshower. Be warned though, staying in this treatment room all day becomes an attractive possibility given the thoughtful inclusion of amenities such as an LCD television and panoramic views out onto

THIS PAGE: A few brisk laps in the hotel's pool will get the heart pumping and blood flowing.

OPPOSITE (FROM LEFT): The Water Garden Room, one of the spa's nine lavish treatment suites; the view of the harbour from the Plateau's guestrooms and suites is breathtaking.

the Victoria Harbour. Fortunately, the features to be found in the rest of the spa outweigh those installed in the suite.

Plateau's nine treatment rooms are theatres of indulgence, where the finest natural spa products are given the stage by expert therapists who direct every moment of the drama with steady hands. The renowned Carita company has granted Plateau the exclusive right to its products in Hong Kong, and the spa's aestheticians have been trained by representatives from the Parisian 'House of Beauty'. The June Jacobs skincare range is another exclusive coup that has won the spa many fans due to its reputation for powerful botanical antioxidants. Products from Aesop and Decleor are also used throughout the extensive menu of treatments.

Facials such as the Renovateur Hydration Intense and the Ideal Controle employ advances in modern science and chemistry to effectively restore health and radiance to tired skin, lifting and firming without the need for surgery. Men have their own exclusive selection of anti-ageing and moisturising procedures, including circulation-boosting facial treatments and body wraps with balms made from semi-precious gemstones.

A veritable United Nations of massage techniques is available, with the supreme Plateau Massage ritual easily blending Thai, Swedish and *shiatsu* massages with a choice of specially formulated essential oils named Relax, Flow, Detox and Tonic. A deep-pressure Hong Kong Massage is also available, along with Chinese foot reflexology, four-handed massages, hot stone therapy and a gentle tension-relieving rub for expectant mothers.

Adjacent to the spa's entrance are doors leading out to a terrace that includes the hotel's 50-m (164-ft) pool and comprehensive fitness facilities. A 400-m (1,312-ft) jogging track, golf driving range, tennis courts and five exercise studios fitted with the latest fitness equipment are just some of the ways that Plateau encourages a relationship between relaxation and keeping fit.

china **hong kong**

Plateau caters to those who only have an hour to spare as well as those with a full weekend to devote to themselves. Express treatments range from Anti-Stress Facials to neck and shoulder massages, which can rejuvenate one in just 25 minutes. Longer treatment packages combine procedures to create three- to five-hour journeys that target specific needs, often pausing for tea in the middle and ending with exquisite spa cuisine.

Additionally, the hotel's nine restaurants and bars provide many venues for healthy eating. The Grill is a poolside restaurant where meals are prepared from fresh ingredients, without using additives or excessive fat, while the Courtyard features healthy breakfasts.

The four pillars of Plateau's philosophy are Relaxation, Fitness, Aesthetics and Culinary Excellence. Few can manage the delicate balancing act required to excel in all of these areas, but by applying the resources and knowledge of the Hyatt group, this residential spa performs in each category as if that particular area was its only concern. As a result, since its opening in 2004, the property has earned a slew of accolades, including *Travel+Leisure*'s award for the second best destination spa in the world and recently 'Best Hotel Spa in Hong Kong' at the *AsiaSpa* & Wellness Festival Gold Awards. Don't let the name fool you; in the years to come, this Plateau is destined for even greater heights.

rooms
14 Plateau guestrooms and suite •
9 treatment rooms

food
The Grill: healthy fare by the pool •
The Courtyard: light refreshments

drink
herbal teas

features
steam room • sauna • pool • fitness centre •
jogging track • driving range • tennis courts •
squash courts

nearby
Victoria Harbour • Hong Kong Arts Centre •
Convention & Exhibition Centre • Star Ferry •
Academy for Performing Arts

contact
1 Harbour Road, Wan Chai
Hong Kong, China •
telephone: +852.2584 7650•
facsimile: +852.2802 0677 •
email: hongkong.grand@hyatt.com •
website: hongkong.grand.hyatt.com,
hyattpure.com

spa by mtm

Picture this: a well-regarded skincare firm expands into the spa business, relying on its loyal customer base and scientific expertise to trade retail success for a foothold in custom-blended skincare products, facials and other spa treatments. If the story sounds familiar, it is because many have tried, but ultimately they failed to grasp the nuances of the competitive beauty services industry, and their clients have eventually returned to more traditional spa operations.

If this were about any other company it would be easy to close the chapter here, but the Japan-developed and Hong Kong-based MTM is far from your average skincare company. Since 1991, the MTM name has symbolised skincare that goes above and beyond the industry's standard approach. Recognising the different properties and demands of each individual's skin, their 'custom-blended skincare' system offers products as unique as the customers themselves. Only by meeting the specific needs of each client down to the exact composition of each solution can real results be achieved. In this regard, the personalised style of MTM makes them perfectly suited to do what others cannot.

The first SPA by MTM involved more than merely adding treatment rooms to an existing skincare boutique. Opening in 2005 after months of planning, the first Hong Kong SPA by MTM was considered by many to be a six-star facility, bringing a never-before-seen level of customisability to the category of full-service spas. Every visit begins with a personal consultation and skin analysis, during which clients should specify any preference for refreshments, length of treatments and even the aromatherapy scents present throughout their visits. Today, there are two outlets in Hong Kong, one in the premier shopping district of Causeway Bay, and the other in Tung Chung, a newly developed area in the northwest of Lantau Island.

The Causeway Bay property features five treatment suites, each named after a mood evoked by their décor schemes. Happiness, Health, Wisdom, Beauty and Energy all include provisions for baths, scrubs and massages but also specialised facilities appropriate to their themes. The Energy Suite is equipped with a

THIS PAGE (FROM LEFT): *The sleek reception is like a portal to another world; sake baths are a unique offering of SPA by MTM.*

OPPOSITE (FROM LEFT): *Each of the treatment suites are tailored for different therapies; with custom-blended skincare products and a host of trained therapists, SPA by MTM will leave one feeling refreshed.*

china **hong kong**

rooms
5 mood treatment suites

drink
tea and refreshments

services
custom-blended skincare and spa products •
massages • wraps • facials • hydrotherapy •
shiatsu • colour therapy

nearby
shopping • restaurants

contact
Shop A, Ground Floor
3 Yun Ping Road, Causeway Bay
Hong Kong, China •
telephone: +852.2923 7888 •

Tung Chung:
Shop 118, Citygate Outlets
Tung Chung, Lantau Island
Hong Kong, China •
telephone: +852.2923 6060 •

email: cs@mtmskincare.com •
website: www.spamtm.com

Cromolight Colour Therapy system, the first in Hong Kong, that bathes the room in soothing washes of coloured light to stimulate the mind and create a deeper state of relaxation. The Wisdom Suite pays homage to MTM's Japanese roots with traditional wooden soaking barrels, in which luxurious *sake* baths may be enjoyed. The minimalist layout of the Wisdom Suite is also appropriate for receiving one of the spa's *shiatsu* massages.

On the other hand, the Tung Chung SPA by MTM distinguishes itself from its predecessor with a focus on hydrotherapy and an abstract-Oriental design aesthetic that is as modern as it is timeless. All five mood suites are also available here, along with their full array of body treatments and facials, but SPA by MTM Tung Chung also promises Vichy shower tables, saunas and a signature Aroma Shower area that will refresh and revitalise.

MTM's efforts have not gone unnoticed; in fact, the company has garnered much praise. *Cosmopolitan* magazine included the MTM spas in their 'Best of the Best' feature for three consecutive years, and just one year after opening, both the prestigious *SpaAsia* Crystal Awards and the Baccarat *AsiaSpa* Awards rewarded them with nominations. The SPA by MTM branches in Shanghai and Beijing have also proven to be a hit, and plans for more spas across the Asia-Pacific are well underway. All from a skincare company, imagine that.

anantara dhigu resort + spa, maldives

THIS PAGE: *Lie back by the infinity pool at the spa's relaxation area and watch the sun descend into the water as night approaches.*

OPPOSITE (FROM LEFT): *The spa, which sit on stilts above the water, has six plush treatment suites; immediately upon arrival at Anantara Dhigu Resort, while stepping off the boat and onto the jetty, one cannot help but feel that they have found somewhere special.*

Arriving in the Maldives, the first thing one notices is how much horizon is missing from everywhere else, congregated here in the form of almost boundless ocean waves. Given the importance of this visual spectacle, it seems natural that any five-star resort should seek to present it as their greatest asset, but perhaps none have done so as convincingly as Anantara Dhigu Resort & Spa.

Situated on the edge of Dhigu Island in the South Malé Atoll, just half an hour from the airport by speedboat, the property includes 70 villas built on a pristine stretch of private beach. If the views from the windows of the villas aren't close enough, an additional 40 over-water suites are also available, with infinity baths and pools joined seamlessly to the glittering seascape.

In the midst of this peerless setting is the Anantara Spa, Maldives, a standalone over-water sanctuary featuring nine luxurious treatment suites, each fitted with glass floors allowing their occupants unobstructed views into the depths below as they benefit from therapies that span the breadth of Asian and Polynesian healing knowledge.

Very nearly as captivating as the marine sights are the spa's architectural touches. The architecture blends Maldivian traditions, as directed by the renowned local architect Mohamed Shafeeq, and elements of interior design from the homeland of the Anantara group, artfully provided by the Abacus agency of Thailand. Together, these creative minds have designed a harmonious style that defers to authenticity when prudent, such as in the dedicated treatment rooms for Ayurvedic and Thai massage. Regardless of whether one occupies a single treatment room or a larger double treatment suite with an al fresco lounge and jacuzzi, it is clear at all times—thanks to an abundance of light and the soothing sound of lapping waves—that one is in the world's most enviable position.

In its pursuit of wellness from a wide and diverse range of sources, the spa's impressive treatment menu promises to bring blissful stress relief to the spa's guests. Thai and Oriental massage techniques join Hawaiian, Indian and Indonesian treatments, as well as aromatherapy, yoga and superb steam and sauna facilities in loosening up tired bodies.

The Anantara Detoxifying Signature Treatment even brings vitamin- and mineral-rich Moor mud into the mix, applied directly on the skin for an infusion of moisture and essential ingredients before a light lymphatic draining massage and steam bath. Other signature baths have a variety of beneficial effects; the Green Tea Bath, for example, utilises the antioxidant qualities of freshly steamed tea leaves to purify the body. On a similarly natural note, those with dry or sensitive skin will find the White Sesame Body Treatment a godsend—one may be surprised at how crushed sesame seeds, yoghurt and rich oils can fully restore moisture to the skin in just over an hour.

Should guests have more time, the spa's Rituals of Wellbeing are a treat for sore or stressed-out bodies, as in the case of the 145-minute Asian Ritual. This treatment package includes a bath, back massage and foot reflexology massage. Going even further, the decadent three-, five- and seven-day Voyages of Wellbeing are some of the most life-affirming, need-fulfilling experiences one can hope to have. Each involves days of pampering, and can be customised to suit one's needs.

rooms
resort: 70 beachfront villas,
40 Over-Water Suites • spa: 6 treatment suites

food
Fushi Café: international buffet •
Fuddan Fusion Grill: fusion cuisine •
Terrazzo: Italian • Aqua: light lunch

drink
Aqua: pool bar

features
in-room treatments • beachside treatments •
Ayurvedic and Thai treatment suites •
private consultations • spa journeys •
fitness studio

nearby
Malé • cruises • fishing • island tours

contact
PO Box 2014, Dhigufinolhu
South Malé Atoll, Malé, Maldives •
telephone: +960.664 4100 •
facsimile: +960.664 4101 •
email: dhigumaldives@anantara.com •
website: dhigu-maldives.anantara.com

conrad maldives rangali island

THIS PAGE (FROM LEFT): *Guests can enjoy views of tranquil, blue waters from the large windows of their villa; the resort's Ithaa Undersea restaurant is the first undersea restaurant in the world.*

OPPOSITE (FROM LEFT): *The villas are furnished with the best the resort can offer, providing tasteful, luxurious lodgings; perched on stilts out over the water, the Spa Water Villas are an alternative option for guests who prefer seclusion.*

The Conrad Maldives Rangali Island is really three resorts in one, spread out over two bridge-connected islands in the open stillness of the Maldivian seascape. All around this peaceful, perfect setting lie miles of pristine lagoons and colourful coral reefs. In addition to the Water Villas and Beach Villas, each with their own distinct characteristics, 21 Spa Water Villas, located up to 500 m (1,640 ft) from shore, offer the feeling of having one's own private island paradise, albeit one equipped with a private treatment room and gym.

The villas are part of the resort's Spa Retreat, a complete destination spa which comprises nine treatment suites, an exquisite spa cuisine restaurant, a herbal dispensary, hair salon, aromatherapy courtyard, juice bar and boutique. All of these stand on stilts over water, providing guests with incredible views into the lagoon from many vantage points, including the restaurant's outdoor dining platform. Every one of the treatment suites has ample space for couples, and contains its own changing area. The central cluster of spa villas also provides an additional four private pavilions with steam, sauna and jacuzzi facilities. The Retreat even employs a resident naturopath and nutritionist.

Therapies at the Spa Retreat are designed around the Philosophy of Five Elements which identifies different needs and helps guests achieve the results they desire. Air treatments, for instance, inspire energy by using heat or organic ingredients that invigorate skin and improve circulation. Earth treatments heal with the application of pure essential oils and unique exfoliation techniques. Fire involves cleansing, the removal of toxins from the body and stress from the mind. A must-try, the Organic Sugar Plum & Spice Wrap draws its power from Hungarian thermal mud and cinnamon, which naturally detoxify, while the plum extract infuses the skin with nutrients. Water treatments are all about bringing one to a peaceful state, often with the help of hydrating marine ingredients and cool aloe vera—a lovely contrast to the sunny climate of the Maldives. Treatments of the fifth element, Plant, feature exotic herbs, fruits and vegetable oils to rejuvenate the body. The treatments all use premium products from Eminence, Terrake and ghd spa, three of the best names in organic and natural wellness.

Complementing the resort's Spa Retreat is the Over-Water Spa, a romantic sanctuary dedicated to couples in its own private corner of the resort. Three of its treatment villas feature glass flooring so every lavish session doubles as an exploration of the ocean floor. Seven is the magic number here, with seven rituals offered to match the seven *chakra* of the human body. Each is identified by a different colour, with an associated gemstone, massage, essential oil and herbal tea, all specially selected to work in harmony. Even the colours play a vital part, through the use of illuminated colour therapy throughout the suite. Two special treatments—Allure and The Art of Love—are recommended for couples. Considering the latter involves champagne and a luxurious bath with views across the ocean, it's not hard to see why.

Fitness and yoga enthusiasts will find more to enjoy on the main island of the resort, where a two-storey complex offers state-of-the-art exercise equipment, an open-air yoga pavilion and a team of expert trainers to help transform mind and body. Far away from prying eyes, suspended in the midst of the world's most tranquil seascape, the Conrad Maldives Rangali Island resort makes every other option seem overcrowded.

rooms
21 Spa Water Villas • Retreat: 9 treatment suites • Over-Water Spa: 3 treatment suites with glass-bottomed floors

food
Mandhoo: healthy meals

drink
juice bar

services
fitness centre • yoga pavilion • steam saunas • jacuzzi • hair and beauty facilities • boutique • herbal dispensary • resident naturopath and nutritionist

nearby
Huruelhi Island (picnics) • Malé • museums • markets • mosques

contact
Rangali Island, 2034 Maldives •
telephone: +960.668 0629 •
facsimile: +960.668 0619 •
email: maldivesinfo@conradhotels.com •
website: www.conradmaldives.com

four seasons resort maldives at kuda huraa

From the moment a traveller touches down at Malé International Airport, the world begins to feel like a different place. The capital of the Maldives may be no larger than 2 sq km (0.4 sq miles), but there's a lot of life packed into its busy streets and markets. On the way over to Four Seasons Resort Maldives at Kuda Huraa—where *kuda huraa* means 'little village'—the noise dies down, and one is left only with the faint whirr of the speedboat as it makes its way across still blue waters.

Designed in the style of an enchanting Maldivian village, the 5-hectare (12-acre) resort's 96 stylish pavilions and bungalows are divided into sunrise- and sunset-facing rooms, with some built directly on the soft, feathery sands of the beach and others suspended on stilts over the sea. The design of each five-star accommodation borrows from the influences present in the Maldives' diverse cultural framework. Architectural touches which originate from the Maldives, India and the Middle East find themselves recreated in white stone, wood and thatch, all assembled by the finest native craftsmen utilising traditional techniques.

Inspired by a Moorish oasis with a central tented reception, the Island Spa is detached from the main body of the resort in a delightfully unusual manner. Picturesque desert islands are in no short supply here in the Maldives, and so the Island Spa resides on its very own, spanning just 0.2 hectares (0.5 acres). A charming traditional wooden boat ferries guests over in about a minute, but for all intents and purposes, the Island Spa feels like its very own resort. Rustic thatched pavilions project out over clear blue waters and reflect the sun as waves gently wash against their supports, which creates a very unique and soothing soundtrack to accompany the spa's intensely relaxing menu of body and beauty treatments.

The Island Spa philosophy embraces the natural and wholesome, so of course, the luxury spa products used during treatments are always pure and chemical-free. Prominent environmentally supportive brands—ILA, Sodashi and A W Lake—supply the spa's exclusive range of body- and facial-care products. Experience the indulgent two-and-a-half-hour Sea Escape Ritual or a nurturing multi-day spa package, which utilises only the highest-quality ingredients such as pure botanical extracts, the finest essential oils and organic products.

THIS PAGE (FROM LEFT): *A dhoni, a traditional wooden boat, ferries guests over to the Island Spa, located in tranquil seclusion on its own island; wholesome natural ingredients form the basis of the products used at the spa.*

OPPOSITE (FROM LEFT): *Soak up fantastic views of crystal-clear water, while experiencing any of the host of spa treatments available; some treatment rooms include spacious bathing pavilions, built with couples in mind.*

maldives **kuda huraa island**

rooms
resort: 96 pavilions and bungalows •
spa: 7 over-water treatment pavilions

food
Baraabaru: Indian • Reef Club: Italian •
Kandu Grill: barbeque • Café Huraa: Asian and Western specialities

drink
Sunset Lounge: cocktails • Poolside Bar

features
yoga pavilion • in-room spa service • spa shop • salon services

nearby
Malé • tranquil beaches

contact
North Malé Atoll, Maldives •
telephone: +960.664 4888 •
facsimile: +960.664 4800 •
email: reservations.mal@fourseasons.com •
website: www.fourseasons.com/maldiveskh

Each of the seven double treatment rooms is self-contained and enjoys its own steam room and private outdoor garden with shower. Three are larger than the others and include luxurious bathing pavilions with extra-large soaking tubs—ideal for couples. All boast underwater viewing panels fitted beneath their massage tables, so one can observe the movement of colourful marine life while indulging in a treatment session indoors. The spa also provides in-room massages, manicures and pedicures.

In a peaceful place such as this, it would be impossible to avoid the suggestion of meditation and, by extension, yoga, and so Four Seasons has a huge open-air platform on the edge of the water (and a resident yogi) to meet these needs. Surrounded by so much space and a clear, blue horizon, the slower pace of life cultivated by every aspect of this unique resort village envelopes one in an unforgettable feeling of relaxation, an experience that feels oceans away from the cares of the rest of the world.

four seasons resort maldives at landaa giraavaru

The flight over from Malé International Airport is the first memorable moment offered by Four Seasons Resort Maldives at Landaa Giraavaru. As the seaplane heads over the remote Maldivian atolls and the turquoise waters of the Indian Ocean below, it feels like the start of an adventure. Thirty minutes later, as the aircraft skims to a stop alongside Baa Atoll and makes its way to the Maldives' most pristine lagoon, the first of the resort's beachfront villas comes into view, and the second memorable moment begins.

Comprising 102 exclusive thatched villas on the beach and over water, the premier island resort is inspired by traditional architecture from the Maldives and Sri Lanka with 45-degree pitched thatched roofs and coral walls. Beach Villas have expansive outdoor living spaces and are surrounded by ample, verdant indigenous foliage that provides maximum privacy.

One of the highlights of the resort is its Marine Research Centre, which is responsible for running a host of environmental projects. Guests are invited to enrich their vacation experience with educational insights into the breathtakingly beautiful yet fragile ecosystem of the Maldives by participating in some of the many green activities on offer.

If the main resort is sufficient reason to pack one's bags and head straight for the Maldives, then imagine the joy of discovering an entirely separate resort on the same island—a visitor's third memorable moment.

As a matter of fact, with a compound measuring a total of 1 hectare (3 acres) over both land and water, The Spa and Ayurvedic Retreat is closer to three spas in one.

The first area is composed of three pavilions inside a dedicated Ayurvedic retreat, a first for the Four Seasons group. The second section is a collection of three more pavilions ensconced in a tropical garden. The third is a cluster of four thatched huts built over the water on stilts. All of the 10 treatment pavilions occupy a site that cuts a spectacular swathe from the centre of the island down to the open sea.

In the serene garden pavilions, rituals are performed by devout Tantrikas, trained in both Tantric philosophy and the science of Ayurveda. In the over-water pavilions, the signature treatment Giraavaru Sacred Water Ritual, is performed—a sumptuous seven-step ritual that harks back to the days of the Maldivian queens, where bathing was an art form as well as an act of devotion.

THIS PAGE (FROM LEFT): *A resident yoga guru is on hand to teach classes in the most picturesque of settings; the signature Giraavaru Sacred Water Ritual is one of the spa's must-try treatments.*

OPPOSITE (FROM LEFT): *Devout Tantrikas perform rituals based on both Tantric and Ayurvedic principles in the garden pavilions; the all-natural ingredients used during treatments, which include herbs and spices, make one's spa experience both fragrant and wholesome.*

maldives **landaa giraavaru island**

While the garden pavilions have steam rooms as well as outdoor showers and the over-water pavilions have soaking tubs that look out over the ocean, no matter the spa pavilion, all treatments are designed to nourish the body, mind and spirit.

A resident Ayurvedic physician works in tandem with an Ayurvedic chef to prepare special meals that meet each guest's unique dietary requirements on the road to physical and spiritual rejuvenation. In the meantime, experienced therapists work magic in the three pavilions with herbal baths, mud treatments, steam benches and the many fragrant oils of the healing discipline. Longer treatment packages may last from seven to 28 days, for those seeking more intensive changes in their physical and spiritual states. For example, the Panchakarma Detox Package takes a minimum of two weeks, and involves a special diet, yoga lessons with the resident *guru* and various cleansing procedures. The programme helps to promote better health and re-establish essential balance.

Other facilities at the spa include a floating yoga pavilion, a herb garden that supplies fresh produce, a juice bar, a beauty salon and a spa shop full of supplies to help one relax. It's hard to leave at the end of it all, but with that feeling comes a vow to someday return: the last and possibly most inspiring moment to remember.

rooms
resort: 102 villas • spa: 10 treatment pavilions

food
Blu: Italian • Al Barakat: Lebanese and Moroccan • Fuego Grill • Café Landaa: Asian and Western • Ayurvedic Retreat: healthy, customised Ayurvedic meals

drink
Blu Bar: coconut drinks, cocktails and alcoholic beverages • Shisha Bar • Poolside Bar • Five Degrees North

features
Marine Research Centre • Ayurvedic Retreat • Vedic Wisdom Centre • yoga pavilion • resident Ayurvedic physician • Ayurvedic chef • herb garden • spa shop • in-room spa service • salon services • juice bar

nearby
colourful coral reef • powder-soft, white-sand beaches • Kudarikilu Fishing Village

contact
Baa Atoll, Maldives •
telephone: +960.660 0888 •
facsimile: +960.660 0800 •
email: reservations.mal@fourseasons.com •
website: www.fourseasons.com/maldiveslg

soneva gili by six senses, maldives

THIS PAGE: *The Soneva Gili Crusoe Residences stand apart from each other, ensuring privacy.*

OPPOSITE (FROM LEFT): *The spa's five over-water treatment rooms are outfitted to allow guests to wallow in luxury as they indulge in one of the many treatments on offer; a good night's rest in one of the well-appointed bedrooms is a perfect ending to the day.*

Six Senses resorts don't do things by halves, and the over-water villas at Soneva Gili in the Maldives are no exception. The entire resort is arranged around a small secluded island in one of the region's largest lagoons; there is little here to disturb the peace or even send a stray ripple through the azure waters that lead out to the Indian Ocean.

Designed to establish a rich sense of place with traditional architectural forms, all painstakingly built by hand, the luxurious villas allow a holistic pampering experience that could only happen here at Soneva Gili. The extensive spa treatment menu is the result of an international team of therapists coming together and includes massages, rejuvenating physical therapies and Ayurvedic practices from the spa's resident specialist. Beneath each massage table is a glass panel that looks down to the ocean floor, so even when relaxing, there's never a dull moment.

Signature Six Senses treatments such as the four-handed Sensory Journey are available for those seeking the new benchmark in spa bliss: a facial and body massage performed at the same time, accompanied by a footbath and a stress-relieving scalp massage. Special programmes target specific needs in the

maldives lankanfushi island

areas of beauty, wellbeing and body; for example, Southeast Asian specialities such as Balinese coffee scrubs and Javanese *lulur* (a body rub made from turmeric and other spices) do wonders for the skin.

Those seeking to go further in the pursuit of wellbeing may engage the services of a resident yoga specialist, experiment with the ancient Chinese art of *tai chi* or the Japanese healing energies of *reiki* or participate in quiet meditation journeys with an instructor.

Of the resort's 45 villas, the 29 Soneva Gili Villa Suites each measure a generous 210 sq m (2,260 sq ft), while the Crusoe Residences, which number seven, are larger and include kitchen facilities and other extravagant extras such as mini wine cellars. One villa from each category features an adjoining spa suite, so treatments can be undertaken in the comfort and privacy of guests' own accommodation. In air-conditioned rooms large enough for two, sensuous spa pleasures await, with musical accompaniment provided by state-of-the-art sound systems. Each suite also includes an en-suite bathroom, a steam room, gym, relaxation deck and a wooden jacuzzi with rooftop views of the surrounding water.

In addition to the plethora of spectacular dining opportunities at the water's edge, a PADI dive centre, several cruises and a host of other leisure facilities, the five-star Soneva Gili resort by Six Senses provides all the ingredients necessary for nourishing mind and body. One simply has to arrive.

rooms
hotel: 45 villas • spa: 5 treatment rooms

food
Restaurant on the Beach • Sense by the Sea • Over-Water Bar & Lounge • Gourmet Cellar • organic garden dining • poolside dining • in-villa dining • desert island picnics •

drink
Over-Water Bar & Lounge • Gourmet Cellar

features
yoga/*tai chi* champa • steam rooms • chill rooms • sauna • over-water gym

nearby
diving • snorkelling • cruises

contact
Lankanfushi Island
North Malé Atoll, Maldives •
telephone: +960.664 0304 •
facsimile: +960.664 0305 •
email: reservations-gili@sixsenses.com •
website: www.sixsenses.com/soneva-gili

como shambhala estate

A holistic retreat like COMO Shambhala Estate differs markedly from the standard-issue beach resorts and spa getaways that promise hours upon hours on a massage table, relaxing under skilled hands—not that there's anything wrong with such indulgence, of course. The Estate, as the flagship COMO property is fondly referred to, is happy to assemble an army of its skilled therapists outside one's villa door if requested, but to do so would be a waste of a rare opportunity.

The Estate espouses a philosophy of balance and self-discovery. By offering its guests a well-rounded selection of activities, therapies and learning experiences in a private and secluded environment, the retreat lays vital foundations that allow visitors to retain a lasting sense of peace upon their return to their regular lives.

Set upon the steep slopes that form a valley over the Ayung River, The Estate's five-star facilities appear to flow gently down over the thick cover of leafy treetops. The views from even the lowest points by the river banks rival those from the highest, where miles of surrounding country are clearly visible at all times of the year. An hour from the airport and a short 15-minute drive from Ubud, the property enjoys privileged tranquillity while remaining conveniently accessible.

Only a few guests share The Estate at one time, in five exclusive residences composed of just four to five suites each. Each residence has its own pool and a generous lounge area, and is richly furnished with Balinese woods, antiques and stone carvings. A variety of room configurations easily accommodates different requirements, from basic Garden Rooms to the extravagant COMO Shambhala Suites, which come with private jacuzzis. Entire residences may also be reserved at once, but most will agree the four Private Villas are a satisfactory alternative. Offering between two to three bedrooms, these houses are perfect for families and groups.

THIS PAGE: *Ensconced in the midst of lush vegetation, The Estate is an island of modern luxury.*
OPPOSITE (FROM LEFT): *Breathtaking views of the landscape can be admired from virtually every corner of the property; catch up on lost sleep in one of the grand four-poster beds.*

indonesia **bali**

Once settled in, therapy begins. Worn-out bodies are soothed, salved and stimulated by the exclusive organic Ayurvedic treatments, skincare, facials, baths, massages, hot stones, wraps and pulsing streams of water. True to the COMO 360° approach, even the psyche is accepted as part of the equation; certified psychologists utilise acupressure techniques as well as offer traditional counselling.

These relaxing aspects of rejuvenation are balanced with guided physical training meant to increase fitness and energy levels. Yoga, pilates, martial arts, gym training and whitewater rafting are just some of the activities that tone the body while cultural classes endeavour to enrich the soul.

To nourish oneself during the revival process, COMO Shambhala's world-renowned spa cuisine is served at Glow, a restaurant resting high on the forested hillside; its lofty perch provides the perfect complement to the open kitchen's fresh, healthy fare. For a taste of authentic Indonesian cuisine, guests may wish to visit the Kudus House restaurant. It is set in a century-old transported Javanese mansion and serves breakfast and dinner.

rooms
hotel: 30 rooms and villas
spa: 9 treatment rooms

food
Glow: healthy meals • Kudus House: Indonesian

drink
beverage list • organic, freshly squeezed juices

features
lap and therapy pools • yoga pavilion • pilates studio • counselling • hydrotherapy • shop • rock climbing • biking trails • tennis court

nearby
Ubud

contact
Banjar Begawan, Desa Melinggih Kelod,
Payangan, Gianyar
80571 Bali, Indonesia •
telephone: +62.361.978 888 •
facsimile: +62.361.978 889 •
email: res@cse.comoshambhala.bz •
website: cse.comoshambhala.bz

dala spa

THIS PAGE (FROM LEFT): Contemplate the meaning of life as skilled therapists work their magic; the Ixora Room is one of the seven lavish treatment suites.

OPPOSITE (FROM LEFT): The Midori Room allows couples to enjoy a session in the company of their significant other; chandeliers are featured in the treatment rooms, adding to the opulent décor.

Local wisdom, global cultures and their ideals of luxury come together in Bali's DaLa Spa to create an exclusive destination spa. Travellers coming to enjoy themselves here usually have an image of tropical paradise in mind—one that goes hand in hand with the beach and palm tree aesthetic found in most spas. But where others stop at traditional treatments and a single design philosophy, DaLa Spa explores an entirely new concept of its own.

There are seven treatment suites in total, but 'treatment suite' seems too paltry a name for such luxurious spaces. Each one is richly decorated in a decadent, last-century style that lies somewhere between a Parisian boudoir and the palace of King Louis XIV. The lush havens are named after exotic flowers and have been individually appointed to display their own personalities, brought out with unique furnishings, carefully selected colour schemes and design motifs. Of the seven suites, two are single occupancy, four are ready to accommodate couples and the last is the Sonya Treatment Room, which is fully equipped to allow guests to indulge in manicures, pedicures and foot treatments.

DaLa—which means 'leaf'—comes from ancient Sanskrit, and is a fitting name since all of the therapies rely on wholly natural ingredients and essential oils. The one-of-a-kind spa menu is the result of countless hours of research, including the formulation of DaLa Spa's own range of body and beauty products. One example of the care that went into the process can be found in the blended massage oils which use only Australian sweet almond oil as a base; this oil is far superior in adapting to the needs of different skin types.

Newlyweds will certainly appreciate the signature Royal Wedding Ritual treatment, which was originally reserved for brides of the royal family in Central Java. It begins with a footbath with lavender and eucalyptus, and segues into a blissful, hour-long Balinese massage. *Lulur*, a Javanese paste of turmeric, sandalwood and ground rice powder, is then used as an exfoliating agent to nourish and soften the skin. A floral-infused milk bath and yoghurt body polish will also be experienced by the end of the ceremony. A cup of warm chrysanthemum and ginger tea brings the hedonistic treatment to a close after a well-spent two and a half hours.

The four-hour Divine Pampering is the ultimate indulgence. Including a break for a light meal of spa cuisine, the full programme of foot and body massages, scrubs, masks, baths and facials is a relaxed, all-day affair.

Having a strong brand identity has helped DaLa Spa win some notable accolades after just a year in the business. In October 2008, it was declared 'Best Boutique Hotel Spa' at the *SpaAsia* Crystal Awards, and that's not likely to be the last we'll hear of it. With its location in Villa de daun resort, it's a breeze finding some incredible lodging to go with the spa date.

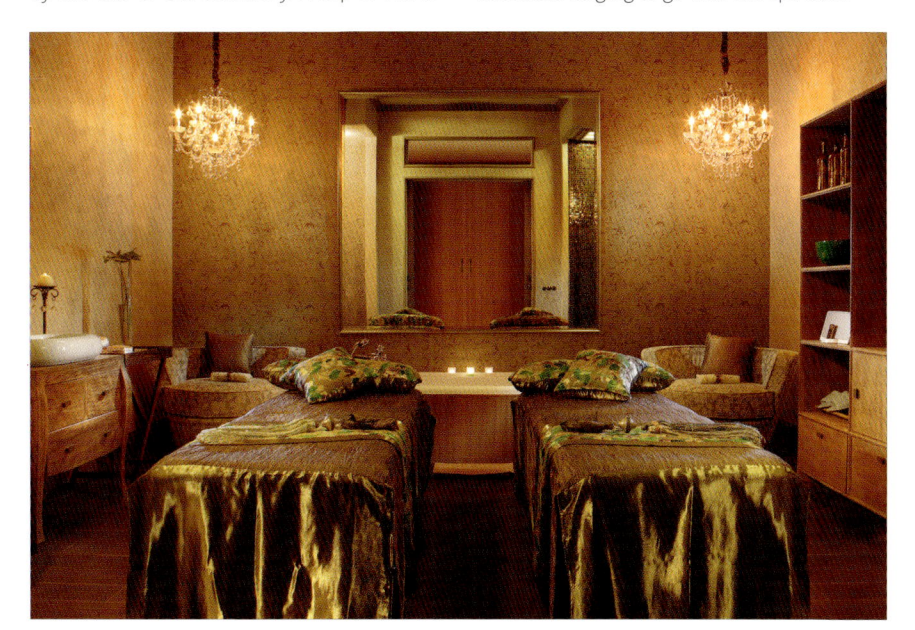

rooms
7 treatment rooms

food
de daun restaurant: international

drink
beverage list

features
spa lobby • post-treatment lounge • gift store

nearby
Kuta • beach • shopping • airport

contact
Raya Legian, Kuta, Bali, Indonesia •
telephone: +62.361.756 276 •
facsimile: +62.361.750 643 •
email: dalaspa@villadedaun.com •
website: www.villadedaun.com

four seasons resort bali at jimbaran bay

THIS PAGE: *Each villa is designed to remind visitors that they are holidaying in the quiet, restful countryside of Bali.*

OPPOSITE (FROM LEFT): *The soothing sound of the ocean makes an ideal soundtrack for any of The Spa's treatments; to preserve the modesty of female guests, The Spa is equipped with separate jacuzzis for men and women.*

The map of Bali's most popular tourist areas can be read as a compartmentalisation of the very different needs and desires that visitors to the island have. Kuta is where beach-lovers and merrymakers flock to during surf season; Seminyak is known for having some of Bali's best food; Ubud is more remote and favoured by those seeking some quiet, while Nusa Dua supplies high-end luxury and is the domain of multimillion-dollar hotel brands. There is, of course, a select breed of traveller that rejects the notion of having to choose between two or more equally attractive attributes, and it was for this group that Four Seasons Resort Bali at Jimbaran Bay was created.

Nestled in a corner on the southern end of Bali, Four Seasons Resort Bali at Jimbaran Bay combines five-star luxury with fine gourmet dining, a beachside location amidst lush greenery, and convenient access to all major attractions. Kuta Beach and its bars and restaurants are close by, and the international airport is only a 15-minute drive away.

Here, a rarely seen side of Bali emerges. Designed around a traditional village model, the property consists of 147 standalone villas organised into seven clusters. However, the structures blend so easily into the landscape, and are arranged with such consideration to privacy, that one easily forgets that this is an island constantly inundated with visitors. Instead, it feels like an secluded paradise with an exceptional sea view.

The restorative benefits of such a place are numerous. The ocean breeze invigorates the spirit, while indigenous plants and herbs are used to make natural spa products. The three deluxe spa suites—equipped to cater to couples—feature Swiss showers and separate body treatment areas; they also open out to a garden with soaking tubs and showers. Smoothies made from local fruit are another of The Spa's healthy benefits.

Regardless of guests' desired therapy or outcome, The Spa's extensive menu is varied and enticing. Guests may try out specialised

indonesia bali

alternative procedures, such as *reiki* natural healing and *watsu*, or one of the many treatments ideal for couples. The Sodashi Water Valley Ritual, for example, takes place at the most romantic of settings, a private waterfall on the edge of the Java Sea.

Many treatments use exotic ingredients which stimulate the senses. During the Coco de Mer aromatic bath treatment, a heavenly-scented body wash is used to cleanse and exfoliate the skin with crushed mother-of-pearl. After a rainshower, a kukui nut *muru-muru* butter rub and a blue reef and algae body wrap, guests can linger over tea and sweets in a soothing milk bath.

Other treatments, the Sodashi Crystal Facial among them, employ a variety of holistic methods to increase circulation and improve skin tone. In this all-organic facial, warm carnelian, rose quartz and green aventurine crystals are massaged gently over the just-cleansed face, then a pure mask of chemical-free clay is applied.

Alternatively, guests may pursue physical excellence with a fully-equipped gymnasium and other sporting facilities, supplemented by the spectacular 7-m (23-ft) cascading infinity pool. The influence of the sea and nature is not only seen everywhere at Four Seasons Resort Bali at Jimbaran Bay, it is also felt.

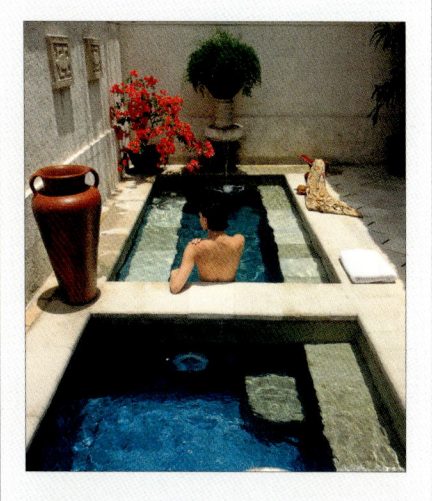

rooms
hotel: 147 villas, 9 private residences •
spa: 6 treatment rooms, 2 spa suites,
1 Royal Spa Suite

food
Pool Terrace Café: light meals •
PJ's: international • Taman Wantilan: Italian •
Warung Mie: traditional Indonesian and Balinese, Asian noodle dishes

drink
Spa Bar • Terrace Bar and Lounge

features
aerobics studio • gym • infinity pool • tennis

nearby
golf • surfing • beaches

contact
Jimbaran Bay, Denpasar 80361, Bali, Indonesia •
telephone: +62.361.701 010 •
facsimile: +62.361.701 020 •
website: www.fourseasons.com

four seasons resort bali at sayan

Entrance to this one-of-a-kind resort, the Four Seasons Bali at Sayan, is via a suspended bridge that brings guests straight to the very top of the hotel. Here, they are greeted by the placid surface of a levitated pond, complete with water lilies. They then descend a flight of stairs situated in the middle of the water feature to the reception area on the level below. The journey down beneath the water signifies the purification that is to follow.

It is hard not to feel a sense of reverence here, as one stands looking into the majestic Ayung Valley, held sacred by the Balinese. Just breathing the bracing air, cooled by the altitude and an abundance of trees, refreshes the body in anticipation of the spa treatments to follow. Each one draws on the distinctive qualities of the resort's location, using plants, herbs, spices and even clay of the surrounding regions to heal and energise.

Near the town of Ubud, an area known for its tranquil seclusion and far-reaching views, the village of Sayan marks a special spot along the Ayung River. It is here amidst tall tropical trees that a unique architectural entity rises from the lush greenery like a giant Zen garden ornament. Saucer-shaped levels float above one another, the spaces formed between their absent walls laid open to the elements.

The wholly immersive experience is not only a matter of Eastern scents and liniments, but also includes lavish attention to the spa environment. A total of three luxurious spa villas cater to the needs of guests, and all are built in the traditional Balinese style, with Indonesian silks, specially designed teak furnishings and exquisite details. Two of the villas feature outdoor pavilions with steam showers and soaking tubs, while the Cendana Villa boasts showers over its two massage beds and a private outdoor pool. Additionally, the main spa has four treatment rooms equipped with baths.

THIS PAGE: *With its luxurious lodgings, renowned spa and lovely far-reaching vistas, the resort is the perfect spot for a rejuvenating vacation.*
OPPOSITE (FROM LEFT): *Some of the villas come with jacuzzis; the suites and villas provide havens away from home.*

indonesia **bali**

Once in the hands of an experienced therapist, there is nothing left but to enjoy the full complement of pleasures that the acclaimed Four Seasons spa menu offers. From Ayurvedic treatments—such as Suci Dhara, which improves circulation with a scalp massage and a warm herbal oil rub, and Chakra Dhara, in which two therapists clear blockages with a back, scalp, hand and foot massage—to full body wraps with volcanic mud from the mountains, every need is taken care of. Even beauty treatments and pedicures are done with a twist, such as the clove-and-ginger massages that accompany the latter.

When it comes to the time to rest after all that kneading and scrubbing, retreat to one of the 18 suites and 42 villas scattered over the gradated terraces of the 6.9-hectare (17-acre) estate. Each is a haven of handwoven fabrics, soft down pillows and jungle views. The single Royal Villa is a resort unto itself, with the same rooftop pond concept as the main building, this time spread over two levels of residential luxury and a 43-sq-m (462.8-sq-ft) plunge pool. Whether staying in a one-bedroom suite or a three-bedroom villa, alone or with family, the most important thing is not to miss this experience for the world.

rooms
hotel: 18 suites, 42 villas •
spa: 3 spa villas, 4 treatment rooms

food
Ayung Terrace: modern Asian and Indonesian •
Riverside Café: poolside restaurant, wood-fired pizzas and seafood

drink
Jati Bar

features
fitness centre • split-level outdoor pool •
24-hour business services

nearby
Ubud • golf • hiking • watersports

contact
Sayan, Ubud
Gianyar 80571, Bali, Indonesia •
telephone: +62.361.977 577 •
facsimile: +62.361.977 588 •
email: reservation.fsrb@fourseasons.com •
website: www.fourseasons.com

jimbaran puri bali

Created by the Orient-Express group on the southwestern edge of Bali, Jimbaran Puri Bali could not be any more different from its sister property, Ubud Hanging Gardens. Where that inland paradise is encircled by the heavily forested walls of a river valley, with views of miles of leafy treetops all around, this sibling's location in the traditional fishing village of Jimbaran provides no end of wide-open vistas which comprise sand, sea and clear skies.

Guests of Jimbaran Puri Bali have the opportunity to enjoy spectacular sunsets from one of its eight exclusive beachside cottage accommodations or a dip in their own private pool in one of the 22 pool villas. The remaining 42 cottages of the resort stand on the margins of the beach in the shade of palm trees, each boasting Balinese design and a private walled garden for a greater sense of privacy.

This natural setting is very conducive to the recovery of one's spirits, as the sights, sounds and scent of nature envelop the estate in the illusion that the outside world has ceased to exist. If the modern amenities and flat-screen televisions in the rooms ever bring something of that former life to mind, a visit to the resort's Beach Spa will reinforce the fantasy in no time. Amid the sound of lapping waves, a full menu of spa treatments is available throughout the day and evening; the latter hours are an extremely atmospheric delight. Three treatment suites constructed in the form of Balinese terraces, or *balé*, offer couples a romantic space in which they may experience the enchanting view together while experienced therapists work another sort of magic with all-natural herbs and oils.

Most of the treatments on the menu are inspired by traditional Southeast Asian techniques, particularly Balinese massage—characterised by long strokes and the rhythmic application of rolling pressure on the skin, which causes it to stretch with the release of tension. However, Indian Ayurvedic treatments are also available in the wet room. The classic Abyhanga Oil Massage is a real treat, but the Shirodhara Oil Flow treatment—where a stream of pure oil is soothingly applied to the forehead—is also popular. If the choice induces undesired stress, simply request the Best of Ayurveda treatment package, which combines the two into a blissful 90-minute experience.

To really soak up the essence of being in Bali, body scrubs using local ingredients are a good way to leave a lasting impression on one's skin. The Balinese Coffee Scrub involves volcanic pumice from Mount Agung along with fine-ground coffee beans, while the Jasmine Javanese Lulur treatment is a beauty ritual that originated in the Javanese royal court. Its secret combination of powdered spices makes for an effective exfoliation session, soon followed by a moisturising dollop of yoghurt.

Contrary to the popular saying, you can never have too much of a good thing, especially when it comes to the resort's Beach Spa. If the plan was to only stay three nights, take this advice and consider four, or even more.

THIS PAGE: *Relax in the seclusion of one's own well-furnished cottage and enjoy the breeze.*

OPPOSITE (FROM LEFT): *Pause a moment to admire the lovely pond and fountain while strolling through the garden; all guests can expect to be pampered with the best that Jimbaran Puri Bali has to offer.*

indonesia **bali**

rooms
hotel: 8 beachfront cottages, 22 pool villas, 2 two-bedroom cottages, 32 one-bedroom garden cottages • spa: 3 treatment suites

food
Nelayan Restaurant: Mediterranean and seafood • Tunjung Café: Indonesian and Balinese • breakfast buffet

drink
Puri Bar

features
Beach Spa • in-room massages • yoga • *tai chi* • watersports • horizon-edge pool • high-speed Internet access • private garden

nearby
Seminyak area • golf courses

contact
Jalan Uluwatu, Jimbaran, 80361 Bali, Indonesia • telephone: +62.361.701 605 • facsimile: +62.361.701 320 • email: info@jimbaranpuribali.com • website: www.jimbaranpuribali.com

kayumanis bali

THIS PAGE: *Kayumanis Ubud makes the most of the region's breathtaking landscape with its restaurant by the pool.*

OPPOSITE (FROM LEFT): *Four-poster beds ensure that one gets a restful night to complement the effects of the therapies; skilful hands soothe away tension with the assistance of fragrant essential oils.*

Every destination has a story, and to ensure that Bali never gets distilled down to just a single, convenient anecdote, the team behind Kayumanis created three distinct properties. Distributed across the geographically varied landscape, each one offers a unique point of view on what Bali has to offer, while providing uncompromising five-star luxury in the form of private villa accommodations.

The forested river valley of Ubud, the hidden coves of Jimbaran Bay and the international beachfront resort atmosphere of Nusa Dua are all equally represented by the Kayumanis collection. Among the three properties, no two are alike in design and execution, and even within each one, every villa is its own individual entity. An observant eye will only note that their architectural style pays tribute to traditional Balinese buildings, with thatched roofs covering the many sumptuous pavilions that make up each secluded holiday enclave.

In accordance with local beliefs, the exclusive Kayumanis Spa places the balance between inner and outer beauty above all, which results in a series of treatments that waste no time in getting results. That is not to say, of course, that time is not spent leisurely and in the most enjoyable of ways. Each resort has a very similar spa menu, but as the saying goes, a change in scenery can make all the difference. A strong focus on authentic local techniques ensures that every massage, body treatment and facial has the pedigree to match the spectacular sights. Whether marvelling at the cascading terraces and flourishing trees over the Ayung River at the Kayumanis Ubud, listening to the gentle lapping of waves and swaying of palm trees at the Kayumanis Jimbaran, or wondering how the palatial Kayumanis Nusa Dua manages to feel like its very own island, things have a way of feeling just right at that very moment.

All products and ingredients used are derived from natural sources, many of them drawn from Bali's own store of miraculous compounds—in the pursuit of health and sensual enlightenment, there can be no other

indonesia **bali**

way. As in the Balinese tradition, expert fingers apply pressure and massage rich aromatic essential oils directly into the skin, with all therapies involving a human touch. The staff members are remarkably versatile, friendly and helpful when communicating with guests, and so respectfully reserved at other times that they almost vanish.

Kayumanis' signature Moods at a Glance treatment sounds like the title of one of Duke Ellington's fantastic compositions, and going by the sensations, may well be the spa equivalent of one. Starting with a luxurious warm footbath, the ritual continues with a flurry of palm and finger acupressure movements over the entire body. In the end, there is only complete surrender.

Returning to one's villa after the first treatment, it is a pleasure to discover that every effort has been made to ensure the absolute comfort of guests. From the refined interiors and plush furnishings, to the wealth of amenities that include fully equipped kitchens, private pools and a personal butler service available all around the clock, there is little to ask of the Kayumanis Villas that they have not already anticipated.

Regardless of whether one stays in Ubud, Jimbaran Bay or Nusa Dua, the Kayumanis experience is guaranteed to include a phenomenal setting to engage all of one's senses, backed up by a menu of simple yet potent spa therapies. To see Bali in any other light would be wasting an opportunity.

rooms
hotels: 20 villas (Nusa Dua), 19 estates (Jimbaran), 23 villas (Ubud) •
spas: 2 treatment rooms (Nusa Dua), 2 treatment rooms (Jimbaran), 6 treatment pavilions (Ubud)

food
Tetaring: contemporary Asian (Nusa Dua) • Piasan: Italian (Nusa Dua) • Tapis: Indonesian (Jimbaran) • Dining Corner: Thai (Ubud)

drink
Wine Corner: fine wines (Ubud)

features
massages • body scrubs • facials • treatment villas with bath and shower facilities

nearby
beaches • temples • shops

contact
The Sales and Marketing Corporate Office at:
Kayumanis Jimbaran Private Estate and Spa
Jl Yoga Perkanthi, Jimbaran 80364
Bali, Indonesia •
telephone: +62.361.705 777 •
facsimile: +62.361.705 102 •
email: info@kayumanis.com •
website: www.kayumanis.com

kupu kupu barong villas + mango tree spa by l'occitane

THIS PAGE (FROM LEFT): Soaking in a floral bath surrounded by scented candles is a decadent multi-sensory experience; the spa facility peeks out among the boughs and leaves of verdant mango trees.

OPPOSITE (FROM LEFT): The view of the treetops makes the wonderful spa treatments even more memorable; the spa's open design allows one to appreciate the lush greenery before, during and after treatments.

For as long as Ubud has been the destination of choice for travellers seeking Bali's spiritual side, away from the hedonism and surf-jockeying of areas such as Kuta and Seminyak, there has been the Kupu Kupu Barong Villas & Mango Tree Spa by L'Occitane. Although Ubud is known today as the island's cultural capital, where scores of traditional arts and crafts are offered for sale, the area was once unknown to outsiders. This changed 20 years ago, when Kupu Kupu became the first five-star boutique hotel to set up beyond the limits of the town, in the heart of acres of dense forest surrounding a magnificent river valley, today still virtually untouched.

Named after the many large, colourful butterflies that inhabit Ubud's rainforest ecosystem, the resort has recently undergone a metamorphosis of its own, emerging from a cycle of continuous upgrades over the past five years. Six new villas put the number of luxurious Balinese-style lodgings at a total of 34, all of them built on terraces with views over the verdant canopy and the Ayung River below. Constructed from traditional building materials, with some villas standing two storeys tall, they create an exquisite sense of place with exteriors just as beautiful as the redwood-panelled bedrooms and living areas outfitted with handcrafted furnishings. A number of villas even enjoy their own private plunge pools on an outer sun deck, with the water kept at a comfortable 29°C (84°F) at all times by means of eco-friendly solar power.

If the new villas were the *kupu-kupu* emerging from its cocoon, then the unveiling of the Mango Tree Spa by L'Occitane would be the spreading of its wings. As the very first outpost of the renowned Provençal spa and skincare brand in Bali, the Mango Tree Spa by L'Occitane had to be truly unique to live up to the high expectations, and thankfully it really does. Suspended high above the ground in sturdy branches belonging to the denizens of a mango grove, the two bamboo, treehouse-style treatment rooms offer a majestic view and matching soundscape of birds, flowing water and soft rustling of leaves all around to put every beach massage cabin to shame.

indonesia **bali**

Beginning with a personal consultation session, spa visits are tailored to meet the needs of each individual, with therapies being a blend of L'Occitane's signature treatments and time-honoured local healing traditions. The relaxing effects of all massages, facials and other therapies are now complemented by a new steam room which lays claims to being the largest on the island. Carefully designed to be a multi-sensory experience with lights, heat and aromatherapy, the *hammam*-style bath will induce effects that are both refreshing and soothing.

Try the signature treatment, Tree Top, during which one can enjoy a massage with a massage oil made of grape seeds and fresh mango juice followed by a mango body scrub. The whole experience is designed to be good for the skin and smell so delicious that it just might whet your appetite. However, appetites will surely be satisfied by the healthy French-Asian fusion cuisine at the resort's restaurant, outfitted with a terrace and private infinity pool dining area for two.

Set on more than 3 hectares (7 acres) of woodlands, the Kupu Kupu Barong Villas & Mango Tree Spa by L'Occitane makes an excellent argument for the power that natural landscapes can have in enhancing the effect of therapeutic treatments. So, if anyone asks where to find one of Ubud's best spas, the reply should be 'up in the trees'.

rooms
hotel: 34 Balinese-style lodgings •
spa: 6 treatment rooms

food
French-Asian fusion

drink
beverage list

features
L'Occitane spa products • steam room • exclusive mango spa treatments • boutique

nearby
Ubud Palace • Monkey Forest • Bali Bird Park • Elephant Safari • Ubud town • shopping • restaurants • temples

contact
Kedewatan, PO Box 7
Ubud 80571, Bali, Indonesia •
telephone: +62.361.975 478 •
facsimile: +62.361.975 079 •
email: spabyloccitane@kupubarong.com •
website: www.kupubarong.com/spabyloccitane

maya ubud resort + spa

In decorating Maya Ubud Resort & Spa, its creators did not cover its walls with the usual Balinese paintings, masks and iconography. Instead, the proud structure atop a peninsula of land between two parallel river valleys honours its location with authentic local architecture. Ingrained in its 10 hectares (24.7 acres) of land is a reverence for the natural surroundings—Bali's true heritage.

The winner of numerous international awards for its overall experience, design and spectacular location, the spa at Maya Ubud Resort & Spa, nestled at the bottom of the peninsula along the Petanu River, is a unique creation which defies every expectation. Reaching the spa entails a 30-m (98.4-ft) descent down the side of a forested slope in a purpose-built elevator. Soon enough, a cluster of charming thatched roofs comes into view.

The best of these are the Riverside Pavilions. Made using only natural materials such as teak, marble and natural stone, the treatment suites boast interiors that are both functional and ecologically responsible. Each features a generous amount of space, and some are made to house two people. These come with twin tables, a dressing room, a bathroom with a shower and stainless steel soaking tub, twin outdoor rainshowers and a daybed area suspended over the river. All through the enclave, the sound of water lends a sense of calm to the sensuous proceedings.

THIS PAGE (FROM LEFT): Immerse yourself in a bath of fragrant flowers and herbs at one of the spa's treatment pavilions; five of the eight pavilions are equipped to accommodate two persons at one time.

OPPOSITE (FROM LEFT): An amazing view of the verdant environs is available from the pool outside the spa; scrubs and other therapies on the menu take advantage of the natural properties of an array of herbs and spices.

indonesia **bali**

rooms
5 double riverside spa pavilions •
3 single riverside spa pavilions

food
River Café: healthy, light meals

drink
beverage list

features
private spa pavilions • reflexology deck • manicures and pedicures • 2 pools • yoga • tennis court • cooking classes

nearby
Ubud • shops • restaurants

contact
Jalan Gunung Sari Peliatan
Ubud 80571, Bali, Indonesia •
telephone: +62.361.977 888 •
facsimile: +62.361.977 555 •
email: info@mayaubud.com •
website: www.mayaubud.com

The riverside Spa at Maya also pays tribute to Balinese culture with its embrace of natural remedies. Treatments such as the Balinese Boreh make use of powdered cloves and cinnamon, while others employ various herbs and spices along with Balinese massage techniques. Male guests benefit from the spa packages designed with their needs in mind. For example, the Refined Man programme comprises a massage followed by foot therapy and a soak in a bath of herbal essences.

Derived from ancient Thai practice, the Hot Compress Herbal Treatment uses a blend of 11 local ingredients including ginger, galangal, betel and turmeric in medicinal pouches. Steamed and applied directly to the skin, the compresses act to soothe muscles, revitalise the skin, kill germs, increase blood circulation and reduce inflammation.

Local spices also find their way into the body through the excellent spa cuisine served at the al fresco River Café. The café lets diners design their own meal plans based on caloric content and other nutritional data available in the menu. Vegetables are organically grown, and many ingredients such as sea salt are handmade and unprocessed to reap the benefits of their freshness.

Upon reaching the Maya Ubud Resort & Spa, one might catch a glimpse of Bali's soul, but to really, truly feel it—that calls for a short trip down a long slope.

nusa dua beach hotel + spa

Take the most attractive tropical island paradise that comes to mind, with long, white sandy beaches, leafy gardens and exotic dining opportunities. Then, imagine one end of it hides a secluded beachfront enclave so exclusive that it makes everything else seem a little commonplace. That would just begin to describe the Nusa Dua Beach Hotel & Spa's 9-hectare (23-acre) estate of five-star guestrooms, facilities and restaurants hidden away on Bali's southern tip.

Offering the kind of convenience where guests are immediately whisked into the lap of luxury just minutes after arriving at Bali's Ngurah Rai International Airport, with privacy and a peaceful location to match, the resort has famously hosted various royalty, foreign dignitaries and international celebrities over the years. Playing as large a part in this success as the superb service and luxurious amenities is the hotel's Nusa Dua Spa.

This sanctuary embraces long-lasting traditional wellness and the power of natural environments over 5,000 sq m (53,820 sq ft) of landscaped greenery and reflective plunge pools. The modern spa complex blends a contemporary interior style and the latest equipment with elements of ancient Balinese

THIS PAGE (FROM LEFT): *A scented flower bath ends the Javanese Royal Body Polish Treatment on the perfect note; having a foot massage on the beach makes for an unforgettable experience.*

OPPOSITE (FROM LEFT): *The pool and the spa's sauna, steam room and jacuzzi, are the ideal places to relax and refresh; try one of the exotic body scrubs that blend native herbs, flowers and spices.*

indonesia bali

design and architecture for an experience that features both global appeal and a distinctive local approach.

Likewise, the treatments that are on offer originate from around the world, including a variety of beauty therapies, massages and facials, performed with the same techniques and meticulous attention to detail as at any world-class spa—but with the addition of a few secrets from the Indonesian region.

The special village tradition of *boreh* is represented in the hour-and-forty-five minute Balinese Spice Body Wrap, in which the warming spice mix is freshly crushed and applied to the body after a massage.

Lulur, another traditional preparation made of rice, turmeric and sandalwood, is also used during the Royal Javanese Body Polish treatment. A full-body massage prepares the skin for the *lulur* exfoliation which is followed by the application of a rich yoghurt. Then, a frangipani-scented floral bath completes the ancient detoxification ritual.

Not only are all spa products blended from natural ingredients in accordance with the traditions gleaned from centuries of Indonesian culture, they are also available for purchase at the on-site Spa Essentials Shop. The entire exclusive range of body oils, flowers, spices and herbs are prepared in much the same way as they always have been, so any souvenir purchased from the shop is guaranteed to be both authentic and environmentally friendly.

A total of 12 thoughtfully outfitted treatment rooms are available, with some of the rooms dedicated to facials, others to traditional wet treatments and some reserved for couples. In addition, the Nusa Dua Spa boasts three double-storey Spa Villas, each with its own steam room, sauna, jacuzzi and plunge pool, as well as two Balinese *balé* huts on the beach that serve as outdoor massage pavilions.

The incredible features of the spa in combination with the resort's picture-perfect tropical surroundings make for a beautiful escape that anyone, not just kings and queens, can appreciate.

rooms
hotel: 381 rooms and suites •
spa: 12 treatments rooms, 3 spa villas

food
Spa Café • Wedang Jahe Restaurant • Raja's Balinese Cuisine • Sandro's Pizzeria • Maguro Asian Bistro • Chess Beachfront Restaurant • Budaya Cultural Theatre

drink
Spa Café: wholesome beverages • Chess Bar • Pool Bar • Lobby Bar • Santi Lounge

features
lap pool • sauna • steam room • jacuzzi • hair and beauty salon • gym • aerobics studio • squash and tennis courts • mountain bikes • Spa Essentials Shop • Players Games Room

nearby
beaches • Bali Golf and Country Club • shops • Ngurah Rai International Airport

contact
PO Box 1028, Denpasar, Bali, Indonesia • telephone: +62.361.771 210 • facsimile: +62.361.772 621 • e-mail: spa@nusaduahotel.com • website: www.nusaduahotel.com

st regis bali

The New York Astors' legendary St Regis name has finally arrived on Bali's sandy shores, and by the look of it, this resort may change how travellers view Indonesia's island paradise. With personal butlers, world-class fine dining and over a hundred five-star luxury suites and villas, it's rich living even by the already high standards of Nusa Dua, Bali's southern enclave of exclusive international resorts.

All other features aside—and there are many that are worth mentioning, such as the long stretch of beach shared by no other resort and the immense swimmable lagoon which doubles as a pool—the St Regis Bali's most exciting contribution might be its 2,800-sq-m (30,139-sq-ft) Remède Spa, a veritable institution in the group's American properties, and one rarely found elsewhere in the world. Created with the renowned spa and beauty product company, Laboratoire Remède, this latest effort calls upon every dimension of St Regis' experience to provide superlative comforts, gourmet spa cuisine and body and beauty treatments customised for each and every guest.

First impressions count, and before the Balinese-style spa reveals itself, the first thing one notices is a tranquil koi pond. Inside are 12 treatment rooms, two spa suites and a salon, all lit and decorated in a manner reminiscent of an enchanted forest. Clever technology animates the flutter of butterfly silhouettes behind softly-lit panels, creating a mood inspired by the 13th-century Indian poet, Kabir, who wrote 'the moon shines in my body'. Those carefully chosen words, like a mantra, embody Remède Spa's desired effect on tired, stressed or otherwise needful bodies.

Visits to the spa always begin with personalised consultations to determine the needs of the individual. Treatments are customised by each expert therapist to compensate for differences in skin type, preference and unique features.

In typical St Regis style, however, there's always time before and after treatments to indulge in a glass of champagne, juice or some traditional Indonesian herbal tea outside at the Gazebo. And then it's time to lie back and enjoy one's choice of any one of

THIS PAGE (FROM LEFT): *A stint in the aqua vitale pool will bring relief to tense muscles; relax in a traditional hut after an invigorating treatment.*

OPPOSITE (FROM LEFT): *Every part of the hotel exudes a sense of sleek elegance, and this effect only increases in the evenings; traditional therapies such as this herbal poultice massage are available at Remède Spa.*

indonesia **bali**

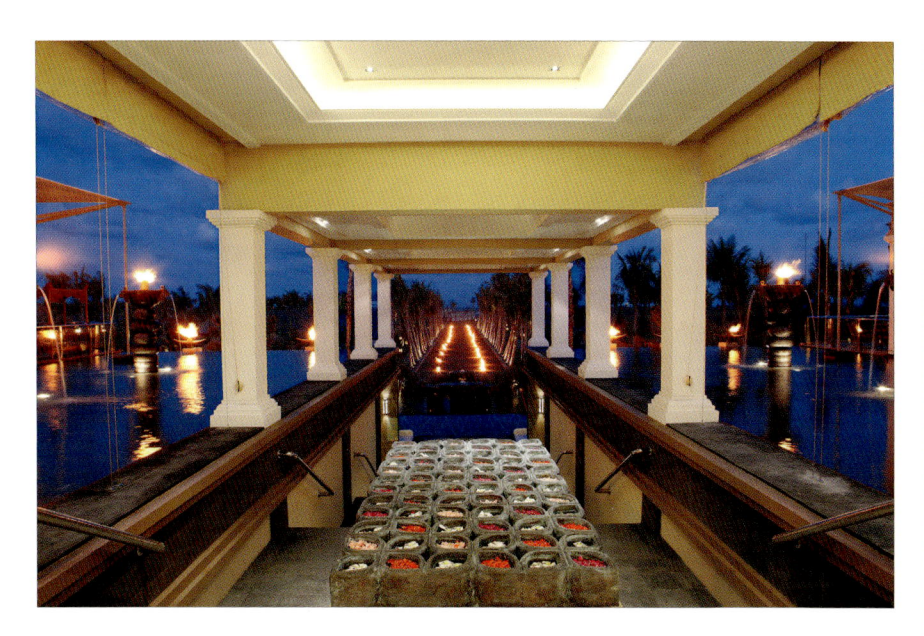

several massage styles, ranging from *shiatsu* to Swedish, luxurious facials, rich moisturising wraps or hand and foot therapy.

For an experience that is wholly unique amongst Remède Spas, indulge in the Lulur Experience of Indonesia ritual. An exotic combination of turmeric, sandalwood and groundnuts is prepared as a paste for use with an exfoliating rice scrub. The skin-renewal regime is a true Indonesian tradition, followed here by a rich yoghurt mask and the slow, kneading strokes of a Balinese massage.

An interesting contrast with the ways of the ancient East can be found in the Remède Spa's signature Bloody Mary spa package, inspired by the famous cocktail that was an original St Regis' creation. In this luxurious affair lasting two hours, the energising properties of tomatoes, pineapples and *wasabi* are deliciously combined with vodka, vermouth and mineral salts for a wrap, bath and massage like nothing else on earth.

Other highlights of Remède Spa at the St Regis Bali include an aqua vitale pool where one can experience underwater massages; sauna and steam room facilities; a fitness centre stocked with all the equipment one could possibly need or want; and—if between mouthfuls of exquisite Jacques Torres truffles, one should spare a thought for friends and family back home—a spa boutique. Here, one can select from a range of Laboratoire Remède's coveted skincare products in order to purchase souvenirs that will surely incite envy.

rooms
hotel: 123 suites and villas •
spa: 12 treatment rooms, 2 spa suites

food
Gazebo: light, healthy meals •
Kayuputi: seafood • Bonek: Continental •
Gourmand Deli: baked goods

drink
Gazebo: fresh juices, mocktails, Indonesian herbal drinks, champagne • Vista Bar •
King Cole Bar

features
aqua vitale pool • fitness centre • yoga •
sauna and steam room • boutique • salon •
locker rooms • pedicure room

nearby
beach • watersports • Bali Golf & Country Club

contact
Kawasan Pariwisata, Nusa Dua Lot S6
P.O. Box 44, Nusa Dua 80363, Bali, Indonesia •
telephone: +62.361.847 8111 •
facsimile: +62.361.847 8099 •
email: remedespa.concierge@stregis.com •
website: www.stregis.com/bali

indonesia 157

ubud hanging gardens

THIS PAGE (FROM TOP): The Ayung Spa blends indoor and outdoor spaces with elegance; the pool overlooks a dramatic hillside and lush greenery.

OPPOSITE (FROM LEFT): Coming back to one's villa is the perfect end to a day of spa treatments; natural ingredients make for wholesome spa products.

Given its longstanding association with sandy beaches, spectacular sunsets and tropical charm, Bali has long enjoyed a reputation for being one of the world's premier vacation destinations. For most visitors, the draw of a full-body massage on a private stretch of one of the island's beaches is unquestionable, and more than satisfactory.

Away from the crowds, however, nestled deep in Bali's verdant green heart, is a resort of an altogether different temperament in the altogether different town of Ubud. Known as the island's centre of culture, Ubud is home to a bohemian mix of artists, craftsmen and an array of ancient temples. As its name implies, Ubud is a place of healing, where time is marked by quiet contemplation and self-discovery. In this serene environment, the Ubud Hanging Gardens hotel offers 38 private villas of delightfully unusual construction.

High amongst the treetops, on cascading terraces cut into the sloping sides of the gorge above the Ayung River, the resort appears to defy gravity. Each villa features a private infinity pool built over the edge that opens out to an unobstructed view down the hillside and over the forest beyond, flanked on all sides by the canopy vegetation swaying in the breeze. Temperature controls for the water mean that even as night falls, guests can enjoy drifting under the stars amidst the sounds of a pure, natural landscape.

indonesia bali

rooms
hotel: 38 villas • spa: 3 pavilions

food
Beduur: Asian and French • Di Atas Pohon Café: healthy light meals on a terrace

drink
Bukit Becik Bar

features
3 spa pavilions • yoga deck and instruction • 2 infinity pools • cooking and painting classes • outdoor excursions • landscaped gardens • hillside cable lifts

nearby
Ubud town centre • shops • golf • rafting • trekking trails

contact
Desa Buahan, Payangan
Ubud, Gianyar 80571, Bali, Indonesia •
telephone: +62.361.982 700 •
facsimile: +62.361.982 800 •
email: ubud@orient-express.com •
website: www.ubudhanginggardens.com

The Ayung Spa facility at Ubud Hanging Gardens is wholly dedicated to extending that sensual experience with techniques and ingredients native to Bali. Built on the banks of the Ayung River, the spa consists of three private pavilions constructed in traditional style, with local materials and designs sensitive to the area's intrinsic beauty. Each pavilion houses two massage beds and a sofa for relaxing, as well as a bath area that seamlessly harmonises with the river's moving water.

The spa offers a series of treatments tuned to the needs of both genders—from the relief of effects caused by stress, to lavish indulgences that leave the skin more radiant. Ayung Spa's essential oils and products, which are created from local organics, are among the finest of their kind. They are used in therapies such as Balinese massages, foot reflexology, body scrubs and facials, which are available to both men and women. Men may also indulge in a signature package that incorporates a special herbal wrap and finishing bath.

Children, too, may have the pleasure of their very own Ayung treatments. Following a light massage that releases tension, young guests will enjoy a strengthened sense of wellbeing and sleep more soundly at night.

Once refreshed, one may then properly savour the award-winning cuisine of French chef Renaud Le Rasle. At Beduur, his candle-lit dinners prove that romance and relaxation go hand in hand here. Afterwards, all that awaits is a bedroom at the top of the world.

four seasons hotel tokyo at chinzan-so

New York may have Central Park, but Tokyo has the gardens of Chinzan-so. The beautiful and varied traditional Japanese design puts this garden in heated competition with the best metropolitan gardens in the world. Sheltered from the capital's noise and neon haze, Chinzan-so exists in a different realm.

Opened in 1992, the Four Seasons Hotel's façade blends harmoniously into this lovely environment, but inside, one is greeted by an atmosphere of grand luxury that combines European furnishings and grace with the delicate sensibilities of Japanese art. That alliance of design also finds its way into each of the 259 rooms, where form and function meet in spacious, high-tech accommodation with superb views over Chinzan-so.

The hotel's YU, THE SPA is a great example of what can happen when old and new are allowed to work together. Traditional healing treatments from both Eastern and Western cultures complement modern facilities and such niceties as a heated swimming pool with a roof that retracts in fair weather. The theme is predominantly Japanese, revealed by the inclusion of an *onsen* bath chamber, and the spa's indulgent use of fine hardwoods and natural stone goes hand-in-hand with such features as an outdoor water garden.

Outdoor views may also be enjoyed from the 115-sq-m (1,238-sq-ft) VIP treatment suite and two 60-sq-m (646-sq-ft) twin rooms, which have private bathtubs set in Japanese courtyard gardens. In addition, the residence-like VIP suite features lounge areas both inside and out, so couples may go straight from a relaxing massage to a welcoming sofa furnished with plenty of throw cushions. Six single treatment rooms, a steam room, a dry sauna and jacuzzis round up the offerings.

Chinzan-so's beautiful gardens do more than just set the mood for an afternoon of pampering in the sun, they also serve as the source of several botanical ingredients used in YU's exclusive seasonal treatment oils. Each one is formulated with the herbs and flowers representative of a particular season and will protect the skin with powerful antioxidants.

Many of the therapies here are unique. For instance, choose the signature Fire and Water Purification Ritual, based on a 12th-century Buddhist tradition. The water portion involves a Vichy shower and steam room, while fire comes in the form of a massage and wrap, along with a long soak and hot tea. At the end of the three-hour affair, one should feel that much closer to enlightenment, and a lifetime away from modern Tokyo.

THIS PAGE (FROM LEFT): The cleansing, invigorating water spray treatment is a must-try; spectacular views of the city's skyline or the garden are available from the guestrooms and suites.
OPPOSITE (FROM LEFT): In the VIP treatment suite and the two twin treatment rooms, one will find private bathtubs set in a serene Japanese garden; twin treatment rooms offer an ideal environment for couples to relax together, during and after their treatments.

japan **tokyo**

rooms
hotel: 259 rooms, including 44 suites •
spa: 6 single treatment rooms, 2 twin rooms, 1 VIP suite

food
Miyuki: classic Japanese • Seasons Bistro: Mediterranean • Il Teatro: Italian

drink
Le Jardin • Le Marquis

features
Japanese gardens • indoor *onsen* bath with water from the Izu Peninsula • steam room • sauna • indoor and outdoor jacuzzis • Elemis UK, Aromatherapy Associates & Beyond Organic spa products • Guerlain salon products • fitness centre • indoor pool with retractable roof

nearby
gardens • restaurants • central Tokyo

contact
10–8, Sekiguchi 2-chome
Bunkyo-ku, Tokyo 112–8667, Japan •
telephone: +81.3.3943 6958 •
facsimile: +81.3.3943 2300 •
email: tokyo.spa@fourseasons.com •
website: www.fourseasons.com/tokyo

the westin tokyo

Subject to the ever-turning tides of fashion and external influence, Tokyo's modern cultural landscape is a riveting pastiche of remixes and revivals that continually astonishes any visitor, while remaining uniquely Japanese.

Take The Westin Tokyo hotel, for instance. Set in the middle of Yebisu Garden Place—the former site of a giant beer brewery which has been turned into a downtown entertainment district—this five-star business hotel bears more than a few elements of modern European design across its 438 rooms. The hotel's recently opened spa facility, Le Spa Parisien, further develops the Continental theme with lush, intimate interiors based on the imperial French aesthetic.

All things French have always held a certain appeal for the Japanese, and it's not hard to see why as one enters the boudoir-like reception area, where every visit begins with a personalised consultation amidst classical refinement. From there, guests may either proceed to the relaxation lounge for a special blend of herbal tea, or the Aqua Area, which includes hydrotherapy jet pools, a steam sauna with the aromatherapy benefits of lavender and eucalyptus and a dry sauna reserved for men. The central feature here is the Aqua Sound pool, where reverberations of a distinct frequency are transmitted through the water into the body, creating a massaging sensation that tempts one to go no further.

THIS PAGE (FROM LEFT): *Enter the Aqua Area and it is impossible to miss the Aqua Sound pool; the spa's copper bathtubs exude old-world charm.*

OPPOSITE (FROM LEFT): *Each of the 11 treatment rooms is decked out in elegant luxury, creating soothing spaces where expert therapists work their magic; guests are spoilt for choice with Le Spa Parisien's wide range of body and beauty treatments, many of which serve specific purposes.*

japan **tokyo**

However, to stop there is to miss out on the full menu of treatments. Everything from Swedish massages and Monticelli mud wraps, to candle and hot stone aroma body therapies can be found on offer. The latter is a seasonal special that improves blood circulation and is especially delightful in the winter months.

When it makes sense to do so, Le Spa Parisien has no qualms about fusing its Eurocentric approach with traditional Japanese wisdom. Shokusai no Kyuujitsu is a ritual that begins with a Japanese meal rich in natural skin-enhancing nutrients, followed by a lavish European-style facial treatment. Other special facials—such as anti-ageing, whitening and rejuvenation—cater to specific desires, and they are performed with imported skincare products found nowhere else in the country.

One can expect to enjoy all procedures in the comfort of 11 exquisite treatment areas, each named for a place in France. Six luxury suites are richly appointed in classic palatial style, with three boasting handcrafted copper soaking tubs for a decadent bathing experience. Most of the rooms readily accommodate couples and feature privileged views over the city.

In addition, The Westin Tokyo provides several ways to enhance a stay. For one, an in-room spa service caters to those with busy schedules, or those who prefer more privacy. Each evening, the Unwind(SM) event at the Lobby Bar brings guests together over food and drink, featuring snacks prepared with herbs from the hotel's garden. With its unique take on European spas, even Francophiles will discover unexpected joys at Le Spa Parisien.

rooms
hotel: 438 rooms • spa: 11 treatment rooms

food
relaxation lounge snacks

drink
herbal teas

features
Aqua Sound pool • sauna • steam room • hydrotherapy jet spa • in-room spa service

nearby
Yebisu Garden Place Shopping Complex • Shibuya • Roppongi • Tokyo Tower

contact
1-4-1 Mita, Meguro-ku
Tokyo 153-8580, Japan •
telephone: +81.3.5423 7002 •
facsimile: +81.3.5423 7600 •
email: wetok@westin.com •
website: www.westin-tokyo.co.jp

cyberview lodge resort + spa

THIS PAGE (FROM TOP): **A moisturising bath in rich milk and fresh flowers will bring a healthy glow to one's skin; the carefully prepared cuisine available at the spa demonstrates that healthy food can be delicious as well.**

OPPOSITE (FROM LEFT): **Groups of friends or family may wish to request the Tasik Suite, which can accommodate up to four guests at one time; skilled hands will gently coax tension from a guest's body.**

Malaysia's Multimedia Super Corridor (MSC), an area designated for intensive development as the country's answer to Silicon Valley, is the last place one would expect to find a world-class spa retreat, but then Cyberview Lodge Resort's Sembunyi Spa defies expectations. Located in the futuristic town of Cyberjaya, just 20 minutes from the capital city of Kuala Lumpur and the famed Sepang racing circuit, Cyberview Lodge Resort & Spa is shrouded from all the commercial activity of the MSC by nearly 12.1 hectares (30 acres) of greenery and award-winning landscaping, so that work and play are always clearly separated for the hotel's many business visitors.

At the centre of the grounds, behind countless palm trees, winding footpaths and murmuring water features, the resort's main building forms the heart of a five-star village. In keeping with the atmosphere of a rural getaway, accommodation comes in the form of 74 exclusive suites, bungalows and deluxe chalets, all furnished with rustic hardwood and local artefacts. The best suites have their own jacuzzis with splendid views of the surrounds, better enjoyed with one of the unique floral bath treatments available on order.

Nowhere else on the premises does one feel more at the centre of attention than at Sembunyi Spa. Recipient of the 'Best Spa Concept' and 'Best Spa Experience' Platinum Awards (2005/2006) from *Hospitality Asia*, the huge 929-sq-m (10,000-sq-ft) facility is in a class of its own. Standing at the doorstep of its sprawling thatched-roof complex, looking out over an idyllic scene of lakes and gentle green fields that the best championship golf courses can only hope to challenge, one gets an inkling of the pampering that awaits.

Take a step into the complex and the craftsmanship of the spa's stone wall-tiling and carved wooden features immediately becomes apparent—a traditional design style reigns here. Many of the body treatments and facials on offer draw from a well of Southeast Asian traditions, although more contemporary therapies are also given a place on the menu. All-natural ingredients are used exclusively; *kemiri* nuts and a *lulur* rub made from ground rice powder, turmeric and tamarind seeds are just some of the exotic tools at the spa's disposal. Seven treatment rooms, a Mayang Sari Suite for couples and an immense Tasik Suite that can house four guests are where a visit ends or begins, depending on one's preference. Some may wish to visit the fitness centre first, or experience an invigorating scrub followed by a long session in the steam room and a dip in the icy plunge pool.

Healthy spa cuisine is served in a private gazebo overlooking the lake, but the resort also features five other bars and restaurants, all offering further indulgence. Whether on business at an MSC convention, or purely for pleasure, visiting Cyberjaya no longer involves the clinical images that its name suggests, and that's all due to a little taste of paradise at the Cyberview Lodge Resort & Spa.

malaysia cyberjaya

rooms
hotel: 74 suites and chalets •
spa: 9 treatment rooms and suites

food
healthy meals • Bistro Cascata: Italian fusion •
Verandah Restaurant: Pan-Asian •
Xing Zhu: Chinese

drink
Atap Lounge • Tree Haus Fun Pub

features
lap pool • sauna • cold plunge pool •
landscaped gardens • fitness centre •
high-speed Internet access

nearby
Multimedia Super Corridor • Kuala Lumpur •
Sepang Circuit

contact
Persiaran Multimedia
63000 Cyberjaya, Selangor, Malaysia •
telephone: +60.3.8312 7000 •
facsimile: +60.3.8312 7001 •
email: spa@cyberview-lodge.com.my •
website: www.cyberview-lodge.com

four seasons resort langkawi

It's clear that rest and rehabilitation are taken very seriously on the Malaysian island of Langkawi—the weekends begin on Friday, exactly when much of the working world wishes it could be on a beautiful beach overlooking the Andaman Sea. The Four Seasons Resort Langkawi embodies that feeling of escape with more than a mile of incredible beaches and world-class spa facilities nestled in tropical greenery.

Built to the same high standards as the rest of the 90-room resort, the spa forgoes having any single dominant style for an inspiringly original scheme that melds local Malay forms with elements of Mughal and Moorish architecture. The result is a collection of serene spa pavilions that resonates with ancient Eastern knowledge but also contains all the five-star amenities of the modern age. Constructed from carved local wood and perched over a reflecting pond, the six private buildings form a very picturesque scene set against 19 hectares (48 acres) of lush gardens and sheer limestone cliffs.

Each spa pavilion is luxuriously spacious and allows couples to enjoy their time together thoroughly with such extravagant indoor facilities as celadon soaking tubs, as well as outdoor gardens outfitted with rainshowers and lounge areas. Completely

THIS PAGE (FROM LEFT): *Malay-inspired treatments are the speciality of the spa, but the staff's expertise extends to Ayurvedic treatments as well; with white sand and ocean waves just a few steps away, each Beach Villa also features a private spa room.*
OPPOSITE (FROM LEFT): *Three striking structures offer a beautiful, tranquil space for relaxation and contemplation after one's luxurious spa treatments; the spa's expert yoga teachers share their extensive knowledge with guests.*

malaysia **langkawi**

separate from one another, the pavilions are the ultimate in private indulgence where guests can savour a moment of true peace.

The extensive treatment menu of the spa focuses on the unique traditions of the region, leaving its team of expert practitioners to hone their craft instead of accommodating techniques from around the world.

Some of the novel therapies include the Putra Laksamana for men, which involves a herbal foot soak, an exfoliating scrub with ginger and kaffir lime and a spicy massage with cloves, nutmeg and other traditional ingredients, and the Seri Pesona for women, which starts with an invigorating coconut oil scalp massage, and then continues with hydrating hair treatments, a Malay-style body massage, herbal steaming, a floral bath and ends with a warm cup of *jamu* elixir. Others, like the Bulan Madu, are geared for couples, but also employ techniques that reap the benefits of the local botany, such as cinnamon body brushing and *boreh* spice wraps.

As an alternative to the standalone spa, the 20 Beach Villas, the two-bedroom villa and the Royal Villa have private treatment rooms built in as a key part of the accommodation, each one large enough for two. There, guests may choose to have any one of the four signature Asian treatments performed as an exclusive in-room spa service. Even without these extras, these beachfront villas already boast views that would make anyone out there jealous on a weekday afternoon.

rooms
hotel: 68 Melaleuca Pavilions, 20 Beach Villas, 1 two-bedroom villa, 1 Royal Villa •
spa: 6 spa pavilions

food
Serai: Italian • Kafe Kelapa: Asian and Western • Ikan-Ikan: Thai, Chinese and Malay cuisine

drink
The Spa Juice Bar • Rhu Bar •
Kafe Kelapa Bar • Ikan Ikan Bar

features
yoga pavilion • in-room spa service for villas • traditional speciality treatments • boutique • kids' bath menu • beauty salon

nearby
beaches • Kilim Nature Park • crocodile farm • Gunung Raya mountain • Air Hangat Village

contact
Jalan Tanjung Rhu
07000 Langkawi, Kedah Darul Aman, Malaysia •
telephone: +60.4.950 8603 •
facsimile: +60.4.950 8899 •
email: reservations.lan@fourseasons.com •
website: www.fourseasons.com

shangri-la's tanjung aru resort + rasa sayang resort

In just a few years, the Shangri-La group's CHI, The Spa has expanded to over 16 locations worldwide. Based on the healing rituals and ways of life in the Himalayan regions and China, its unique 'spa within a spa' design philosophy, use of premium organic products and expert therapists have established CHI as a leader in traditional holistic wellness.

CHI's Malaysian properties go one step further, weaving strands of local culture into both their architecture and offerings.

Shangri-La's Tanjung Aru Resort + Spa

Shangri-La's Tanjung Aru Resort sees a private island devoted entirely to housing the 4,161-sq-m (44,789-sq-ft) CHI, The Spa facility. The compound comprises eight Island Villas, each equipped with exclusive treatment areas, steam rooms and gardens, so guests never have to leave except to appreciate views of the South China Sea and Himalayan-inspired buildings. Elements such as the Sanctum's bronzed roof, modelled after a Himalayan *stupa*, and the red earth bricks used in the central water feature were contributed by Himalayan craftsmen, but local knowledge also played a large role: all villas were constructed from indigenous hardwood and adorned with traditional carvings.

The spa also utilises ingredients derived from Sabah's rainforests. The Borneo Volcanic Mud Wrap is a signature treatment that aids

THIS PAGE (FROM LEFT): *Inspiring settings for yoga are available at both of the spas; the design of the Sanctum at CHI, The Spa at Shangri-La's Tanjung Aru Resort reflects a medley of Asian influences.*

OPPOSITE: *Shangri-La's Rasa Sayang Resort, Penang is immersed in lush greenery.*

malaysia **kota kinabalu + penang**

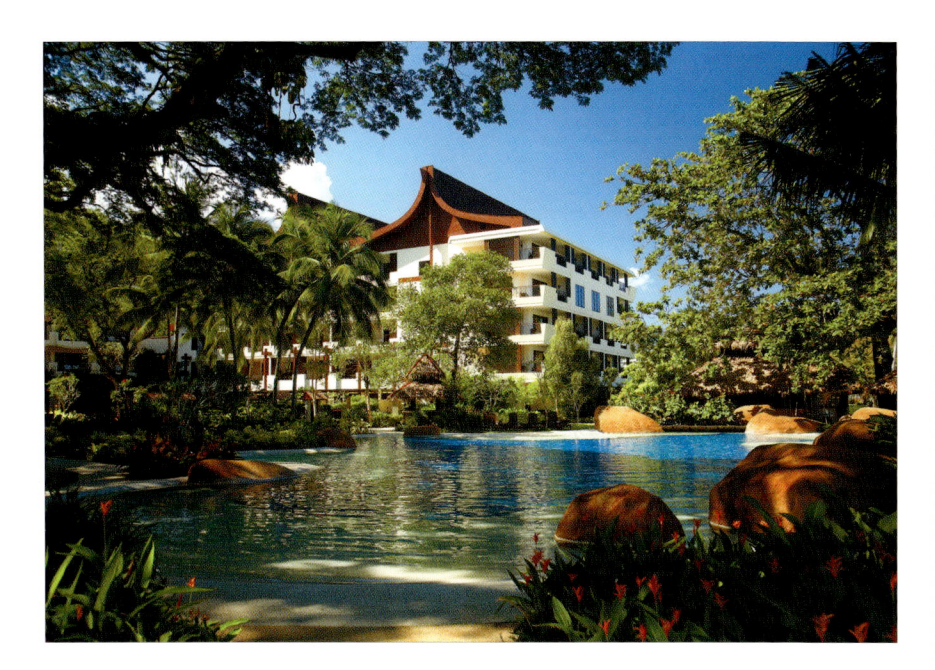

detoxification with a blend of minerals found in the clay of the Lahad Datu region. Overexposure to the sun is countered with a Cooling Bayu Wrap that calls upon aloe vera, mango, avocado and various other fruit extracts that have long moisturised and soothed the local populace.

Shangri-La's Rasa Sayang Resort + Spa
A similar benefit is offered in the Rasa Sayang Resort's Rasa Nyaman Body Wrap, but the ingredients vary in reflection of its westerly location in Penang. Being on the Malaysian peninsula, the spa at Shangri-La's Rasa Sayang Resort incorporates a more diverse range of Asian influences. The architecture pays tribute to Peranakan style with a combination of timber flooring and granite walls, while techniques from regions along the ancient spice route feature alongside Malay disciplines on the spa menu. To experience the sensations on offer, try the Rasa Asmaradana, a full-body massage that includes a warm herbal pound, Malay essential oils, Thai massage, Chinese acupuncture and deep Ayurvedic strokes, reflecting Penang's multicultural influences.

Designed in the form of a hidden village, the 3,800-sq-m (40,903-sq-ft) sanctuary is an oasis of gardens and rustic treatment villas close to the sea, including a yoga pavilion that embodies the phrase: 'a place of peace'. Each of the 11 villas features CHI's integrated spa design, with a treatment room, soaking tub and a plethora of other facilities.

rooms
Kota Kinabalu: 492 rooms and suites • 8 spa villas
Penang: 304 rooms and suites • 11 spa villas

food
Kota Kinabalu: Café TATU • Coco-Joe's • Peppino • Shang Palace
Penang: Feringgi Grill • Spice Market Café • Pinang Bar & Restaurant

drink
Kota Kinabalu: Blue Note • Sunset Bar • Borneo Lounge & Bar
Penang: Feringgi Bar • Lobby Lounge • Pinang Restaurant and Bar • Tepi Laut Restaurant and Bar

features
private spa villas • traditional treatments with local ingredients and practices • CHI boutique • yoga pavilions • steam rooms • pools

nearby
Kota Kinabalu: snorkelling and diving • nature reserves • shopping
Penang: beaches • restaurants • bars • museums • shopping • night markets

contact
Kota Kinabalu:
20 Jalan Aru, Tanjung Aru
88100 Kota Kinabalu, Sabah, Malaysia •
telephone: +60.88.327 888 •
facsimile: +60.88.327 878 •
email: tah@shangri-la.com •
website: www.shangri-la.com

Penang:
Batu Feringgi Beach
11100 Penang, Malaysia •
telephone: +60.4.888 8888 •
facsimile: +60.4.881 1800 •
email: rsr@shangri-la.com •
website: www.shangri-la.com

st gregory spa

THIS PAGE: *Parkroyal Penang is one of the most sought-after accommodations in Penang.*

OPPOSITE (FROM LEFT): *Designed to allow couples to share private, romantic spa sessions, every inch of the VIP treatment room is furnished in luxury; guests are spoilt for choice with a menu of more than 30 body and beauty treatments.*

For over a decade, residents in neighbouring Singapore have regarded the St Gregory name as a leader in holistic health and wellness. Successful expansion has led to a current total of 11 spas across the Asia-Pacific region, with six of those in health-conscious Japan. However, unlike most spa and beauty establishments, the company places equal emphasis on fitness—with the provision of fully featured gym facilities—as well on its concept of 'Active-Ageing', which enables clients of all ages to lead balanced lifestyles and practise intelligent weight management. St Gregory's treatments and programmes are inspired by a combination of traditional Asian techniques as well as Western advances in aesthetics and science. Thus, it is not unusual to see Javanese massage techniques enjoyed in tandem with Ayurvedic therapies here.

St Gregory at the five-star Parkroyal Penang is ideally situated, and it takes full advantage of its location amidst palm trees and landscaped gardens by incorporating elements of Malay design common to coastal

malaysia **penang**

rooms
7 treatment rooms, including VIP/couple room

features
facial treatments • body massage rituals • Hydrobath treatments • children's spa • manicures and pedicures

nearby
Batu Feringgi Beach • city centre • shops • tourist attractions • Penang International Airport

contact
Parkroyal Penang, Batu Feringgi Beach
11100 Penang, Malaysia •
telephone: +60.4.881 1133 or +60.4.886 2288 •
facsimile: +60.4.881 2233 •
email: enquiry@pen.parkroyalhotels.com •
websites: www.stgregoryspa.com,
parkroyalhotels.com

areas, as well as a number of refined Persian features. Simple, uncomplicated interiors are wisely employed in keeping the mood light and relaxed. Throughout the seven treatment rooms, it can be clearly seen that comfort comes first. One room is dedicated to hand and foot massages, while another is reserved for Hydrobath therapy, a highly recommended half-hour-long spa jet massage in a bath of essential oils and atomised Thalgo seaweed extracts. Concluded by a brief but effective neck and shoulder massage, it's ideal for alleviating the aches of travelling and jet lag.

The remaining five rooms are open for any of the full menu of over 30 treatments. A few popular choices are the Aromatic Body Bliss Massage, which uses the gentle motions of Swedish massage to infuse healing oils; the Balinese Massage, which will flush out toxins; and the invigorating Yoghurt Body Glow Scrub. Honeymooners will appreciate that all these and a range of customised couple packages can be enjoyed together in a spacious VIP treatment room overlooking the sea.

In a nod to the hotel's popularity with families, a Kids Spa package is available for those aged seven to 12. Precocious children can have a Mini Manicure/Pedicure, a Milk/Flower Bath, or a Chocolate Body Mask while their parents are elsewhere. No wonder St Gregory won the title of 'Best Service Spa in Asia' from *The Ultimate Spa Guide* and obtained its 'Leading Spa' certification in Singapore from The Leading Hotels of the World group.

the st regis singapore

Think spa treatments accented by a glass of chilled champagne, a handful of handcrafted chocolates and exotic teas grown in the south of France. That's what to expect from Singapore's newest and most opulent health and beauty experience, the Remède Spa at the incomparable St Regis Hotel.

Unveiled in late 2008, the property is Southeast Asia's first branch of the legendary American hotel collection. Positioned at the highest end of the market, the 299-room St Regis is all about luxury without compromise. For instance, guests can indulge in retail therapy, touring the shops of Orchard Road in style with their pick from a fleet of custom Bentleys, and then return for therapy of another kind at the Remède Spa.

Developed by the dedicated skincare laboratory Laboratoire Remède, the lavish facility makes use of the same exclusive body and skincare products so popular with the spa's loyal clients in New York and San Francisco. Furthermore, every visit is prefaced with an in-depth consultation to tailor every procedure specifically to the client's unique dermatological needs.

As one leaves the shimmering, crystal-studded reception area to unwind in a relaxation lounge, personal iPods are provided to help create the desired atmosphere. The individuality of each visitor is acknowledged in the varied music selection; everything from opera and jazz to natural soundscapes and world music is available.

THIS PAGE (FROM LEFT): The sparkling reception area hints at the treasures within the spa; guests relax with a glass of champagne and chocolates after their treatments.

OPPOSITE (FROM LEFT): Water is an integral element of both the treatments and the facilities, as evidenced by the spa's inviting wet lounge; Vichy shower tables reinvent the traditional hammam experience with an added touch of luxury.

singapore

rooms
hotel: 299 guestrooms •
spa: 6 treatment rooms, 1 Jade Couple Suite, 2 wet lounges, 2 Vichy shower rooms

food
Brasserie Les Saveurs: international •
Yan Ting: fine Cantonese • LaBrezza: light meals and Mediterranean cuisine

drink
Astor Bar: cocktails • The Drawing Room: teas • Decanter: fine wines

features
ice fountain • Vichy showers •
steam marble chambers •
spa garden with pool and aqua reflex path •
cedarwood sauna • heated wave loungers

nearby
Orchard Road shopping district •
Singapore Botanic Gardens

contact
29 Tanglin Road
Singapore 247911 •
telephone: +65.6506 6892 •
email: spa.singapore@stregis.com •
website: www.stregis.com

That same diversity is also present in the spa menu. Designed to encompass the breadth of healing knowledge, it includes elements from as far back as the Roman Empire and the dynasties of ancient China, while spanning the globe so far as to include the *hammam* of the Middle East.

The traditional *hammam* is reinvented here with marble Vichy shower tables heated with infrared technology and the use of decadent ingredients such as eucalyptus black soap, rose or orange blossom-scented water, Dead Sea salts and scented milk.

One of the spa's signature treatments is the Warm Jade Stone Massage which uses the semi-precious Oriental gemstone as a thermal implement. Over a series of long strokes, essential oils are infused into the skin while muscles receive a relaxing deep tissue rub that leaves one feeling renewed and cleansed, with the pleasant lingering scent of Himalayan cedarwood, vetiver and cypress. These harmonise well with the distinctive, custom-blended 'St Regis scent' that is diffused throughout the spa to create a mood of warmth and balance.

Offering countless extravagant options, the Remède Spa makes it easy to find the ultimate indulgence, even for someone with the most discriminating of wishlists. With peerless facilities and products, it's a five-star experience worthy of the St Regis Singapore.

malaysia+singapore 173

plantation bay resort + spa

Over the last few decades, the word 'resort' has become somewhat trivialised. The resort hotels today rarely deviate from the standard template of beach, pool and collection of low-rise structures. However, to discover a place such as the Plantation Bay Resort & Spa is to restore meaning to a term that once described singular destinations.

Located only 30 minutes from Cebu City, Plantation Bay enjoys comfortable seclusion in a tropical plantation setting, complete with authentic colonial-style architecture and an expansive, privately owned waterway running through the 11-hectare (28-acre) estate.

The spa takes things a step further. Mogambo Springs is a separate entity, a fact which becomes apparent at first glance. If one experienced a sense of awe upon arriving on Plantation Bay's charming front steps, then the 18th-century Japanese Tokugawa village design in the spa promises to have an even more dramatic effect. With its wooden huts, pagodas, Zen gardens, creeks and other carefully reproduced details, the design direction is nothing if not ambitious, and the final product achieves the effect of inducing an almost otherworldly calm upon visitors.

These Japanese features do not just set the mood but also make for an impressive list of amenities that can be enjoyed before and after treatments. For instance, guests can take hotspring baths or indulge in hydro-massages under a waterfall. Other facilities include a dry sauna, steam room, Thalassic pool and private

THIS PAGE (FROM LEFT): *The refreshing spray and the picturesque surroundings make the needle shower nook an idyllic spot; herbal or floral baths help to relax mind and body.*

OPPOSITE (FROM LEFT): *Plantation Bay offers one of the largest privately owned waterways in the world, along with the clean elegance of colonial-plantation architecture, allowing one to decompress from life's pressures in the healing tranquillity of an environment that truly feels 'away from it all'; a soothing cup of herbal tea after a treatment is the perfect way to conclude a relaxing day at the spa.*

the philippines **mactan island**

rooms
hotel: 256 rooms and suites •
spa: 3 Spa Indulgence Rooms

food
Palermo: Italian • Fiji: Pacific Rim cuisine •
Kilimanjaro Kafé: international and Filipino •
Savannah Grill: fast food

drink
power drinks • herbal teas

features
indoor and outdoor hot pools with jacuzzis •
Thalassic pool • outdoor pool with cascading falls for hydromassage • needle shower nook • sauna and steam room

nearby
Mactan airport • beaches • Cebu City

contact
Marigondon, Mactan Island
Cebu 6015, Philippines •
telephone: +63.32.340 5900 •
facsimile: +63.32.340 5988 •
email: spa@plantationbay.com •
website: www.plantationbay.com

rooms for a wide range of massages, facials and body treatments. Mogambo Springs also features the German 'Dorn Method' of spinal alignment to treat back ailments—a first for any spa in Asia.

In addition to the traditional Filipino *hilot* massage—a deep-tissue massage that uses fast and long strokes—the spa's other massage options include *shiatsu*, Swedish, fusion or traditional Thai massages. The spa's signature massage is an hour-long odyssey that employs a variety of techniques. It's called Skinful Pleasures, but what it should really be called is addictive. An original creation of the spa, it involves stretching, squeezing, straightening and other soothing motions that are applied to skin and muscles.

Loving Life is the wellness programme at Mogambo Springs, not based on any single fad but on the most effective findings related to wellbeing and health. Loving Life is not a fad diet but is a programme that includes a balanced diet, moderate exercise, meditation, daily spa pampering and colon cleansing.

Guests who want to experience a complete spa pampering treat should try the Ultimate Mogambo Springs Experience, a six-hour-and-30-minute package that includes a pool massage, body scrub, foot therapy, facial, aromatherapy oil massage and nail care. After experiencing such top-of-the-line spa treatments, along with Plantation Bay's superb dining and leisure facilities, lesser resorts may never satisfy again.

shangri-la's boracay resort + spa

THIS PAGE: In addition to its private lap pool, Pool Villa Balani has an outdoor shower, a pergola for outdoor dining, and a daybed that is perfect for having a massage.

OPPOSITE (FROM LEFT): The CHI Couples Villas offer couples a chance to relax and reconnect; experience the rejuvenating, relaxing effects of traditional Filipino massage techniques.

The island of Boracay is arguably the hottest tourist destination in the Philippines, walking the fine line between commercialism and conservation with ease. The 18-hole, par-72 championship golf course, a plethora of bars and restaurants, and the throng of activity surrounding the aptly named White Beach do little to detract from the island's appeal, in part because many of the reasons why Boracay was so desirable before the world came to holiday here still hold true today.

However, from 2009, Boracay is set to take back some of what was lost—that elusive undiscovered vibe—between the arrival of the first tourists and the building of some 350 beach resorts across the island.

Shangri-La's Boracay Resort & Spa, far from just another hotel, is the first five-star international resort development on the island, striving to protect Boracay's natural beauty and showcase it for discerning travellers. Spanning a total of 12 hectares (30 acres) in a protected nature reserve in the hitherto untouched north of the island, beside a private stretch of beach that measures more than 350 m (1,148 ft), the resort is effectively isolated by its hillside location and a wall of greenery. Guests share this spectacular address with some 75 species of plants, 36 recorded species of birds and even fruit bats—some of these are rare and unique to this corner of the world.

The resort is also home to the latest CHI, The Spa development, which represents the culmination of the Shangri-La group's varied experience in building award winning spa concepts. All CHI spas start from a template of ancient Chinese and Himalayan traditions, and their elements inform everything from the design of the buildings to the recipes and techniques used in healing rituals. On top of that, painstaking research into the history of each location adds little details to make each spa an individual entity, in addition to putting exclusive local treatments on the menu.

At CHI, The Spa on Boracay, four special treatments are offered, each one reason enough to book a second visit to the spa immediately upon finishing the first. The Palina Hilot Four Hand Massage blends

the philippines **boracay island**

traditional Filipino massage techniques with the privileged bliss of having two therapists at once. Additionally, muscle relief comes in the form of the Hot Dinu-ot treatment, ideal for anyone whose body is fatigued from hours of trekking on the many nature and wildlife walking trails surrounding the estate. Lastly, for guests who must have everything—and who have more free time—the three-day Boracay Wellness package includes a huge range of treatments, complemented by the use of local all-natural ingredients.

These and all the other CHI signature therapies—such as the Himalayan Healing Stone Massage and the Mountain Tsampa Rub—take place in an elevated spa village built on a rocky promontory overlooking a private bay. The 5,714-sq-m (61,505-sq-ft) enclave features its own pool, scenic yoga pavilion and numerous spa villas, each with its own 'spa within a spa' facilities ideally suited for both single guests and couples.

It's not often that the opening of a resort can be celebrated as a return to a region's exclusivity, but with careful environmentally conscious planning, that's exactly what the new Shangri-La's Boracay Resort and CHI, The Spa have allowed. A chance to discover new pleasures in such a natural and 'undiscovered' spot is just too good to be missed.

rooms
hotel: 219 rooms and villas •
spa: 1 Grand Villa, 3 Couple Villas,
5 Garden Suites, 1 CHI Pavilion

food
Vintana • Rima: Italian • Sirena: seafood •
The Lobby Lounge • Cielo Poolside Restaurant

drink
Solana Bar • Alon Bar

features
spa treatments unique to Boracay •
reflexology lounge • yoga pavilion •
CHI boutique • pool • reception sanctum •
separate male and female lockers and
relaxation lounges • 15-m lap pool

nearby
White Beach • shops • restaurants • nightlife •
diving • fishing • nature reserve

contact
Barangay Yapak, Boracay Island
Malay, Aklan 5608, Philippines •
telephone: +63.36.288 4988 •
facsimile: +63.36.288 5088 •
email: slbo@shangri-la.com •
website: www.shangri-la.com

shangri-la's mactan resort + spa + edsa shangri-la, manila

It is said that Cebu's golden age began in 1993 with the Shangri-La's Mactan Resort & Spa's creation, for the five-star retreat not only raised hospitality stakes across the famously friendly province, but also the entire country. Part of this was due to the Mactan's status as the first Philippine property to host the hotel group's renowned CHI, The Spa.

Not a single expense was spared in the execution of the spa's finer details, and its popularity made the opening of another branch at the Edsa Shangri-La in central Manila an inevitability. Today, the treatment menus at both properties borrow from the best of local traditions to supplement CHI's famous signature massages and therapies.

Shangri-La's Mactan Resort + Spa

Designed as a village of one luxurious grand spa villa, six villas for couples and eight garden suites, Mactan's CHI, The Spa is one of the largest of its kind, at a double take-inducing 10,000 sq m (107,640 sq ft). Virtually all of the space is dedicated to the enjoyment of the spa's treatments and Cebu's tropical environment, seen in the acres of gardens around each villa. Inspired by the culture of the Himalayas, CHI, The Spa features Himalayan architectural motifs, but one will also find Philippine elements. Locally mined stone forms the base of construction, while interior fittings are the work of local artisans who use materials from the region.

THIS PAGE (FROM LEFT): *The serene atmosphere of the Karakal Vitality Pool at Shangri-La's Mactan Resort & Spa invites relaxation and contemplation; take a refreshing swim in the beautiful pool at Shangri-La's Mactan Resort & Spa.*

OPPOSITE: *The Himalayan and Filipino design elements give each of the CHI treatment rooms a distinctive flair.*

the philippines manila + mactan island

It is also a CHI tradition to bolster its menu of treatments, largely influenced by ancient Chinese and Himalayan traditions, with secrets from each local community. And so the Mactan resort's spa experts utilise barako coffee, pito-pito herbs, virgin coconut oil, sampaguita flowers and various tropical fruit extracts. An example of this heady fusion can be found in the Philippine *hilot* massage, which combines time-tested local herbs with Chinese and Ayurvedic techniques to enhance one's general wellbeing.

Edsa Shangri-La, Manila

Located in Ortigas Centre, a vibrant commercial district, the Edsa Shangri-La, Manila manages to shroud itself in the cool calm of tropical greenery, which sets the scene for an experience that feels miles away.

At 3,000 sq m (32,292 sq ft), it is the city's most spacious spa facility, and like the Mactan, it offers treatments that feature traditional Philippine healing practices and use all-natural indigenous ingredients.

In the opulent cocoons that are its treatment suites and relaxation lounges, such pleasures as the Hayahay (a fresh coconut scrub followed by the richness of a mayo butter wrap that is then finished off with an hour-long *hilot* massage) and the Dagdagay Foot Therapy (a treatment that uses a method pioneered by highland tribes) ease one into a state of total relaxation.

The benefits of yoga, hydrotherapy and fitness are also readily available within the spa's facilities, putting it in a class of its own among urban day spas.

rooms
Mactan: 547 rooms and suites • 1 grand spa villa • 6 spa couples' villas • 8 spa garden suites
Edsa: 632 rooms and suites • 11 spa treatment suites

food
Mactan: Acqua • Cowrie Cove • Tea of Spring • Buko Bar • Tides
Edsa: HEAT • Paparazzi • Summer Palace • Senju • The Bakeshop

drink
Mactan: Beach Bar • Chill Out Bar • Lobby Lounge
Edsa: e's Bar • Lobby Lounge • Pool Bar

features
Mactan: spa pool • CHI cuisine • *watsu* pool • Water Garden Vitality Tubs and Body Scrub • Reflexology Lounge • yoga studio • Hilot Massage Pavilion • Windsong Meditation Pavilion
Edsa: private off-street entrance and parking • couples suite with green verandah • Himalayan Wet Rooms • yoga studio and library

nearby
Mactan: beaches • diving • snorkelling • sailing
Edsa: SM Megamall • Greenhills Shopping Centre • Tiendesitas Shopping Village

contact
Mactan: Punta Engaño Road, Lapu-Lapu Cebu 6015, Philippines •
telephone: +63.32.231 0288 •
facsimile: +63.32.231 1688 •
email: mac@shangri-la.com •
website: www.shangri-la.com

Edsa: 1 Garden Way, Ortigas Centre Mandaluyong City 1650, Philippines •
telephone: +63.2.633 8888 •
facsimile: +63.2.631 1067 •
email: esl@shangri-la.com •
website: www.shangri-la.com

absolute sanctuary

THIS PAGE: *Spend a weekend, or better yet an entire week, at Absolute Sanctuary detoxing and rejuvenating.*

OPPOSITE (FROM LEFT): *The 38 rooms are painted in striking colour palettes and outfitted with a host of modern amenities; the use of high-quality spa ingredients combined with the therapists' skill ensure that guests leave satisfied.*

Following the explosive success of Absolute Yoga studios in Singapore and Thailand, the Absolute group has now begun introducing the wonders of detoxification programmes to those in need of a healthy reset in their lives.

Enter Absolute Sanctuary. Situated on the island of Koh Samui, Absolute Sanctuary is a complete residential spa, detox and yoga destination. The resort's design takes its cues from exotic Moroccan architecture, with the final result forming a remarkable interplay between the shape of the complex and the organic entropy of its tropical surroundings.

Even if a guest can only spare a weekend, one of the Detox Centre's custom-designed programmes will replace toxins, fat and waste with nutrients. The Ultimate Detox is the most effective, involving structured fasting and colon hydrotherapy, while the Living Foods and Vegetarian Detox programmes focus on the

thailand **koh samui**

benefits of raw foods and healthy, vegetarian cuisine. Manual lymphatic drainage, an alternative to colon hydrotherapy, is also offered. Every visit begins with a consultation with a wellness consultant who will tailor the programme according to each guest's needs.

Yoga still forms the core of the Sanctuary experience; and in building the new Yoga Centre, the group has created their most impressive studio yet. Not only equipped with a heating system for Hot Yoga classes and separate male and female facilities, the large indoor studio is also fitted with floor-to-ceiling windows for a beautiful view of the peaceful greenery. A wide spectrum of yoga styles is taught here by some of the most respected instructors in the yoga world.

The third pillar of any Absolute Sanctuary rejuvenation is the pampering offered at the Absolute Spa. The signature massage, Tropical Indulgence, is a four-handed procedure that lasts an hour; it will knead out any trace of one's stressed-out life. Also popular is the 90-minute Healing Hands Massage, which is an exclusive Absolute Sanctuary creation that blends a sports or medical massage with *reiki* healing techniques for a spiritual boost.

Those not staying at the resort can sign up for the One Day Spa Sampler, and everyone can try The Love Kitchen, where vegetarian fare is served with healthy drinks. Nutritious meat and seafood dishes are now in the pipeline too. At the Absolute Sanctuary, the road to feeling good is finally as enjoyable as the results.

rooms
hotel: 38 rooms and suites •
detox: 8 private rooms with colon hydrotherapy equipment •
spa: 4 indoor treatment rooms, outdoor massage area for 6

food
The Love Kitchen: healthy meals, fruit juices, smoothies, 'Smart' Drink Boosters

drink
Pool Juice Bar: Super Juices, shakes, 'Smart' Shooters

features
Detox Centre • Spa Centre • Yoga Centre • steam room • infinity pool • mini theatre • wireless Internet access

nearby
Cheong Mon • Chaweng Beach • Samui International Airport • Crocodile Farm • Monkey Theatre

contact
88 Moo 5, Tambol Bophut
Amphur Koh Samui
Suratthani 84320, Thailand •
telephone: +66.77.601 190 •
facsimile: +66.77.601 209 •
email: info@absolutesanctuary.com •
website: www.absolutesanctuary.com

anantara hua hin

Designed to offer a five-star tropical experience, the luxury retreat is surrounded by 6 hectares (14 acres) of leafy gardens and lagoon pools, while its 187 guestrooms and suites enjoy elegant traditional touches such as high ceilings, hardwood floors and terracotta soaking tubs. Nearby, waves gently wash against the edges of a long stretch of beach. It is a fitting location for a sanctuary as transcendent as the Anantara Spa, the resort's centrepiece.

While part of the property's lush estate, the spa feels like an even more remote destination, cocooned from the noise of the outside world. Perhaps it's the fact that getting to some of the suites involves crossing a body of water on a wooden jetty lined with oil lamps. Or perhaps it's the high courtyard walls that grant couples complete privacy once they pass through the heavy doors of each spa suite.

The resort comprises seven treatment areas, each graced with distinctive designs and personalised gardens, while the facilities such as the twin outdoor rainshowers are common to all. Ingeniously, each suite's central treatment room can be sealed off from the courtyard area with a sliding glass door, which allows for body treatments in total air-conditioned comfort.

The award-winning landscape architect Bill Bensley may have given it form—and what glorious scenery the little spa village has—but all credit for the day-to-day miracles performed here must go to an attentive team

THIS PAGE: *The double massage rooms are ideal places for couples to share the relaxing experience of a spa treatment.*
OPPOSITE (FROM LEFT): *The luxurious Lagoon Suites cater to all the needs of the guests; be treated like royalty with traditional massages in a private garden pavilion.*

Distinguishing this resort's locale from the scores of postcard-like settings one finds clustered around Thailand's hot spots is, oddly enough, its location. Instead of an offshore island or a purpose-built holiday town, the scene of this Anantara property is the northern seaside town of Hua Hin, home to glorious beaches and authentic cultural expressions that have remained the same for decades. Favoured by the country's royal family, this scenic haven of sunsets, gardens and well-preserved Buddhist temples is the perfect antidote to today's hectic city life.

of expert therapists and assistants. From the moment one arrives, the professionalism on display sets every nerve at ease.

Traditional Thai techniques are well represented, with the aid of many ancient herbal concoctions to bolster the effects of the modern treatments. Ayurvedic medicine also plays a large part by contributing such ideas as the balancing of one's internal *dosha* energies with the use of rich essential oils. These all come together in the spa's signature treatment, the Culture of Anantara. Over the course of three hours, one experiences Ayurveda during a 'massage of the third eye', also known as a *shirodhara* massage, a stress-relieving back rub and a soothing and decadent bath of pure milk and honey. Other offerings include facials, steam rituals, spa packages that target specific needs such as full-body detoxification and a selection of therapies performed with the internationally renowned Elemis brand of products. With Elemis, both modern science and natural ingredients come together to create unique products with real, lasting benefits. Some of the most popular products are Japanese silk masks for sensitive facial skin, Vitamin C serums and wraps with the unique restorative powers of frangipani flowers and coconut.

Whether accompanied by friends or a loved one, few things in life can equal an afternoon spent in this exotic spa, being pampered by the wisdom of the ancient traditions of an entire continent, capped off with a long rewarding soak in the open-air terracotta tub of a sea-facing pavilion.

rooms
hotel: 187 rooms and suites •
spa: 7 spa suites

food
Issara Café: international and Thai •
Sai Thong: international • Rim Nam: Thai •
Baan Thalia: Italian •

drink
Sala Siam • Loy Nam • lagoon

features
Ayurvedic treatments • rainshowers •
multi-day spa journeys • steam rooms •
outdoor sea-facing tubs •
hair and beauty salon

nearby
beaches • Hua Hin Night Market • parks •
Khao Takiap Vantage Point • royal palace

contact
43/1 Phetkasem Beach Road
Hua Hin 77110, Thailand •
telephone: +66.3.252 0250 •
facsimile: +66.3.252 0259 •
email: huahin@anantara.com •
website: www.huahin.anantara.com

anantara phuket resort + spa

THIS PAGE: *Eighty-three well-appointed villas, each with a private pool such as this, are on offer.*

OPPOSITE (FROM LEFT): *The treatment suites can easily accommodate two, so couples may luxuriate in spa sessions together; enjoy a soak under the stars in the villa's outdoor jacuzzi.*

Famed for immersing guests in the ways and traditions of local culture with a host of activities such as various cooking classes, market tours and interactive demonstrations, Anantara resorts are known for offering a deeper sort of holiday experience. With its roots in Thailand, it seemed inevitable that this luxury hotel group would create something special for the popular island destination of Phuket. However, it took over seven long years from the founding of the first Anantara resort in the city of Hua Hin in Thailand before the new Anantara Phuket Resort & Spa was unveiled in October 2008.

That time was most certainly well-spent. Each of the 83 guestrooms takes the form of a private villa equipped with a pool and vistas of the surrounding landscape. A view of the Andaman Sea stretches far to the north, including an exclusive expanse of Mai Khao Beach that borders coral reefs and offers hours of engaging watersports. In the other direction, a landscape of forest-covered hills conceals the property from the more heavily touristed areas. For all its seclusion, however, the resort does not involve a difficult journey; after one's arrival at the international airport, it is only a 15-minute drive.

Drawing from architecture found in southern Thai villages, all of the resort's low-lying structures feature breezy spaces and soaring, arched ceilings that permit their occupants to enjoy a close kinship with nature at all times. The understated, yet luxurious, interior design bridges the gap between contemporary style and the local flavour of traditional Thai art, materials and handicrafts.

That very same approach to creating places of relaxation was adopted for the resort's Anantara Spa. Amidst gardens filled to the brim with colourful orchids and other native flora, the facility distils everything the Anantara group has learnt from years of building unmatched spas down to 1,000 sq m (10,764 sq ft) of lavish Thai hospitality and transcendental treatments. Inspired by the lotus flower, as all Anantara spas are, the sanctuary embodies the serenity of the associated Buddhist teachings and the purity of its form—just as the lotus is nourished by nature, so are all guests by the spa.

The treatments on the spa menu make use of an exclusive collection of custom-blended skincare products and essential oils, which are derived from local herbs and plants, and are prized for their quality and potency. These products give off soothing aromas and provide tingling sensations when placed in the hands of the resident therapists. These experts are also trained in the ways of Ayurveda and other healing disciplines from across the globe. The signature Anantara massage, for instance, blends a variety of these techniques into a sensual medley, involving pressure point stimulation, fragrant natural essential oils and the traditional Eastern philosophy of meridian lines.

For those who wish to effect a real transformation, the spa also features 'journeys' that last either three or five days. These comprehensive programmes include training for a healthier lifestyle and spa treatments specifically designed to refresh one's body from the inside out. Also, the services of expert yoga trainers are on hand to complement any guest's experience. Regardless of a traveller's intentions for a trip to Phuket, with such qualities as those of the newest Anantara, the weight of having to choose from one of the island's many resorts has now been lifted.

rooms
hotel: 83 pool villas • spa: 5 treatment suites

food
La Sala: Italian and Thai specialities •
The Tree House: cocktails and canapés •
The Tasting Room: wine cellar private dining •
Sea.Fire.Salt: grills and sea views

drink
Infinity: poolside chill-out bar

features
landscaped gardens • yoga *sala* • spa journeys •
Ayurvedic treatment suite • fitness studio

nearby
Koh Phi Phi • Phuket town • Similan Islands •
Koh Sireh • golf • elephant trekking • yachting

contact
888 Moo 3, Tumbon Mai Khao
Thalang, Phuket 83110, Thailand •
telephone: +66.76.336 100 •
facsimile: +66.76.336 177 •
email: phuket@anantara.com •
website: phuket.anantara.com

anantara si kao resort + spa

THIS PAGE: *The sun decks boast stunning views of the resort and its natural surrounds.*

OPPOSITE (FROM LEFT): *The interiors are outfitted in a mix of modern and traditional Thai style, and as a result, the resort is trendily elegant; the resort offers plenty of stunning locations for those seeking a romantic interlude.*

In ancient Sanskrit, *anantara* describes the Zen concept of an experience 'without end'. At the secluded Anantara resort in the Thai province of Trang, visitors are given a chance to see this concept in constant practice.

For starters, the setting is possessed of a timeless beauty. An hour south of Krabi International Airport, in a location that has eluded much of the commercialisation seen in other areas, the Anantara Si Kao Resort & Spa is part of the protected Hat Chao Mai National Park, which extends in all directions, encompassing long, white sandy beaches, flourishing tropical greenery and numerous untouched islands. The view of the Andaman Sea from all of the resort's 138 rooms and suites also appears to be without end. This is not surprising, considering the area is one of the most sought-after diving spots in the world. Over 20 spectacular nearby reefs are served by a dedicated dive centre twice a day, with private expeditions available to other locations farther afield.

Throughout the property, natural foliage grows beside landscaped gardens designed by Bill Bensley, creating an otherworldly atmosphere. In the heart of this green cocoon lies the Anantara Spa Si Kao, a place of meditation and healing that seems to exist outside of time zones, busy schedules and conference calls. Peace accompanies guests from the minute they first lay eyes on the floating pavilions to the time they leave, detoxified, revived and reborn.

The humble lotus flower informs much of the spa's award-winning style. From the aquatic environment the plant thrives in, to its context in Buddhist teachings as a symbol of enlightenment, the lotus motif finds a home in the Anantara. Four double treatment rooms are equipped for a range of exclusive lotus-inspired treatments, as well as other massages, wraps, facials and even hot stone therapies. Each room features soft lighting, private baths and steam rooms for two, so couples can enjoy the spa rituals together.

If one has to choose just one treatment, it should be the signature Meridian Lines Massage. Drawing from the teachings of

thailand **si kao**

Oriental medicine, this massage stimulates the flow of energy throughout the body with the help of aromatic oils, leaving behind a sensation of vitality and deep relaxation.

Those with the luxury of time may wish to embark on one of the holistic spa journeys. Encompassing inner and outer wellbeing, they are similar to the packages offered by the spa's Wellness 360° centre, which span anywhere from one day to two weeks. These more involved treatments harness the power of Ayurveda, yoga, meditation and other such naturopathic practices to help control weight, reduce the effects of stress and detoxify. Under the close supervision of a resident doctor and nutritionist, visitors are empowered to forge their own paths to better health. All practices are designed to be sustainable upon leaving so the benefits, too, can be without end.

Whether for just a day or for an entire month, between the gorgeous scenery and the superb services of its full-featured spa, there's reason enough for everyone to pay the Anantara Si Kao Resort a visit this lifetime.

rooms
hotel: 138 guestrooms and suites •
spa: 6 treatment rooms, 1 spa suite

food
Leelawadee: organic spa cuisine •
Acqua: Italian •

drink
beverage list

features
Wellness 360° holistic lifestyle centre •
spa journeys • on-site Ayurvedic doctor •
landscaped gardens • fitness studio •
beauty salon

nearby
beach • airports • Trang town

contact
198–199 Moo 5
Had Pak Meng, Changlang Road
Maifad, Sikao, Trang 92150, Thailand •
telephone: +66.75.205 888 •
facsimile: +66.75.205 899 •
email: sikao@anantara.com •
website: www.anantaraonline.com

the barai

THIS PAGE: *Nightfall and the warm lighting that follows give the spa an air of mystery.*

OPPOSITE (FROM LEFT): *The many benefits of staying in THE BARAI's residential spa suites include daily 60-minute massages, in-suite treatment areas, plunge pools and a uniquely tranquil atmosphere; tension accumulated over months of stress slips away under the ministrations of a highly trained therapist.*

Those hoping to embark on a journey of physical and spiritual rejuvenation will be pleased with THE BARAI, a destination spa on beachfront land adjacent to Hyatt Regency Hua Hin. THE BARAI'S customised journeys of experience, as they are called, exceed all expectations, and the elegant surrounds are capable of making such an impression that Crystal Awards and *AsiaSpa* presented the award for 'Spa Design of the Year' to THE BARAI at the 2008 *AsiaSpa* Awards.

The first thing one notices is the amount of land devoted to just eight residential spa suites and 18 private treatment rooms. At over 18,500 sq m (199,132 sq ft) in all, they are some of the most generously proportioned facilities of their kind in Thailand, built to seclude guests from the troubles of the outside world. Designed by Lek Bunnag, one of the finest architects and interior designers in the country, the serenity of THE BARAI's spaces is enhanced by the use of rich, warm tones—maroon paired with brass, stained glass and terrazzo, intended as an interpretation of the varied cultures and traditions in the region.

Based on Thai concepts of health through the balance of four essential elements, all the treatments fall into one of the following categories: Water, Earth, Fire and Air. Water programmes relieve stress, and Earth rituals cleanse and detoxify, usually with the aid of botanical extracts. Fire therapies increase energy by strengthening the body, revitalising the mind and brightening the spirit, while Air treatments focus on beauty and radiance.

The treatment rooms feature indoor and outdoor areas with soaking tubs, rainshowers and Thai beds. Some come with Vichy shower tables and steam rooms, which are quite a treat after a body scrub experience. One especially notable experience is the Compress Massage, which combines the ideals of Thai herbalism with the healing power of touch. A warm compress, filled with herbs and flowers, is used during an oil massage to improve circulation and relieve stress.

THE BARAI provides not only spa facilities, but also eight residential spa suites. A stay at one of THE BARAI Suites is the best way to experience everything on offer. The suites are expansive and boast built-in treatment areas and private steam rooms. Some guests enjoy private plunge pools, while others have far-reaching views. Every BARAI Suite also comes with the services of an attentive butler, a daily 60-minute massage, a separate dining area and a host of modern conveniences such as high-speed Internet access.

Another of THE BARAI's winning features is the Tranquility Court, with its Zen-like gardens, swimming channels and square for meditation sessions and yoga classes. As a bonus, the property is just steps away from a beach that faces the Gulf of Thailand.

rooms
8 BARAI Suites • 18 treatment rooms

food
McFarland House: Thai and Western served *tapas*-style, snacks, light meals

drink
McFarland House

features
Tranquility Court • saunas • steam rooms • pool • high-speed Internet access • butler service • complimentary drinks and snacks

nearby
Sam Roi Yod National Park • Pa-La-U waterfall • Khao Takiap • Kaeng Krachan National Park • Marukhathaiyawan Palace • Khao Wang • Hua Hin Night Market

contact
91 Hua Hin–Khao Takiap Road
Hua Hin, Prachuap Khiri Khan 77110, Thailand
telephone: +66.32.511 234 •
facsimile: +66.32.521 233 •
email: thebarai.hrhuahin@hyatt.com •
website: www.thebarai.com

chiva-som

The resort's tranquil setting is a world of its own, carved from some of Thailand's most spectacular natural landscape, in the royal city of Hua Hin. Upon arrival, all guests are treated to a private consultation at the Health and Wellness Centre, where their individual needs are addressed with a special programme of activities tailored to the length of their stay.

Chiva-Som's holistic approach caters to every aspect of a guest's physical and mental wellbeing. Eastern and Western philosophies are in perfect harmony, with *tai chi* taking its place beside pilates, yoga, gym workouts and physiotherapy. While being attended to by the spa's diverse team of international therapists, one gradually comes to the realisation that healing occurs every step of the way: from the gourmet spa cuisine, to the focus on fitness and the vigorous massages which stimulate the lymphatic system.

Spa facilities include separate male and female saunas, steam baths and jacuzzis, as well as a unisex multi-level steam room. A bathing pavilion provides a comprehensive array of hydrotherapy options; guests may

THIS PAGE (FROM LEFT): *Plunge into the cool depths of the pool at the end of the day's training; a variety of techniques, including such favourites as meditation and yoga, refresh a guest's mind and body.*
OPPOSITE (FROM LEFT): *The Orchid Lounge offers refreshment in the form of juices and tea; highly trained professionals guide guests through every step of their spa journey.*

This aptly named 'haven of life' in southern Thailand has remained at the forefront of global spa resorts for 15 years. Among many other accolades, Chiva-Som has been ranked as one of the top three in the 'Overseas Spa Retreats' category of the *Condé Nast Traveller* Reader's Choice Awards for almost a decade. Given the 2.8 hectares (7 acres) of beautiful tropical gardens the spa resides in, and the unmatched breadth and variety of treatments on offer—over 150 in all—it's easy to see why.

expect to enjoy an exercise pool, Kneipp therapy foot spa, hydro-jacuzzi and *watsu* pool along with a plunge pool.

From facials to body wraps, masks and massages, the treatment menu may at times prove to be overwhelming. In such scenarios, selecting just one of the signature treatments promises a total rejuvenation. Using oils and products made from local plant ingredients, these treatments have long-lasting effects. By soothing tired muscles, renewing the glow of healthy skin and infusing the body with vital nutrients, these treatments are the spa's way of inspiring real life change from the inside out.

State-of-the-art technology is the domain of the Niranlada Medi-Spa facility. Expert practitioners of cosmetic medicine marshal the latest laser and computerised techniques to realise new levels of beauty. Laser techniques are able to tighten skin and remove unsightly veins, while Botox and Restylane procedures are also available and increasingly popular.

At the end of every day, it's a pleasure to return to some of the most opulent lodgings to be found in any hotel. Chiva-Som offers 58 guestrooms, in a mix of Thai-style pavilions and Ocean View rooms. The former cluster around the central lake, surrounded by greenery and water, while the Western-style rooms and suites of the latter overlook the Gulf of Thailand.

In this environment, pleasurable moments lived in good health and companionship go as far in refreshing oneself as all the remarkable treatments that Chiva-Som can offer.

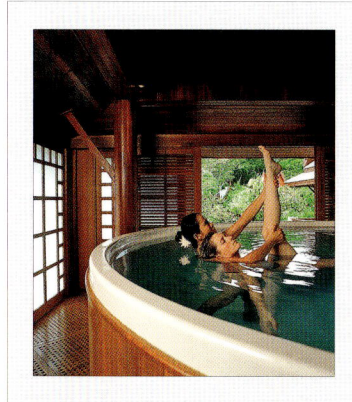

rooms
58 rooms and villas

food
Emerald Room Restaurant: international •
Taste of Siam Restaurant: Thai •
low-fat, low-calorie options available

drink
Orchid Lounge: herbal tea, fruit juice

features
spa and hydrotherapy suites • pools •
physiotherapy • yoga • pilates • fitness classes •
dance classes • holistic treatments •
Niranlada Medi-Spa facility • hair studio

nearby
Hua Hin Beach • Chopsticks Hill • caves •
waterfalls • palaces • golf

contact
73/4 Petchkasem Road
Hua Hin, Prachuab Khirikhan 77110, Thailand •
telephone: +66.32.536 536 •
facsimile: +66.32.511 154 •
email: reservation@chivasom.com •
website: www.chivasom.com

four seasons resort chiang mai

THIS PAGE: *A dip in the pool set in the midst of fields brimming with life is accompanied by an unobstructed view all the way to the distant mountains.*

OPPOSITE (FROM LEFT): *Couples can celebrate a special occasion with a romantic getaway; the fragrance of oils, spices and spa ingredients perfumes the air inside The Spa.*

Four Seasons Resort Chiang Mai almost appears to be an authentic Lanna Kingdom village, so well-executed are its architectural tributes, its terraced rice fields so flourishing and functional throughout the seasons. Encircled by miles of thriving plant life and the distant peaks of the Mae Rim Valley's mountains, the 81-room hotel's 8.1 hectares (20 acres) of landscaped gardens and lakes seem completely natural. But in truth, the five-star resort and spa destination was created before the turn of the millennium, by the Chiang Mai Architects Collaborative and the acclaimed Bunnag Architects of Bangkok, to bring a bygone era to life in the trademark style of the Four Seasons group.

The Spa follows the same Lanna-inspired theme, utilising hallmarks of the 13th-century kingdom's design traditions—a portmanteau of Burmese, Indian, Chinese and several other prominent styles of the region—to produce an impressive structure that looks more like a northern Thai temple than a spa. But beneath its unadorned skin lies a series of luxurious interiors in regal shades of maroon, decorated with gold leaf and fine local art pieces.

Befitting its status as the World's Best Spa, as chosen by the readers of *Conde Nast Traveller* (UK) in 2007, The Spa offers a holistic experience that can hardly be matched by anything else in the country. Here, just seven

thailand **chiang mai**

exclusive treatment suites are available, each completely enclosed for privacy yet open to natural light and fresh air, scented with delicate fragrances from further inside The Spa. Catering to all needs, the suites are equipped with outdoor showers, soaking tubs, double rainshower massage beds, and herbal steam rooms, suited to both single occupancy and couples.

Every procedure and ingredient used at The Spa is informed by centuries of tradition and history, with almost all the therapists trained in such arts as Thai massage and Ayurveda. To this end, The Spa employs three exclusive product lines in conjunction with its treatment offerings: Ytsara, a series of ancient Thai procedures using a range of products made from organically grown local herbs, flowers and fruit for healthier skin; Elemis, a collection of essences imported from England administered with their own unique blend of massage techniques including the Welcome Touch warm foot compress; and finally, the Four Seasons Originals, the acclaimed spa group's scientifically perfected answers to the challenges of modern living.

Stretching enthusiasts have something extra to look forward to in the form of the Yoga Barn. Right in the middle of the resort's serene rice fields, it is ideal for one's daily yoga practices. Even complete novices are welcome to book a private lesson and take in the splendour of this beautiful corner of Thailand, just 20 minutes north of Chiang Mai city.

rooms
hotel: 64 pavilions, 12 pool villas (available from December 2009) • private residence rentals: 17 resort residences • spa: 7 treatment suites

food
Sala Mae Rim: Thai • Terraces: international and Italian • cooking school

drink
Elephant Bar

features
traditional and alternative spa treatments • yoga • retail store • salon • fitness centre • pools • tennis

nearby
Chiang Mai • night market • shops • galleries • golf

contact
Mae Rim–Samoeng Old Road
Mae Rim, Chiang Mai 50180, Thailand •
telephone: +66.53.298 181 •
facsimile: +66.53.298 189 •
email: spa.chiangmai@fourseasons.com •
website: www.fourseasons.com/chiangmai

i.sawan residential spa + club

Never before have there been spa facilities in a major hotel quite like those at the i.sawan Residential Spa & Club of the five-star Grand Hyatt Erawan Bangkok, located in the midst of the city's central commercial district. The i.sawan offers luxurious treatments, beauty services, healthy cuisine, fitness opportunities and its own exclusive accommodation in an enchanting setting among rooftop gardens.

Billed as the 'fifth level of heaven', the spa occupies over 7,000 sq m (75,347 sq ft) of space and is furnished to make the hectic city seem miles away. With a Zen-like design by renowned interior designer Tony Chi, i.sawan Residential Spa & Club is an escape into a world of Thai indulgence and contemporary elegance.

Six 100-sq-m (1,076-sq-ft) residential spa cottages are on offer. Each one features all the modern conveniences of a deluxe hotel suite, with separate bedrooms and living rooms, en-suite bath facilities and a private treatment room so one hardly ever needs to leave. Yoga mats and instructional DVDs are provided, as are iPods filled with custom relaxation music (these are also found in the spa's treatment rooms and salons). The cottages may also be booked for day use, but the temptation to stay a few nights once ensconced in their airy comforts should not be underestimated.

Using only all-natural products, the spa treatments incorporate the best of local and international knowledge. Being in Thailand,

THIS PAGE (FROM LEFT): Fall into the embrace of large comfortable beds covered with crisp sheets after all tension has been kneaded out of one's muscles; each cottage comes with a treatment room where residents can indulge in a therapy session in private.
OPPOSITE (FROM LEFT): Jump into the picturesque 25-m pool for some light exercise; large en-suite bathrooms with deep tubs allow guests staying in the spa cottages to soak their stresses away.

thailand **bangkok**

rooms
6 residential spa cottages •
9 treatment bungalows

food
The Breezeway: healthy Thai and Western

drink
The Juice Bar

features
spa treatments • sauna • fitness centre • yoga • tennis court • squash court • pool • hair salon • nail bar • Power Plate Studio® • retail store

nearby
Erawan Shrine • Siam Ocean World • Central World • Siam Paragon • shops

contact
5th floor, Grand Hyatt Erawan Bangkok
494 Rajdamri Road, Bangkok 10330, Thailand •
telephone: +66.2.254 1234 •
facsimile: +66.2.254 6283 •
email: isawan.bangh@hyatt.com •
website: www.isawan.hyatt.com

one would expect to enjoy authentic Thai massage techniques—and i.sawan certainly delivers. In addition, treatment packages are divided into categories such as Purity, Energy, Harmony and Thai to meet a wide range of needs. The use of Comfort Zone skincare products from Italy ensures the highest level of quality, while facials benefit from exclusive Intraceuticals Oxygen technology.

The Thai Royal Lotus massage regime is popular with couples, while the Executive Energy treatment only takes half an hour and can be done while fully clothed. Men have their own Man Space menu to heal injured muscles and induce tranquillity with hot oil rubs, hot stone therapy and deep tissue massages.

Club i.sawan fitness centre houses a gym, movement studio, squash court, tennis court and Power Plate® studio. Cool down after your workout with a dive into the pool or a dip into one of the icy plunge pools.

The Breezeway restaurant beside the pool serves light meals and healthy renditions of Thai classic dishes throughout the day, and these skilfully prepared favourites are made even more appetising by the idyllic setting.

Winner of the 'Urban Spa of the Year' (*AsiaSpa* magazine, 2006), 'Best Down-Time Spa' (*Lifestyle + Travel* magazine, 2006) and 'Best Spa in Thailand' (*SpaAsia* Readers' Choice Awards, 2007), i.sawan Residential Spa & Club is cloud nine come down to the fifth floor.

kamalaya koh samui

THIS PAGE: *With two inviting ocean-view swimming pools, a lap pool and a leisure pool, there are many beautiful places to take a refreshing dip.*

OPPOSITE (FROM LEFT): *The luxurious accommodation makes the journey to health and self-awareness a pleasant one; massages involving essential oils are sure to leave one feeling calm and relaxed.*

For an industry predicated on peace and relaxation, competition is fierce in the top tier of spa destinations. One might be forgiven for thinking that, as winner of *AsiaSpa*'s 'Best Destination Spa of the Year' 2008 award and the *SpaAsia* Crystal Awards' 'Best Wellness Retreat' title in the same year, the Kamalaya Koh Samui was simply more aggressive in competition than its rivals. But the truth is quite the opposite, and readily apparent from the minute one first sets eyes on this tranquil, laid-back property.

Its location is a marvel of natural beauty on the southern coast of Koh Samui, a scene composed of towering trees, lush vegetation, miles of sandy beach below, dramatic cliffs overlooking the water and a deep green valley. Scattered over this landscape are a number of impeccably designed buildings.

While creating the resort's modern but timeless look, the architect Robert Powell exhibited a sensitivity to the surroundings that few others might have, and in so doing, honoured the history of the site, which is home to an ancient Buddhist monks' cave. As in the past, the cave is open for all who desire a moment of reconnection and reflection.

The philosophy behind Kamalaya is one that goes beyond a system of treatments and luxurious facilities. With the rejuvenation of

thailand **koh samui**

the detox programmes, the improved health and muscle tone brought about by yoga and other holistic fitness regimes, the sense of community that exists between guests and the enduring comfort from the therapies is an awareness of personal growth that builds throughout the entire synergistic experience.

Helping to create this personalised and effective experience, the spa offers a menu of more than 70 services, designed to detoxify, correct ailments, recover from stress, balance emotions, manage weight or increase fitness. Disciplines from around the world are no strangers to the team of John and Karina Stewart, who founded Kamalaya in 2005. Between them are nearly four decades of study in the Asian arts of healing and spirituality; they bring acupuncture and traditional Chinese medicine together with Ayurveda, Western naturopathy and pilates.

As if to prove that the road to health is not necessarily arduous, Kamalaya offers five-star creature comforts, in addition to its miracle work. Including a number of villas with private pools, set along the beach or immersed within the tropical rainforest, 59 luxurious rooms are available in total, and delicious spa cuisine is prepared from the freshest ingredients. Named 'the Lotus Realm', the Kamalaya Koh Samui is a journey that no spa enthusiast can afford to refuse, at the risk of missing out on the elusive bigger picture.

rooms
hotel: 24 rooms, 10 suites, 25 villas • spa: 30 treatment rooms

food
Soma Restaurant: detox menu, vegetarian dishes, fresh seafood and healthy meats, with select wines and desserts • Amrita Café: juices, vegetarian dishes, grilled fish, healthy meats and a detox menu

drinks
Alchemy Tea Lounge: healthy snacks, juices, herbal infusions and a range of teas and wines

features
holistic spa • 2 pools • 2 yoga venues • library • art gallery • fitness centre • plunge pools • steam cavern • Yantra Hall • meditation room

nearby
golf • waterfalls • trekking • beaches

contact
102/9 Moo 3, Laem Set Road
Na–Muang, Koh Samui
Suratthani 84140, Thailand
telephone: +66.77.429 800
facsimile: +66.77.429 899
email: info@kamalaya.com
website: www.kamalaya.com

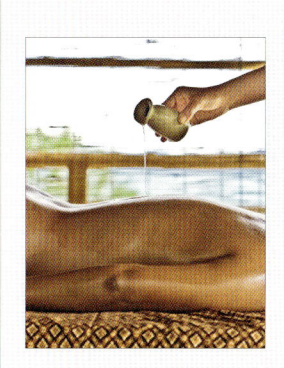

pimalai resort + spa

THIS PAGE: *Sea-facing pool villas have private infinity pools that overlook the bay.*

OPPOSITE (FROM LEFT): *Guests can enjoy a walk in the very romantic natural setting; pamper yourself with in-villa treatments from the comprehensive spa menu.*

One day, Krabi will be a household name, mentioned in the same breath as Phuket, Honolulu or Boracay as one of the world's premier beach destinations. That day has not yet arrived, but recent developments on the province's island of Koh Lanta Yai now mean that first-rate resort accommodation and facilities are available in one of the last remaining bastions of unspoilt natural beauty in Southeast Asia.

Situated on the western coast of the island facing the Andaman Sea, the Pimalai Resort & Spa overlooks a secluded stretch of white beach and pristine waters. Far from other tourist areas on Koh Lanta, the hilltop resort is protected by 40 hectares (100 acres) of rainforest and landscaped greenery, keeping its beach villas, open-air seafront restaurants and magnificent infinity pools from prying eyes.

The atmosphere of privacy is enhanced by the spa's layout, a cluster of seven *sala* huts amid an authentic jungle setting. Arranged around a central pavilion, the *sala* are where one can experience traditional Thai massages outdoors. Guests may rest assured that the valley's geography and abundance of trees create the impression of being alone in an ancient place of healing.

thailand koh lanta

Most of the therapeutic activities—an extensive range of body massages, wraps, treatments and facials—take place in the *sala*, three of which are furnished for double occupancy with their very own jacuzzis. Also, an outdoor jacuzzi with an adjacent herbal sauna is located nearby.

The treatments and beauty salon services, such as hair and nail care, emphasise local specialities in both the techniques and the ingredients used. The pampering two-hour Royal Siam Massage uses finger and palm pressure along energy lines to stretch and renew muscles. The massage is supplemented by a half-hour application of steamed *luk pra kob*, aromatic herbs that awaken the senses and moisturise the skin. Thai-style massage techniques also feature in the Oriental Fusion Massage, a treatment that utilises fragrant essential oils, and the Pimalai Sports Massage and many other body treatments.

Not to be missed are the customised facials, one for each skin type. The Harmonies Extreme Facial for sensitive skin is suitable for those not accustomed to the all-day Krabi sun, using a variety of natural ingredients to cool down and refresh the skin. The facial tailored especially for men does a remarkable job of cleansing blocked pores and comes with a stress-relieving head massage.

The time is ripe for visiting Koh Lanta Yai, as it is fast becoming one of the world's desirable holiday destinations. But even if visitor numbers were to explode, the serene oasis that is the Pimalai Spa should help turn the volume down a notch.

rooms
hotel: 64 deluxe rooms, 39 pool villas, 7 beach villas, 7 Pavilion Suites •
spa: 7 treatment rooms, 1 outdoor spa *sala*, 1 jacuzzi/steam *sala*

food
Spice 'N Rice Thai Restaurant • The Banyan Tree Pool Side Café • The Seven Seas Wine Bar & Restaurant: seafood and Western • Rak Talay Beach Bar & Restaurant • Baan Pimalai Restaurant: Thai and international

drink
Rak Talay Beach Bar • The Seven Seas Wine Bar

services
jacuzzi • steam room • open-air Thai massage pavilion • infinity pools

nearby
beach • Old Lanta Town • caves • Marine National Park • Saladan Market • snorkelling and diving spots (e.g. Koh Haa, Emerald Cave, Hin Daeng and Hin Muang)

contact
99 Moo 5, Ba Kan Tiang Beach
Koh Lanta, Krabi, Thailand •
telephone: +66.2.320 5500 •
facsimile: +66.2.320 5503 •
email: reservation@pimalai.com •
website: www.pimalai.com

pranali wellness spa

An original spa concept from Thailand, Pranali was founded on an idea of total wellness that one often sees reserved for remote retreats and week-long detox adventures, but this now can be found in the heart of downtown Bangkok. That the nurturing of one's mind, body and spirit requires an escape to some yogic encampment will seem like an outdated concept after some time at one of Pranali's two urban facilities.

A return to the basics of plant-based organic healing distinguishes the Pranali line of health and beauty products, which are used in the spas' exclusive treatments and offered in their boutiques. The Scentherapy range of soaps, essences, oils and floral mists is all derived from natural sources, turning away from the heavy reliance on chemical treatments that is now common practice elsewhere, while also retaining a scientific approach in order to extract greater efficacy from such ingredients as apricot kernels, jojoba, wheatgerm and ginseng.

Other products available for sale at Pranali's outlets include aromatic potions made from wild honey blended with essential oils and a line of facial cocoon masks with such ingredients as green tea and purifying medicinal charcoal. One of the most unique offerings is a high-protein formulation made from black rice, which the company's experts have folded into a reviving shower gel along with aloe vera, hydrating body milk and smooth almond oil.

An exclusive L'atelier du Pranali service takes things one step further with skincare combinations blended to the specifications of each guest. This is ideal for repeat visitors who wish to observe a customised skincare regimen, devised carefully by the spa's expert therapists and clinicians.

These elements all come together in several excellent rituals, including the Scent of Pranali which uses light massage techniques with aromatic oils to increase lymphatic flow

THIS PAGE (FROM LEFT): *The many treatments, activities and products available from Pranali aim to help clients find total wellness; looking up at the 'stars' while experiencing a treatment is just one of the benefits that state-of-the-art technology provides Pranali's guests.*

OPPOSITE (FROM LEFT): *The boutique offers a wide range of products made from the finest natural ingredients; compresses filled with herbs and lightly-scented flowers are a wonderful aspect of many of the massages here.*

thailand **bangkok**

and bring deep relaxation to even the most sensitive of skin types. Also, at three hours long, the Pranali Bliss Package—a body polish, a heat blanket body wrap, a warm oil massage and a facial—is an antidote to the most stressful of Bangkok weeks.

The wholly natural approach is also evident in the layout and visual design of Pranali's two spas, one in the high-tech Shinawatra building, and the other at the Siam Paragon Shopping Centre. Both locations incorporate flourishes of greenery such as bamboo stalks and flowers amidst dark wood and clean, white treatment spaces.

As might be deduced from the spa's name, which comes from the words *pran* (breath) and *leela* (rhythm), the focus here is on the affirmation and enhancement of life. For that reason, a wide range of treatments ranging from fitness and slimming, to pilates and beauty, is brought together into the two convenient locations. Developed at the cost of nearly US$2 million, Pranali has some of the country's best equipment. Examples include an 'Aqua Spa', in existence in only two other countries in the world, a 'Huber' exercise machine that targets 80 muscle groups at once and an innovative Slim Fit Stepper that makes use of infrared technology to burn fat.

Superb service is something of a Thai tradition, and it can be unconditionally found at both Pranali branches, whether one just stops in for an express massage or as part of a total wellness effort for a change in life.

rooms
12 treatment rooms • 2 Thai massage rooms • 2 Slim Fit rooms • 3 consultation rooms • 2 hydrotherapy treatment rooms

food
spa cuisine

drink
juice bar

features
hydrotherapy • hair spa • steam rooms • fitness studio with 'Huber' machines • relaxation lounge • Internet services

contact
Shinawatra Branch:
32nd floor, Shinawatra Tower III
1010 Vibhavadi–Rangsit Rd
Ladyao, Chatuchak
Bangkok 10900, Thailand •
telephone: +66.2.949 2400-4 •
facsimile: +66.2.949 2405 •

Siam Paragon Branch:
Unit 334 Siam Paragon, 3rd floor
989 Siam Paragon Tower
Rama 1 Road, Pathumwan
Bangkok 10330, Thailand •
telephone: +66.2.610 9596-8 •
facsimile: +66.2.610 9598 •

email: pranali@pranaliwellness.com •
website: www.pranaliwellness.com

salus per crystal®

After one has travelled the world and braved the fingers, knuckles, elbows, feet and other tools of traditional massage techniques, bathed in mysterious fluids, packed the mud of volcanoes and rivers alike onto bare skin, endured fire, colonic detox clinics and the freezing cold of marble tables in winter, all in search of the ultimate spa experience—and was left wanting—what's next? The Crystal Day Spa by Salus per Crystal® on the northern outskirts of Bangkok comes to mind.

Certainly, Thailand is home to many a five-star haven of knot-loosening deep tissue rubs and traditional herbal treatments, but when an opportunity to venture into the esoteric realm of crystal and colour therapy presents itself, what bona fide spa enthusiast could refuse? Citing centuries of Tibetan practice, the spa's team of Crystal Therapy practitioners subscribe to a unique system that pairs the resonating qualities of certain crystals with frequencies that occur naturally in each human body. By experimenting with one's compatibility with different crystals, they are able to recalibrate areas of one's physicality that may have been disrupted by stress, injury or other causes in a way that is at once holistic and non-invasive. The stones

THIS PAGE (FROM LEFT): *Indulge in an authentic Thai massage in its place of origin; the treatment rooms are divided into singles and doubles, but all of them are equally well-furnished.*

OPPOSITE (FROM LEFT): *Yoga practitioners may choose between having a session outdoors and making use of the spa's indoor studio; amethyst is said to have many beneficial properties.*

trigger minute electromagnetic reactions, auras are magnified, *chakra* are cleansed and recipients wonder how in the world that persistent ache went away.

Similarly, Salus per Crystal's® take on colour therapy is informed by ancient Egyptian research, but perfected through modern-day scientific advancements. If the physical properties of the healing crystals work on the body, it is their colours, then, that have an effect on the mind. The beauty of the Crystal Day Spa's approach is that one doesn't even need to have an opinion on these techniques to appreciate their effects; the philosophy is seamlessly woven into a more traditional menu of expertly executed body treatments and therapies.

Housed within the two double-storey buildings that make up the day spa are a full complement of facilities that include a yoga studio, a Thai massage area, single and double treatment suites equipped with bathrooms, foot therapy stalls and even a library. Each treatment room is named after a crystal, such as Amethyst or Obsidian, and is decorated in the associated colours for maximum effect.

Hot stone and hot chocolate massages are two of the spa's specialities and can be quite an uplifting experience. All body scrubs and wraps, facials, massages and the like are performed with the exclusive use of all-natural products from Pevonia and Phytomer, two renowned professional brands from the US and France respectively. These luxurious, hypoallergenic products, made from top-quality botanical and marine ingredients, ensure a high level of efficacy and tolerance with regard to all skin types.

The Salus per Crystal® company is an ecologically responsible one, and its efforts to conserve energy also enhance conditions within the spa. Heat produced from the labouring air-conditioners goes to keeping water hot, while a reliance on natural light and wind creates an ambience that brings a little of the great outdoors in (and saves energy at the same time).

With its ability to restore a sparkle to the eye of any jaded spa visitor, the Crystal Day Spa is an invaluable step forward that stands out in a landscape of too many spas jostling to do the same old thing.

rooms
10 treatment rooms • 8 Thai massage rooms

features
Crystal & Colour Therapy • facial treatments • Hot Stone Massage • Hot Chocolate Massage • body massages (Aromatherapy and Royal Thai) • body treatments (steam, bath, scrub and wrap) • yoga studio • hair studio • natural spa ingredients

nearby
shopping • restaurants • Bangkok

contact
189/5–6 Moo 7, Liangmuang Road
Bangtarad, Pakkret
Nontaburi 11120, Thailand •
telephone: +66.25.844 804 •
facsimile: +66.25.844 805 •
email: info@saluspercrystal.co.th •
website: www.saluspercrystal.co.th

shangri-la hotel, bangkok + shangri-la hotel, chiang mai

THIS PAGE (FROM TOP): *The relaxing Himalayan Healing Stone Massage soothes even the most stressed of muscles; the private spa suites at CHI, The Spa in Bangkok are spacious and furnished with the best the hotel can offer.* OPPOSITE: *The exterior of the Shangri-La Hotel, Chiang Mai is even more striking at dusk.*

Truth be told, most five-star hotels include spas as something of an afterthought; just one more service on a long list that includes gyms, pools, 24-hour room service and the like. Rarely does a spa actually take on a life of its own, or better yet, extend the philosophy of the hotel behind it. But that is exactly what the Shangri-La group has done with its acclaimed CHI, The Spa.

Taking a page from the hotel's own inspiration, namely the hidden Himalayan utopia of James Hilton's epic novel *Lost Horizon*, all of the CHI spas incorporate ancient Chinese and Himalayan practices into their full-service spa offerings, allowing modern-day travellers to enjoy the natural remedies and the time-tested massage techniques of another age. Adding to CHI's appeal is its unique 'spa within a spa' concept, which makes every treatment suite a private island by equipping each with a range of facilities such as soaking tubs with 'eternity light' colour therapy, herbal steam showers, relaxation lounges and en-suite bathrooms.

Shangri-La Hotel, Bangkok

Located in the heart of Thailand's capital city with the Chao Phraya River directly at its doorstep, the Shangri-La Hotel, Bangkok was an effortless choice for the site of the world's first CHI, The Spa. Opening its doors to guests in 2004, the 1,000-sq-m (10,764-sq-ft) facility became known as the city's largest spa, a title it still holds today.

Inside, a sophisticated interior by the renowned designer Julian Coombs adheres to the original concept of the hotel by observing Himalayan building techniques, including authentic Himalayan features such as split-face stone walls, traditional artworks and sliding screens. The latter are constructed from delicate teak and follow a lattice design unique to Himalayan culture. Sliding across the inside of rooms, they effect changes in function and atmosphere during the different stages of treatments.

Over 35 therapies are offered on the menu, ranging from full-body massages to facials and men's skincare. Two speciality themed suites were added to the facility, in order to facilitate the Himalayan Tsangpo Ritual. Based on a 1,500-year-old technique,

thailand bangkok + chiang mai

this one-of-a-kind treatment makes use of rare Thethys sea salts, red mountain mud and other minerals in a luxurious session involving exfoliation, a wrap and a cleansing bath. Also, just as soothing is the 100-minute Sen CHI Detox. Using a combination of acupressure and Thai abdominal therapy, it relaxes one's internal organs and stimulates meridian pathways to cleanse the system.

Shangri-La Hotel, Chiang Mai

Four years after that first groundbreaking launch in Bangkok, Thailand would receive another CHI, The Spa outlet at the luxurious Shangri-La Hotel, Chiang Mai. A tranquil oasis within the busy centre of Chiang Mai (just five minutes away from the well-known Night Market), the new CHI retains the original Himalayan influences in its design but pays tribute to the history of the area by including elements that originate from the Thai Lanna kingdom; this move has produced a distinctly different—but no less beautiful—aesthetic. The nine villas that comprise the spa compound are decorated with Thai silks and built with the finest local materials.

Fully embracing local traditions in pursuit of the best possible spa experience, this CHI outlet even offers a Thai massage and a Lanna Blend Massage not available anywhere else. Dubbed the King of Massages, the latter combines Thai techniques with Himalayan hot stone healing to stretch tired muscles.

rooms
Bangkok: 799 rooms and suites • 12 spa suites
Chiang Mai: 281 rooms and suites • 9 spa villas

food
Bangkok: Angelini • Horizon River Cruise • NEXT2 • Salathip • Shang Palace
Chiang Mai: Kad Kafé • Silapa Thai Lounge & Bar

drink
Bangkok: Lobby Lounge • Riverside Lounge • Pool Bar
Chiang Mai: At the Pool • The Lobby Lounge

features
traditional spa treatments based on local ingredients and practices • yoga pavilion (Chiang Mai) • individual spa suite facilities

nearby
Bangkok: Patpong Night Market • River City Antique Shopping Complex • Suan Lum Night Bazaar
Chiang Mai: Chiang Mai Night Market • IT Shopping Centre

contact
Bangkok:
89 Soi Wat Suan Plu, New Road
Bangrak, Bangkok 10500, Thailand
telephone: +66.2.236 7777 ext 6072 •
facsimile: +66.2.237 3750 •
email: chi.bangkok@shangri-la.com •
website: www.shangri-la.com

Chiang Mai:
89/8 Chang Klan Road, Muang
Chiang Mai 50100, Thailand
telephone: +66.53.253 888 •
facsimile: +66.53.253 800 •
email: chi.chiangmai@shangri-la.com •
website: www.shangri-la.com

six senses destination spa–phuket

THIS PAGE: *Lounge by the resort's pool and enjoy the balmy weather, or jump in to cool off.*

OPPOSITE (FROM LEFT): *Treatments can be enjoyed both indoors and outside in the fresh air; the talented chefs are able to whip up tasty and healthy meals at a moment's notice.*

The pride of the Six Senses hotel group, and the only one in its portfolio to hold the title of 'Destination Spa', this Phuket property is all about exceeding expectations. It takes health and therapy beyond the confines of spa treatments to include holistic practices and wellness-inspired gastronomy, creating integrated programmes that can last days or weeks as well as providing not just memories, but invaluable lifelong lifestyle changes.

The exclusivity of the resort is apparent from the minute one arrives. Located on the quiet shores of Naka Yai, marked by long, sandy beaches and a distinct lack of other developments apart from itself, the Six Senses Destination Spa–Phuket is virtually its own private island community. An airport transfer service and ferry brings guests over from the northern edge of Phuket, just 10 minutes away, and the arrival of each new guest is marked by the sounding of a gong.

As might be expected from a five-star establishment where mobile phones, laptops and other technological distractions are not permitted in public areas, all 61 lodgings are serene pool villas set either along the water or on a gentle hillside above. All include their own outdoor *sala* where guests may meditate or enjoy a private massage from one of the spa's many expert therapists.

The resort's concept spa is known as The 7th Sense, regulated by a philosophy built upon the pillars of Spa, Holistic Fitness and Integrative Health to provide guests with total support in every physical and emotional sense. The heart of the spa is a 3,000-sq-m (32,292-sq-ft) facility divided into four themed areas, each one based on the knowledge of a traditional Asian culture. Indonesian, Indian, Thai and Chinese practices are represented, with the treatments administered by masters of their respective fields.

Indonesian signature treatments include Surga Manis, with the healing benefits of rose infusions, and the Balinese Inspiration, a mix of scrubs, soaks and massages using ancient techniques. Indian therapies are centred on a range of Ayurvedic Journeys, but other schools such as the Himalayan Hot Stone therapy are also available. The Chinese Spa brings the wisdom of the East together under one roof, offering foot reflexology, acupuncture and *shiatsu*. In addition, Thai Massage techniques are also well represented on the menu.

Many of the lifestyle retreats—or Life Passages—at the heart of the Six Senses Destination Spa experience require greater amounts of time; however, on the road to real change, there can be no shortcuts. And so a three-night journey to recharge, a week-long Life Passage named Maximum Men's Health and a three-week odyssey of fitness, weight management and self-improvement called Body Confidence are welcome blessings.

rooms
hotel: 61 villas •
spa: 44 indoor and outdoor treatment rooms

food
Ton Sai: fishetarian spa cuisine •
Dining at the Point: raw foods • in-villa dining

drink
organic and bio-dynamic wines •
fresh juices • shakes • smoothies

features
Life Passage Lifestyle Retreats • physiotherapy •
yoga • *tai chi* • naturopathic health • pool •
nutritional and wellness consultations

nearby
beaches • kayaking • fishing • mountain biking

contact
32 Moo 5, Tambol Paklok
Amphur Thalang, 83110 Phuket, Thailand •
telephone: +66.76.371 400 •
facsimile: +66.76.371 401 •
email: reservations-naka@sixsenses.com •
website: www.sixsenses.com/Six-Senses-Destination-Spa-Phuket

thann sanctuary gaysorn

Founded in 2002, THANN skincare products have won a large following throughout the world with their focus on all-natural ingredients and unique Asian formulas. True to the brand's Thai roots, the primary ingredient in many products is a rice extract rich in Vitamin E and oryzanol, which have antioxidant and UV-shielding properties. The innovative company has also won global design awards for its environmentally friendly packaging. In addition to being found in boutique hotels, retail stores around the globe have established THANN as one of the leading names in health and beauty.

Opening a series of spa sanctuaries to showcase their wares, then, was a logical move for the young company. Set in Gaysorn, one of Bangkok's leading lifestyle and luxury shopping centres, THANN Sanctuary spa is an excellent example of how thoughtful design and a holistic, results-driven approach to wellbeing can create a haven of calm and tune out the demands of everyday life.

The highly exclusive spa features just six treatment rooms over 160 sq m (1,722 sq ft) of floor area, with soaring 6-m- (19.7-ft-) high ceilings creating a generous sense of space. The number was chosen to coincide with THANN's six product collections—Mediterranean Floral, Shiso, Rice, Aromatic Wood, Oriental Essence and Sea Foam—with each of the beautifully decorated rooms adopting its theme and ambience from one of the collections. The quiet corridors are dramatically lit with candles and directed lighting from above, and an animation wall of soothing graphics catches the eye at the far end. One may also notice the impressive sculpture hanging overhead, made from over 12,000 individual pieces of bamboo.

Some of the spa's signature treatments use such techniques as Ayurveda, Thai massage, healing stones and one recent advancement, Nano Shiso Therapy. Based on the properties of the *shiso* plant—revered by the Japanese people for its hardiness and health-enhancing properties—the THANN Shiso Collection is the result of years of research into harnessing the plant's moisturising and antioxidant effects. This therapy utilises advanced nanotechnology to introduce a *shiso* leaf extract into the guest's circulatory system with an hour-long massage and 70-minute facial.

All the body massage treatments offered incorporate THANN's unique essential oil blend and nourishing rice bran oil. Spa journeys come in Stimulating, Sensual, Exotic and Calming categories, each employing unique ingredients. The Exotic option with invigorating lemongrass and kaffir lime extracts is especially potent and highly recommended.

At the end of every session, a cup of freshly brewed tea from the THANNnative selection of over 20 varieties, served with seasonal local fruits, presents a perfect way to end one's visit. The overall experience is one of carefully orchestrated pleasures. For these reasons, THANN Sanctuary was named one of *Conde Nast Traveler*'s 'Top 55 Hot Spas' in 2006, making it one of Bangkok's hottest destinations.

THIS PAGE: *The themed treatment rooms are havens of peace and quiet, allowing patrons to properly enjoy their therapy.*

OPPOSITE (FROM LEFT): *Dark colours combine with bold lighting to conjure an intimate feel to the interior of THANN Sanctuary; with so many massage treatments to choose from, every guest will surely be able to find something to suit their wants and needs.*

thailand **bangkok**

rooms
5 body treatment rooms • 1 foot massage room

drink
THANNnative Tea Room

features
facials • massages • scrubs • product shop

nearby
Chidlom Skytrain station • CentralWorld • Grand Hyatt Erawan Bangkok

contact
3rd floor, Gaysorn
999 Ploenchit Road, Lumpini, Patumwan
10330 Bangkok, Thailand •
telephone: +66.2.656 1424 •
email: thannspa@thann.info •
website: www.thann.info

the racha

THIS PAGE: *Surrounded by clear blue waters, one cannot help but relax immediately upon arrival at The Racha.*

OPPOSITE (FROM LEFT): *Lush tropical landscaping envelopes the Anumba Spa's nine treatment rooms and suites; yoga is an excellent way to simultaneously focus one's mind and get some exercise.*

Exclusivity lies at the heart of every great proposition; this holds true for haute couture, luxury automobiles, gourmet restaurants and of course, holiday destinations. The more remote, unknown and impossible-to-book a resort is, the more its allure exponentially grows amongst travellers, with the private island getaway being the most exclusive, and therefore most desirable, of all possibilities.

The Racha hotel on Thailand's Racha Yai Island offers all of the above. Located south of Phuket, just a half-hour boat ride from shore, Racha Yai Island is an unspoilt jewel of sandy beaches and clear, coral-studded waters. Part of the Small Luxury Hotels of the World group, The Racha employs modern measures to ensure its presence remains ecologically sustainable for years to come. Even the architectural profile of the resort was designed to blend with the environment, with its construction leaving no discernible footprint so all that one sees is the natural beauty of palm trees—often allowed to grow through buildings instead of being removed.

thailand **phuket**

Just spending time on the island has a rejuvenating quality, but the Anumba Spa's facilities go a long way in complementing the natural vistas. Over an area of 2,320 sq m (24,972 sq ft), the Anumba Spa is designed to deliver the finest in traditional massages, hydrotherapy, fitness training and beauty treatments in a place unlike any other. Four outdoor pavilions allow guests to luxuriate during Thai massages in complete freedom and privacy under the shade of coconut and frangipani trees, while the soft gurgle of flowing water soothes the spirit.

For those seeking other regional speciality treatments and therapies—such as foot massages, Andaman Sea salt scrubs, Moor mud body wraps, Thai herbal wellness facials or the signature Thai Flower Ritual—a total of nine treatment rooms are available, including four couple suites with their own plunge tubs, steam rooms and courtyards with rainshowers.

An integrated OM Studio sees to guests' fitness, yoga and other active needs, but when one has time to spare on Racha Yai Island, there's nothing better than a few hours whiled away on the grassy Meditation Lane beside the Anumba Spa, or on a deck chair beside the gift shop. Here, ginger teas and cereal cookies are served to guests in search of a light, refreshing snack. On an island that even experts have to consult a map to find, the experience of visiting an exotic tropical spa paired with a relaxed five-star beach resort can seem absolutely priceless.

rooms
hotel: 70 villas •
spa: 9 treatment rooms and suites

food
Earth Café: international with al fresco seating •
Fire Grill: casual poolside dining • Sunset Beach Restaurant: barbecued steak and seafood •
Gerardo's Beach Club: Thai and Western fusion

drink
Lobby Bar: sunset cocktails and panoramic ocean views • Ice Bar: live music and karaoke

features
OM Studio mind-body classes • steam room •
Balance Fitness club • Thai massage pavilions •
sauna • pool • gift shop

nearby
diving • snorkelling

contact
42/12–13 Moo 5, Rawai
Muang, 83130 Phuket, Thailand •
telephone: +66.76.355 455 •
facsimile: +66.76.355 637 •
email: reservation@theracha.com •
website: www.theracha.com

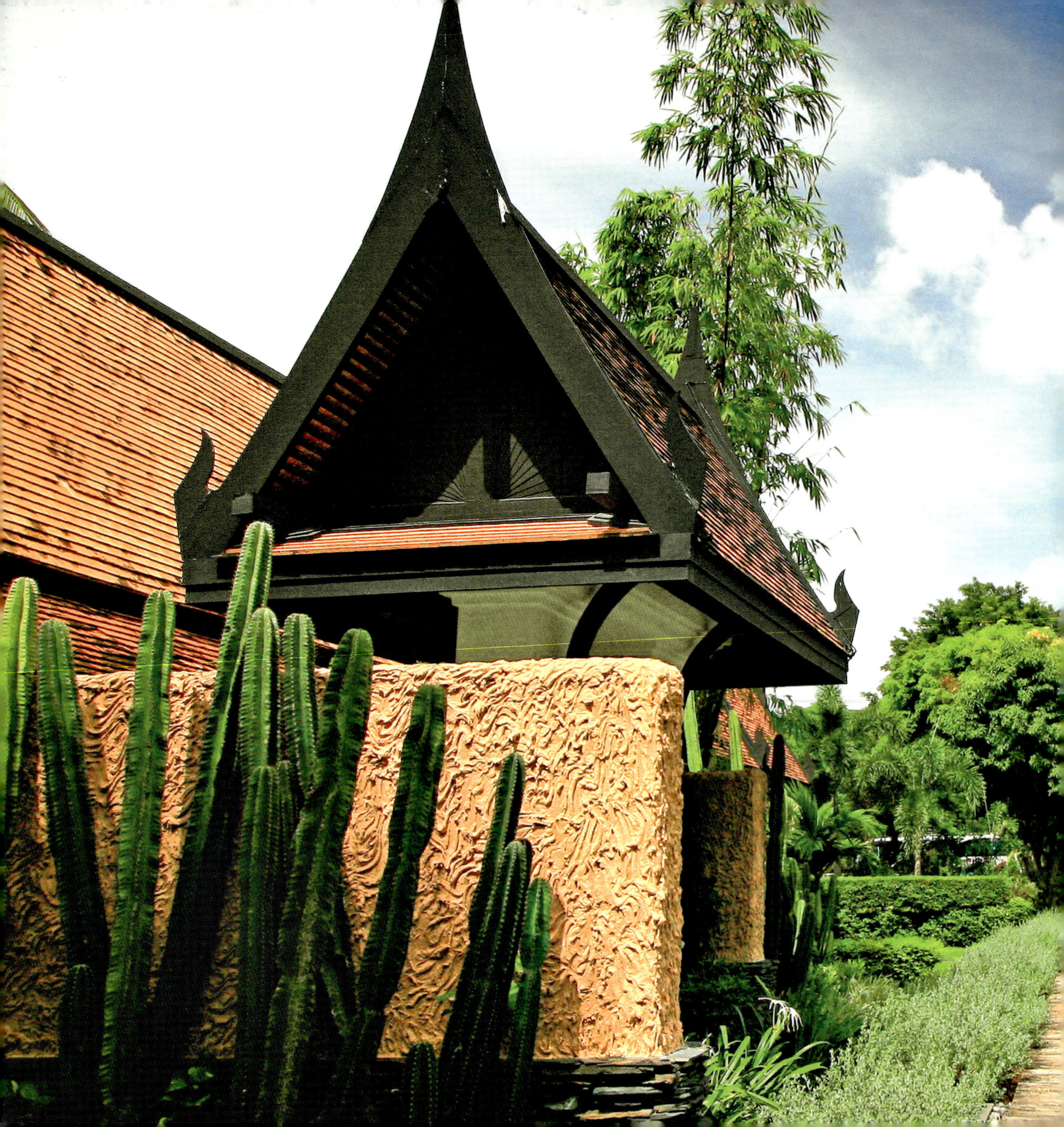

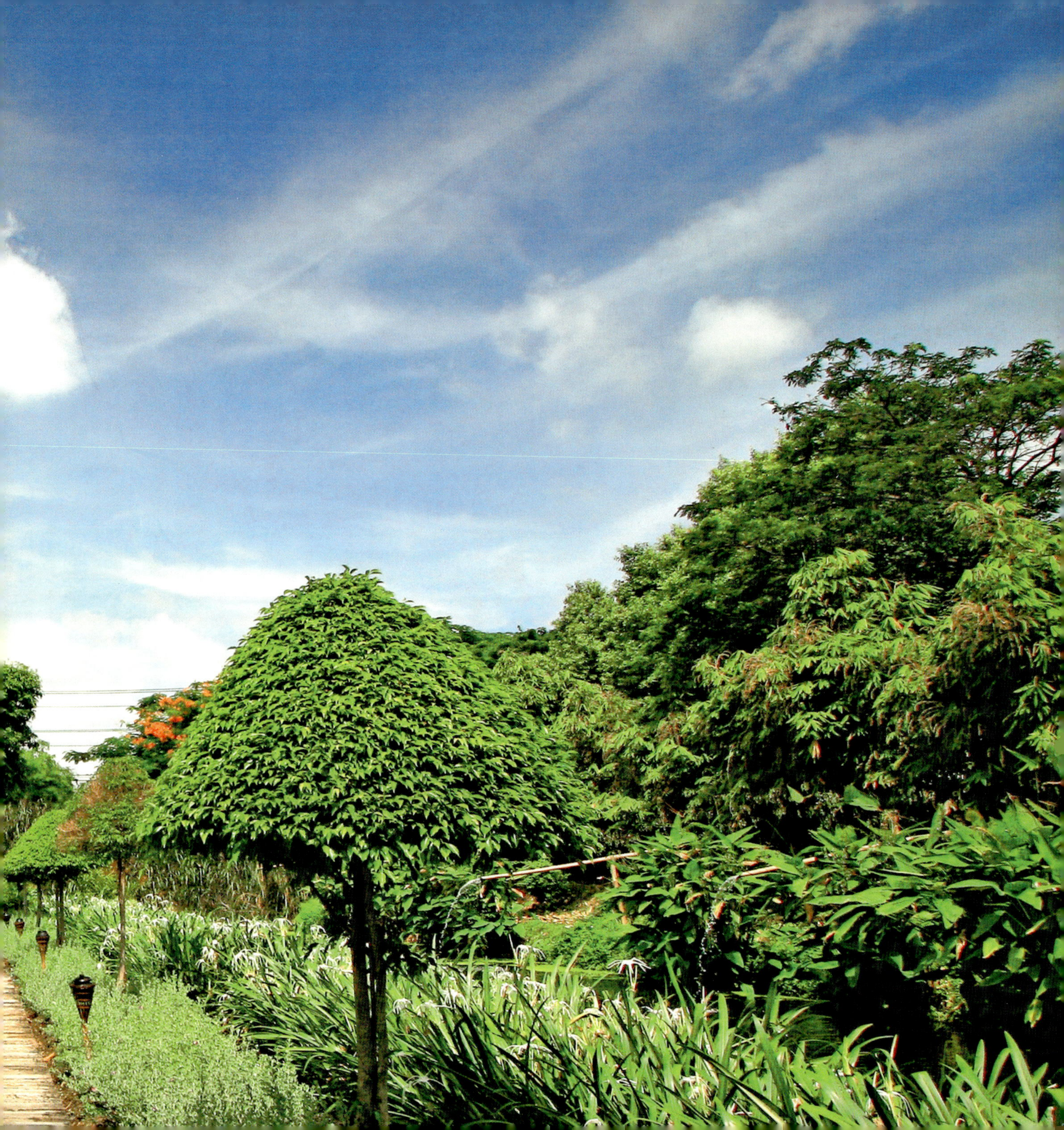

index

Numbers in *italic* denote pages where pictures appear. Numbers in **bold** denote hotel pages.

A
AW Lake products 132
Abacus agency 128
abhyanga massage 47, 53, 57, 70, 146
Absolute
    Sanctuary 26, *109*, **180–1**
    Yoga Studios 180
Active-ageing 170
acupuncture 33–4, *33*, 88, 169, 197, 207
acupuncturists 16
Aesop products 124
Allure 131
aloe vera 50
amalaki 50
Aman
    At Summer Palace, Beijing 41–2
    Spa 56
Amanpulo 99
Amethyst Crystal Steam Room 120
Ananda in the Himalayas 56, 57
Anantara
    Detoxifying Signature Treatment 129
    Dhigu Resort & Spa, Maldives 58, **128–9**
    Hua Hin *109*, **182–3**
    Phuket Resort & Spa *105*, 106–7, **184–5**
    Si Kao Resort & Spa 107, *109*, **186–7**
    cuisine 28–9
Andaman Sea salt scrubs 211
Anumba Spa *106*, 108, **211**
Anti-Stress Facials 125
antioxidants 21, 104, 160
Aqua
    Sound Pool 81, 162
    Spa 201
    vitale pool 157
aquatherapy 120
aromatherapy 68, 69, 109, 121, 129, 130
Aromatic
    Body Bliss Massage 171
    Caress 121
Art of Love 131
Artemisia vulgaris 34
asana 50
Ashtanga yoga 52
Asia Spa & Wellness Festival Gold Awards 125
Asian Ritual 129
AsiaSpa awards 195, 196
Ayung
    massage 69
    Spa 69, *70*, **159**
Ayurveda 15, 47
Ayurvedic
    chef 135
    massage 47, 53, 57, *58*, 129
    medicated oils 49
    philosophies 15
    physician 135
    spa 57
    therapies 47–8, 59, 68, 69–70, 109, 134, 135, 136, 139, 145, 146, 169, 183, 193, 197, 207, 208
Azuki Ritual 81

B
Baccarat *AsiaSpa* Awards 127
balanoy 95
Balinese
    coffee scrub 137, 146
    massage 146, 153, 159, 171
    Spice Body Wrap 155
bamboo tap 96
Barai Spa 106
Bawa, Geoffrey 57
bazilik 54
Beach Spa 69–70
Beduur restaurant 159
bengkung 66
Bensley, Bill 182, 186
beras berseri ritual 91
Best of Ayurveda treatment 146
Bhaccha, Jivaka Kumar 103
bibbitaki 50
Bikram yoga 52
bindi 56
Black and White Seama Scrub with Gold Leaf and Honey 41
Bliss Spa at W Hotel 42
Bloody Mary spa package 157
bobohizan 90
body
    masks 104
    scrubs 15, 70, 146, 159
    wraps 43, 69, 70, 145, 155, 169
Body Confidence 207
bolus treatment 104
Boracay
    island 176
    Sand and Sea therapy 99
    Wellness Package 177
boreh 65–6, 153, 155, 167
Borneo
    Therapy 90
    Volcanic Mud Wrap 168–9
Borobudur 63
Botox procedures 191
brahmi 50
Breezeway Restaurant 195
brownie buffet 42
Buddhism 103
Bulan Madu therapy 167
Bunnag, Lek 188
Bunnag Architects of Bangkok 192
Burmese Thanaka facial 118, *119*
bwa torti 54

C
camellia oil 22
Carita products 124
cekur 88
Centella asiatica 50
Chakra Dhara 145
chakra 57, 131, 202
chamomile 38
champissage 50, *50*
Chan, Emma 123
chavutti pizhichil 47
CHI, The Spa 112, 114, 168, 204
    Bangkok *106*, 107–8, **204–5**
    Beijing 40, *40*, 41, **114–15**

Boracay 99, **176–7**
Chengdu 113
Chiang Mai 108, **205**
Guangzhou 40–1, *41*, **114**, 115
Kota Kinabalu 90, **168–9**
Mactan 98, **178–9**
Manila 98, **178–9**
Penang 90, *90*, **169**
Shanghai 41, **112–13**
Chi, Tony 194
chi nei tsang 37–8
Chiang Mai Architects Collaborative 192
children's treatments 159, 171
Chinese
    acupressure massage 34, 37, 121
    angelica 38
    dispensaries 38
    herbs 121
    spas 40–1, **112–27**
    traditions 33–8
Chiva-Som 15, 24, **190–1**
    cuisine 28
Chocolate Body Mask 171
Cixi, Empress Dowager 41
Cleopatra Milk Bath 118
coco d'amour bath 59
Coco de Mer
    Aromatic Bath Treatment 143
    couples ritual 58
    massage 59
    palm 58
colon hydrotherapy 180
colour therapy 127, 203
Comfort Zone skincare products 194
COMO Shambhala Estate 18, 25, *26*, 64, **138–9**
    cuisine 28
Compress Massage 189
Condé Nast Traveller awards 190, 192, 208
confinement practices 66, 85–6
Conrad Maldives Rangali Island 14, 57, **130–1**
cookery classes 15, 21, 28, 29
Cooling Bayu Wrap 169
Coombs, Julian 204
cosmetic dentistry 18, 27
cowrie shell massage 59
crème bath hair treatment 66
Cromolight Colour Therapy 127
Crystal
    Day Spa **202–3**
    Energising Facial treatment 113
    healers 16
    therapy 109, 113, 143
Culture of Anantara 183
cupping 35, *35*
Cyberview Lodge Resort & Spa 91, **164–5**

D
dagdagay 96, 179
DaLa Spa 70, **140–1**
dang gui 38
Dead Sea salts 173
Decleor products 124
dental clinics 16
deqi 33
Dermalogica
    facial-mapping technique 42

products 117
dermatological surgery 16
destination
    retreats 19
    spas 18–19, 24–7
detoxification therapy 25, 26, 48, 91, 135, 168–9, 180–1, 183, 197, 205
dharana 50
dhyana 50
dinalisay 96
Divine Pampering 141
doctors 16, 18, 26
Dorn Method of spine alignment 97, 99, 175
dosha 47, 50, 183
Double Cho pedicure 42

E
Edsa Shangri-La, Manila 98, **178–9**
Elemis products 183, 193
Eminence products 131
Empress Jade Journey 40
essential oils 49
Executive Energy treatment 195

F
face masks 104
facialists 15
Fire and Water Purification Ritual 160
fitness programmes 18
Five Elements Theory 114, 130
floatation pools 43
four-hand synchronised massage 69
Four Seasons Hotel
    Hong Kong 42, **120–1**
    Tokyo at Chinzan-So 80, **160–1**
Four Seasons Originals 193
Four Seasons Resort
    Bali at Jimbaran Bay **142–3**
        cookery classes 29
        spa 68
    Bali at Sayan **144–5**
        cookery classes 29
        spa 68–9
    Chiang Mai *100*, 107, 108, *108*, **192–3**
        cookery classes 29
    Langkawi 90–1, **166–7**
        cookery classes 29
        cuisine 29
    Maldives at Kuda Huraa 54, 57, **132–3**
    Maldives at Landaa Giraavaru 57, **134–5**
    Seychelles
        spa 58–9
frangipani and coconut body wrap 69
Frégate Island Private 58
Futuresse 113
futon 78

G
geothermal spa 80
ghd spa products 131
ginseng 36, 38
Giraavaru Sacred Water Ritual 134
Glow restaurant 139
gotu kola 50
Grand Hyatt
    Bali 68

index

Erawan Bangkok 106, **194**
Hong Kong 122
Great Wall of China 30, 41
Green Tea
    and Ginger Scrub 41
    Bath 129
    Body Masque 119
gua sha 35, 37

H
hair cream bath 85, 87
hammam 13, 15, 27, 91, 173
harai 75
haritaki 50
Harmonies Extreme Facial 199
Hat Chao Mai National Park 186
hatha 26
Hatha yoga 52
Hayahay 179
head massage 42, 50, 50, 69
Healing Hands massage 26, 181
health farms 21
healthcare professionals 18, 26
herbal
    drinks 88
    Green Tea Body Wrap 43
    medicine 38
    steam rooms 43
    teas and tonics 38
    wrap 85
hilot 95, *95*, 175, 179
Himalayan
    Healing Stone Massage 113, 177, 207
    Tsangpo Ritual 107–8, 204–5
    Water Therapies 113
honey and cucumber facial 104
Hong Kong
    Massage 124
    spas 120–7
Hospitality Asia award 164
Hot
    chocolate massage 203
    Compress Herbal Treatment 153
    Dinu-ot Treatment 177
    stone massage 203
    yoga 26, 181
hotspring
    baths 76, 77–8
    resort 81
Hua Hin 109, 182
Huber exercise machine 201
Hufaven Fushi Maldives 57
Hyatt Regency Hua Hin 106
hydrotherapy 123, 127, 162, 171, 179, 190
hypnosis 18

I
i.sawan Residential Spa & Club 106, **194–5**
ibu pijat 66
Ideal Controle 124
ikal mayang 87
ILA products 132
Imperial Jade Facial 40
Indian
    head massage 50, *50*, 69
    spas 56–7
    traditions 47–52
Indian Ocean
    spas 57–8
    traditions 53–4
Indonesian
    massage 65, *65*
    spas 68–71, 138–59
    traditions 63–6
    wrap 66
Intraceuticals Oxygen technology 195
Island Spa 57, **132–3**
Ithaa Undersea restaurant *130*

J
jade massage 42
jamu 63, 167
    gendong 63, *63*
Japanese
    communal baths *see sentō*
    garden 75
    herbal medicine 77
    spas 80–1, 160–1
    traditions 75–8
jemuju 88
Jimbaran Puri Bali 66, 69, **146–7**
jing 33
June Jacobs skincare range 124

K
Kabir 71, 156
Kadena 25
kalawakan 95
Kamalaya Koh Samui 24, 25, 27, **196–7**
kami 75
kanpo 77
kapha 47
Kayumanis
    Bali **148–9**
    Jimbaran Bay **148–9**
    Nusa Dua 16, **148–9**
    Ubud **148–9**
    spa 69
ki 75, 77
Kiatsu 81
Kids Spa package 171
kisig galing 96
Kneipp-therapy foot spa 191
Kriya Spa 68
Kuda Haraa massage 57
Kudus House restaurant 139
Kundalini yoga 52
Kupu Kupu Barong Villas + Mango Tree Spa
    by L'Occitane 71, **150–1**
kyo-jitsu-ho-sha 75

L
L'Atelier du Pranali service 200
L'Occitane 151
Laboratoire Remède 156–7, 172
laconium 43
Landaa Spa and Ayurvedic Retreat 57
Lanna Blend Massage 108, 205
lapis-lapis 87
Le Rasle, Renaud 159
Le Spa Parisien 81, **162–3**
lempoyang 88
lepa 49
Life
    Long Wellness Programmes 27
    Passage on Maximum Men's Health 207
    Passages 25
Lifestyle + Travel magazine award 195
Lime Spa
    Hufaven Fushi Maldives 57–8
    The Fortress 59
Living Foods Detox programme 180
lomi lomi massage 16
Lotus, Aloe Vera and Pearl Powder Wrap 42
Loving Life 175
lulur 65, 70, 71, 137, 141, 146, 155, 164
Lulur Experience of Indonesia ritual 157
Luxurious
    and Pampering Imperial Jade Facial 115
    Lotus Miilk Bath 115
Lyengar yoga 52
lymphatic drainage 181

M
Madame Dibwa 54, 58
mahendi 56
Malay
    herbal wrap 87
    traditional medicine 85
Malaysian
    spas 90–1, 164–71
    traditions 85–8
Maldives
    healing traditions 54
    spas 57–8, 128–37
Maldivian
    Kurumbaa Kaashi Coconut Rub 58
    Sand Massage 54
male spa products 22
MaloClinicSPA 26–7
Man Space menu 106
Mandala Spa Borocay 95
mandi 66, 87, *87*
    bunga 87, 91
    susu 66
Mango Tree Spa by L'Occitane 68, 71, **150–1**
manicurists 16
marma point massage 49
masseurs 16
Matricaria chamomilla 38
Maya
    Facial 70
    Ubud Resort & Spa 70, **152–3**
medical tourism 16, 18
medicinal herbs 28, 38, 88
medispas 16, 18–19, 24–7
meditation 15, 26, 52, 133, 137, 189
Mercer, Vera 123
Meridian Lines massage 186–7
Milk and Honey Wrap 115
Mogambo Springs Spa 98–9, **174–5**
Monticelli mud wraps 163
Moods at a Glance treatment 149
Moor mud baths 58, 129, 211
Morford, John Edward 122
Morinda citrifolia 54
Mount
    Batok 67
    Bromo 67
    Fuji 72
    Semeru 67
Mountain Tsampa Rub 177
moxa 34
moxa ventoza 96
moxibustion 34, *34*, 88
mud baths 58, 129, 211
mugwort 34
muka berseri-seri 86
mukh lepa 49
mushi-yu 78

N
Namikoshi, Tokujiro 75
Nano
    pearl powder 41, 115
    Shiso Therapy 208
naturopaths 16, 130
naturopathy 197
Ng, David 118
Niranlada Medi-Spa Facility 191
niyama 50
Nuat bo'rarn 103–4
Nusa Dua
    Beach Hotel & Spa 70, **154–5**
    Spa 69, 70–1
nutritionists 18, 130

O
OM Studio 211
Omkaara Tantric Ayurvedic ritual 57
One Day Spa Sampler 181
onsen 13, 77–8, *77*, *78*, 160
    town 79
organic
    gardens 21, 22, 28, 58, 108, 153
    products 16, 22, 23, 106
    Sugar Plum & Spice Wrap 130
Orient-Express group 146
Oriental
    Fusion Massage 199
    Infusion 121
    Jade Ritual 42
    Pearl Radiance Facial 41, 115
oslob 95

P
PADI dive centre 137
paligo 95
Palina Hilot Four Hand Massage 176
panchakarma 48
Panchakarma Detox Package 135
papaya body polish 104
Papyion Body Scrubs 58
Parkroyal Penang 91, **170–1**
passion fruit and coco de mer body cleanse 58–9
Pevonia products 203
Philippine
    resorts and spas 98–9, 174–9
    traditions 95–7
physiotherapy 190
Phytomer products 203
pijat 65
pilates 24, 25, 108, 139, 190, 197, 201

index 215

Pimalai
  Resort & Spa *104*, 108, **198–9**
  Sports Massage 199
pitta 47
pittosporum 22
Plantation Bay Resort & Spa 98–9, *98*, **174–5**
Plateau
  Massage ritual 124
  Residential Spa 42, **122–5**
  cuisine 28
plum and orange blossom foot wash 80
plum blossom and chrysanthemum cream mask 81
protection against pollution 21
Powell, Robert 196
Power Plate® studio 195
prana 47
Pranali
  Bliss Package 201
  products 200
  Wellness Spa 108–9, **200–1**
pranayama 26, 50
pratyahara 50
psychologists 139
Pudong Shangri-La, Shanghai **112–13**
puja 103
purvakarma 48
Putra Laksamana therapy 167

Q
qi 33, 34, 35
qigong 33

R
Radix
  angelica sinensis 38
  panax ginseng 38
ramuan 85, 88
Rasa
  Asmaradana 88, 169
  Nyaman Body Wrap 169
raspays 16, 22, 54
Rasul 91
Red Plum Blossom Mindfulness Ritual 80
Refined Man programme 153
reflexology 34–5, *35*, 88, 124, 159, 207
reiki 75, *75*, 77, 137, 143, 181
Remède Spa, Singapore 71, 91, *91*, **172–3**
Renovateur Hydration Intense 124
Restylane procedures 191
Rituals of Wellbeing 129
River Café 153
Rock Spa 58
rose oil 22
rotenburo 77
Royal
  Javanese Body Polish treatment 155
  Siam Massage with Luk Pra Kob 108, 199
  Thai Floral Bath 118
  Wedding Ritual 70, 141
ryokan 78, 81

S
Sake
  Clay Cocoon 80
  Foot Soak 43
Sakura Revival Therapy 42–3

Salus per Crystal® 109, **202–3**
samadhi 50
samana 50
sambong 95
sangkatauhan 95
Sareerarom Tropical Spa 108
sauna 43
Scent of Pranali 200
Sea Escape Ritual 57, 132
sea kelp and coconut milk foot soak 58
Sembunyi Spa 91, 164
sên 103
Sen CHI Detox 205
Sensory
  Journey 136
  Surrender retreat 69
sentō 13, 77
sepang 88
Seri Pesona therapy 167
Seventh Sense 25, 207
Seychelles
  healing traditions 54
  spas 58–9
Shafeeq, Mohamed 128
shamans 54, 75
Shangri-La Hotel
  Bangkok 108, **204–5**
  Beijing 115
  Chengdu 113
  Chiang Mai 108, **205**
  Guangzhou 115
Shangri-La's
  Boracay Resort & Spa 99, **176–7**
  Mactan Resort & Spa 98, **178–9**
  Rasa Sayang Resort & Spa 90, **169**
  Tanjung Aru Resort & Spa 90, **168–9**
shen 33
shiatsu 75, 98, 124, 127, 175, 207
shirodhara 48, *48*, 53, 57, 70, 109, 118, 146, 183
shiso plant 208
Shokusai no Kyuujitsu 163
SHUI Urban Spa 42, *42*, **116–17**
Siddhartha treatments 131
Signature Massage 107
Singapore spas 91, **172–3**
Six Senses
  Destination Spa-Phuket 20, 24–5, 25, 27, **206–7**
  cuisine 28
  Spa at MGM Grand Macau 43
Skinful Pleasures 175
Slim Fit Stepper 201
sloha shringar 56
snow cabin 43
Sodashi
  Crystal Facial 143
  products 132
  Water Valley Ritual 143
Soneva Gili by Six Senses, Maldives 17, 52–3, 58, 59, **136–7**
Soy Bean Hot Spring 43
Spa at Maya 70
SPA by MTM 42–3, *43*, **126–7**
spa cuisine 15, 21, 28–9
  cookery classes 15, 21, 29
  workshops 18
Spa Essentials Shop 155

spa products 22–3, 28–9
Spa Village Tanjong Jara 91
SpaAsia Crystal Awards 127, 141, 188, 196
SpaAsia Readers' Choice Awards 118, 195
spas 13–16
spice rub 66
Sri Lanka
  healing traditions 54
  spas 59
St Anne Marine Park, Seychelles 55
St Gregory Spa 91, **170–1**
St Regis
  Bali 71, **156–7**
  Singapore 91, **172–3**
Stewart, John 197
Stewart, Karina 197
stress reduction classes 18
Suci Dhara 145
sucimurni 91
superfoods 21
Surga Manis 207
Swedish massage 163, 171, 175

T
tai chi 15, 39, 137, 190
takradhara 48
Taoism 33
tapik kawayan 96
tea bush 54
tea-tree bath and body scrub 69
temu lawak 88
Terrake products 131
Thai
  Flower Ritual 211
  herbal compress 106
  herbal medicine 104
  massage 103–4, *103*, 128, 129, 169, 175, 193, 205, 208
  medicine 103
  Royal Lotus massage 195
  spas 106–9, **180–211**
  traditions 103–4
Thalassic pool 174–5
THANN
  Sanctuary Gaysorn 106, **208–9**
  Shiso Collection 208
THE BARAI **188–9**
The Courtyard restaurant 125
The Grill restaurant 125
The Leading Hotels of the World award 170
The Love Kitchen 181
The Racha 108, **210–11**
The Source 25
The Spa at Mandarin Oriental, Tokyo 81
The Ultimate Spa Guide award 171
The Westin Tokyo 81, **162–3**
Tobira Onsen Myojinkan 80
toxic chemicals
  protection against 21
Traditional
  Chinese Medicine (TCM) 33–8, 88, 197
  practitioners 18
Tree Top treatment 151
triphala 50
Triple Oxygen Facial and Ginger Rub 42
Tropical Indulgence 181

tui na 37, 88
tungku batu 85–6, 91

U
ubat periuk 88
Ubud Hanging Gardens 69, **158–9**
uchi-buro 77
ukup 87–8
ulam 88
Ulpotha 59
Ultimate
  Detox 180
  Indulgence 118
  Mogambo Springs Experience 99, 175
urut 65
  melayu 86, 91
Usui, Mikao 75

V
vata 47
Vegetarian Detox programme 180
Venetian Macao-Resort-Hotel 26
Vichy
  shower and steam room 160
  shower tables 173
Villa de daun 70
virgin coconut oil 22, 98, 99
Vitality
  Lounges 120
  pools 43, 81, 98
Voyages of Wellbeing 129

W
Warm Jade Stone Massage 173
watsu 98, 143
  pools 24, 191
weight management programmes 170
Welcome Touchwarm foot compress 193
wellness
  diagnostics 16
  therapists 26
Wellness 360 28–9, 107, 187
White Sesame Body Treatment 129
whitewater rafting 139
World Health Organisation (WHO) 31
writing workshops 18

Y
yam weed 54
yama 50
yerba buena 95
yin and *yang* 33
Yin Yang Harmonising Massage 40
yoga 15, 24, 50, *51*, 52, 58, 128, 133, 137, 139, 179, 181, 189, 190, 193
  guru 16, 24, 26
  retreats 25, 26
Yoga sutra 50
Yoghurt Body Glow Scrub 171
Ytsara products 193
YU, THE SPA 80–1, **160–1**

Z
Zenspa 41, *41*, **118–19**

picturecredits+acknowledgements

The publisher would like to thank the following for permission to reproduce their photographs:

Absolute Sanctuary 108 (top), 109 (top), 180–181
AFP/Getty Images 95 (bottom)
Ananda-In The Himalayas 56, 57 (bottom left)
Anantara Dhigu Resort & Spa, Maldives 128–119
Anantara Hua Hin 182–183
Anantara Phuket Resort & Spa 105,184–185
Anantara Si Kao Resort & Spa 109 (bottom left), 186–187
Kevin Anderson/Getty Images 38
Hiroshi Ando/Getty Images 81 (top)
Arctic-Images/Getty Images 76 (left)
John W Banagan/Getty Images 39
Werner Blessing/Getty Images 49 (top)
Bethune Carmichael/Getty Images 11
Chave/Jennings/Getty Images 36 (right)
Chiva-Som inside back flap (middle right), 27 (top left), 33 (top), 65 (top), 109 (bottom right), 190–191
COMO Shambhala Estate front cover (top right), back cover (bottom right), 5, 10, 13 (top), 16, 17, 26, 60, 64, 69 (bottom right), 70 (top right and bottom), 138–139
Conrad Maldives Rangali Island 12, 130–131
Cyberview Lodge Resort & Spa back cover (woman carrying dish), 164–165
DAJ/Getty Images 79, 81 (bottom)
DAJ Digital Images/Disc 075 75
DaLa Spa 140–141
Hywit Dimyadi/iStock 89
Hauke Dressler/Getty Images 50 (bottom)
Ahmad Faizal Yahya/iStock 85
Tim Flach/Getty Images 34
Foodie Photography/Getty Images 88 (top)
Four Seasons Hotel Hong Kong front cover (hands holding jade), 21 (bottom), 43 (bottom), 120–121
Four Seasons Hotel Tokyo at Chinzan-So 160–161
Four Seasons Resort Bali at Jimbaran Bay back cover (top right), 2, 29 (top), 142–143
Four Seasons Resort Bali at Sayan 13 (bottom), 144–145
Four Seasons Resort Chiang Mai front cover (bottom right), 100, 107, 108 (bottom), 192–193
Four Seasons Resort Langkawi front cover (bottom left), 29 (bottom left), 166–167
Four Seasons Resort Maldives at Kuda Huraa inside front flap (top), 48, 52 (bottom), 54 (bottom), 132–133
Four Seasons Resort Maldives at Landaa Giraavaru 28, 58, 59 (top left), 134–135
Rene Frederick/Getty Images 103 (top)
GAP Photos/Getty Images 88 (bottom)
Gavin Hellier/Getty Images 72
i.sawan Residential Spa & Club 194–195
Image Source/Getty Images 103 (bottom)
Yutaka Imamura/Getty Images 76 (right)
Jimbaran Puri Bali 66, 146–147
Johannes Kroemer/Getty Images 35 (top)
Jon Feingersh/Getty Images 33 (bottom)
Kamalaya Koh Samui 1, 28–9, 24, 27 (top right), 196–197
Kayumanis Bali back cover (top left), 4, 14 (top), 148–149
Frank Krahmer/Getty Images 67
Kupu Kupu Barong Villas and Mango Tree Spa by L'Occitane 65 (bottom), 68, 150–151
L'Occitane back cover (jasmine), 21 (top), 29 (bottom right)
Linda Lewis/FoodPix/Getty Images 36 (left)
Lynn Johnson/Getty Images 37
Hua Hin Marriot Resort & Spa 212–213
Maya Ubud Resort & Spa inside front flap (massage oil), back cover (spa scrub), inside back flap (top), 14 (bottom), 70 (top left), 152–153
Christian Michael/iStock 87
Hans Neleman/Getty Images 69 (bottom right)
Gerald Nowak/Getty Images inside front flap (bottom), 92
Nusa Dua Beach Hotel & Spa 58 (bottom), 69 (top), 154–155
Michael Paul/Getty Images 50 (top)
Joe Morahan/Getty Images 51 (left)
Kevin O'Hara/Photolibrary 96
PhotosIndia.com/Getty Images 51 (right), 57 (middle)
Pimalai Resort & Spa 104 (bottom),198–199
Plantation Bay Resort & Spa 98 (bottom), 174–175
Plateau Residential Spa 43 (top left), 122–125
Pranali Wellness Spa 200–201
Pudong Shangri-La, Shanghai + Shangri-La Hotel, Chengdu 112–113
Purestock/Photolibrary 55
James D Rogers/Getty Images 77 (top)
Salus per Crystal® 202 –203
Shangri-La Hotel, Bangkok front cover (jade and silver cup), 106, 110–111
Shangri-La Hotel, Bangkok and Shangri-La Hotel, Chiang Mai 204–205
Shangri-La Hotel, Beijing 40, 41 (bottom)
Shangri-La Hotel, Beijing and Shangri-La Hotel, Guangzhou 114–115
Shangri-La Hotel, Guangzhou 41 (middle)
Shangri-La's Boracay Resort & Spa 99 (bottom left), 176–177
Shangri-La's Mactan Resort & Spa + Edsa Shangri-La, Manila 178–179
Shangri-La's Mactan Resort & Spa 98 (top), 99 (top and bottom right)
Edsa Shangri-La, Manila 97
Shangri-La's Rasa Sayang Resort & Spa, Penang front cover (yoga), 82, 86 (top)
Shangri-La's Rasa Sayang Resort & Spa and Shangri-La's Tanjung Aru Resort & Spa 90, 168–169
Shangri-La Tanjung Aru Resort & Spa 86 (bottom)
Shangri-La Villingili Resort & Spa, Maldives 59 (middle)
Vivek Sharma/Getty Images 57 (bottom right)
SHUI Urban Spa front cover (ducks and spa details), 42, 116–117
Six Senses Destination Spa-Phuket front cover (food detail), 18–20, 25, 27 (bottom), 206–207
Soneva Gili by Six Senses, Maldives 15, 44, 52 (top), 59 (top right and bottom), 136–137
SPA by MTM 43 (top right), 126–127
St Gregory Spa 170–171
St Regis Bali 91, 156–157
Tyler Stableford/Getty Images 57 (top)
Yukio Tanaka/Getty Images 77 (bottom)
Luca Invernizzi Tettoni/Photolibrary 45, 47, 49 (bottom)
Ilya Terentyev/Getty Images 30
THANN Sanctuary Gaysorn 208–209
The BARAI 188–189
The Racha 104 (top), 106 (top), 210–211
The St Regis Singapore 172–173
The Westin Tokyo 162–163
Bob Thomas/Getty Images 75 (bottom)
TIMLI/Getty Images 80
Tohoku Color Agency/Getty Images back cover (bamboo pipes and bottom left), 78
Ubud Hanging Gardens 71, 158–159
Westend61/Getty Images 35 (bottom)
Martin Westlake/Getty Images 95 (top)
Zenspa 41 (top),118–119

directory

SPAS

CHINA

Four Seasons Hotel Hong Kong (page 120)
8 Finance Street, Central, Hong Kong, China
telephone: +852.3196 8900
spa.hkg@fourseasons.com
www.fourseasons.com/hongkong

Plateau Residential Spa (page 122)
1 Harbour Road, Wan Chai
Hong Kong, China
telephone: +852.2584 7650
hongkong.grand@hyatt.com
hongkong.grand.hyatt.com or hyattpure.com

Pudong Shangri-La, Shanghai (page 112)
33 Fu Cheng Road
Pudong, 200120 Shanghai, China
telephone: +86.21.6882 8888
slpu@shangri-la.com
www.shangri-la.com

Shangri-La Hotel, Beijing (page 114)
29 Zizhuyuan Road
Haidian District, 100089 Beijing, China
telephone: +86.10.6841 2211
slb@shangri-la.com
www.shangri-la.com

Shangri-La Hotel, Chengdu (page 112)
9 Binjiang Dong Road
610021 Chengdu, Sichuan, China
telephone: +86.28.8888 9999
slcd@shangri-la.com
www.shangri-la.com

Shangri-La Hotel, Guangzhou (page 114)
1 Hui Zhan Dong Road, Hai Zhu District
510308 Guangzhou, Guangdong, China
telephone: +86.20.8917 8888
slpg@shangri-la.com
www.shangri-la.com

SHUI Urban Spa (page 116)
5th floor, Ferguson Lane
376 Wukang Road, Shanghai 200031, China
telephone: +86.21.6126 7800
info@shuiurbanspa.com.cn
www.shuiurbanspa.com.cn

SPA by MTM (page 126)
Shop A, Ground Floor
3 Yun Ping Road, Causeway Bay
Hong Kong, China
telephone: +852.2923 7888
Tung Chung:

Shop 118, Citygate Outlets
Tung Chung, Lantau Island
Hong Kong, China
telephone: +852.2923 6060
cs@mtmskincare.com
www.spamtm.com

Zenspa (page 118)
House 1, 8A Xiaowuji Road
Chaoyang District, Beijing 100023, China
telephone: +86.10.8731 2530
info@zenspa.com.cn
www.zenspa.com.cn

MALDIVES

Anantara Dhigu Resort + Spa, Maldives (page 128)
PO Box 2014, Dhigufinolhu
South Malé Atoll, Malé, Maldives
telephone: +960.664 4100
dhigumaldives@anantara.com
dhigu-maldives.anantara.com

Conrad Maldives Rangali Island (page 130)
Rangali Island, 2034 Maldives
telephone: +960.668 0629
maldivesinfo@conradhotels.com
www.conradmaldives.com

Four Seasons Resort Maldives at Kuda Huraa (page 132)
North Malé Atoll, Maldives
telephone: +960.664 4888
reservations.mal@fourseasons.com
www.fourseasons.com/maldiveskh

Four Seasons Resort Maldives at Landaa Giraavaru (page 134)
Baa Atoll, Maldives
telephone: +960.660 0888
reservations.mal@fourseasons.com
www.fourseasons.com/maldiveslg

Soneva Gili by Six Senses, Maldives (page 136)
Lankanfushi Island
North Malé Atoll, Maldives
telephone: +960.664 0304
reservations-gili@sixsenses.com
www.sixsenses.com/soneva-gili

INDONESIA

COMO Shambhala Estate (page 138)
Banjar Begawan, Desa Melinggih Kelod, Payangan, Gianyar
80571 Bali, Indonesia
telephone: +62.361.978 888
res@cse.comoshambhala.bz
cse.comoshambhala.bz

DaLa Spa (page 140)
Raya Legian, Kuta, Bali, Indonesia

telephone: +62.361.756 276
dalaspa@villadedaun.com
www.villadedaun.com

Four Seasons Resort Bali at Jimbaran Bay (page 142)
Jimbaran Bay, Denpasar 80361, Bali, Indonesia
telephone: +62.361.701 010
www.fourseasons.com

Four Seasons Resort Bali at Sayan (page 144)
Sayan, Ubud
Gianyar 80571, Bali, Indonesia
telephone: +62.361.977 577
reservation.fsrb@fourseasons.com
www.fourseasons.com

Jimbaran Puri Bali (page 146)
Jalan Uluwatu, Jimbaran, 80361 Bali, Indonesia
telephone: +62.361.701 605
info@jimbaranpuribali.com
www.jimbaranpuribali.com

Kayumanis Bali (page 148)
The Sales and Marketing Corporate Office at:
Kayumanis Jimbaran Private Estate and Spa
Jl Yoga Perkanthi, Jimbaran 80364 Bali, Indonesia
telephone: +62.361.705 777
info@kayumanis.com
www.kayumanis.com

Kupu Kupu Barong Villas + Mango Tree Spa by L'Occitane (page 150)
Kedewatan, PO Box 7
Ubud 80571, Bali, Indonesia
telephone: +62.361.975 478
spabyloccitane@kupubarong.com
www.kupubarong.com/spabyloccitane

Maya Ubud Resort + Spa (page 152)
Jalan Gunung Sari Peliatan
Ubud 80571, Bali, Indonesia
telephone: +62.361.977 888
info@mayaubud.com
www.mayaubud.com

Nusa Dua Beach Hotel + Spa (page 154)
PO Box 1028, Denpasar, Bali, Indonesia
telephone: +62.361.771 210
spa@nusaduahotel.com
www.nusaduahotel.com

St Regis Bali (page 156)
Kawasan Pariwisata, Nusa Dua Lot S6
PO Box 44, Nusa Dua 80363, Bali, Indonesia
telephone: +62.361.847 8111
remedespa.concierge@stregis.com
www.stregis.com/bali

directory

Ubud Hanging Gardens (page 158)
Desa Buahan, Payangan
Ubud, Gianyar 80571, Bali, Indonesia
telephone: +62.361.982 700
ubud@orient-express.com
www.ubudhanginggardens.com

JAPAN

Four Seasons Hotel Tokyo at Chinzan-So (page 160)
10–8, Sekiguchi 2-chome
Bunkyo-ku, Tokyo 112–8667, Japan
telephone: +81.3.3943 6958
tokyo.spa@fourseasons.com
www.fourseasons.com/tokyo

The Westin Tokyo (page 162)
1–4–1 Mita, Meguro-ku
Tokyo 153–8580, Japan
telephone: +81.3.5423 7002
wetok@westin.com
www.westin-tokyo.co.jp

MALAYSIA + SINGAPORE

Cyberview Lodge Resort + Spa (page 164)
Persiaran Multimedia
63000 Cyberjaya, Selangor, Malaysia
telephone: +60.3.8312 7000
spa@cyberview-lodge.com.my
www.cyberview-lodge.com

Four Seasons Resort Langkawi (page 166)
Jalan Tanjung Rhu
07000 Langkawi, Kedah Darul Aman, Malaysia
telephone: +60.4.950 8603
reservations.lan@fourseasons.com
www.fourseasons.com

Shangri-La's Rasa Sayang Resort + Spa (page 168)
Batu Feringgi Beach
11100 Penang, Malaysia
telephone: +60.4.888 8888
rsr@shangri-la.com
www.shangri-la.com

Shangri-La's Tanjung Aru Resort + Spa (page 168)
20 Jalan Aru, Tanjung Aru
88100 Kota Kinabalu, Sabah, Malaysia
telephone: +60.88.327 888
tah@shangri-la.com
www.shangri-la.com

St Gregory Spa (page 170)
Parkroyal Penang, Batu Feringgi Beach
11100 Penang, Malaysia
telephone: +60.4.881 1133 or +60.4.886 2288
enquiry@pen.parkroyalhotels.com
www.stgregoryspa.com or parkroyalhotels.com

The St Regis Singapore (page 172)
29 Tanglin Road
Singapore 247911
telephone: +65.6506 6892
spa.singapore@stregis.com
www.stregis.com

THE PHILIPPINES

Edsa Shangri-La, Manila (page 178)
1 Garden Way, Ortigas Centre
Mandaluyong City 1650, Philippines
telephone: +63.2.633 8888
esl@shangri-la.com
www.shangri-la.com

Plantation Bay Resort + Spa (page 174)
Marigondon, Mactan Island
Cebu 6015, Philippines
telephone: +63.32.340 5900
spa@plantationbay.com
www.plantationbay.com

Shangri-La's Boracay Resort + Spa (page 176)
Barangay Yapak, Boracay Island
Malay, Aklan 5608, Philippines
telephone: +63.36.288 4988
slbo@shangri-la.com
www.shangri-la.com

Shangri-La's Mactan Resort + Spa (page 178)
Punta Engaño Road, Lapu-Lapu
Cebu 6015, Philippines
telephone: +63.32.231 0288
mac@shangri-la.com
www.shangri-la.com

THAILAND

Absolute Sanctuary (page 180)
88 Moo 5, Tambol Bophut
Amphur Koh Samui, Suratthani 84320, Thailand
telephone: +66.77.601 190
info@absolutesanctuary.com
website: www.absolutesanctuary.com

Anantara Hua Hin (page 182)
43/1 Phetkasem Beach Road
Hua Hin 77110, Thailand
telephone: +66.3.252 0250
huahin@anantara.com
www.huahin.anantara.com

Anantara Phuket Resort + Spa (page 184)
888 Moo 3, Tumbon Mai Khao
Thalang, Phuket 83110, Thailand
telephone: +66.76.336 100
phuket@anantara.com
phuket.anantara.com

Anantara Si Kao Resort + Spa (page 186)
198–199 Moo 5, Had Pak Meng, Changlang Road
Maifad, Sikao, Trang 92150, Thailand
telephone: +66.75.205 888
sikao@anantara.com
www.anantaraonline.com

THE BARAI (page 188)
91 Hua Hin–Khao Takiap Road
Hua Hin, Prachuap Khiri Khan 77110, Thailand
telephone: +66.32.511 234
thebarai.hrhuahin@hyatt.com
www.thebarai.com

Chiva-Som (page 190)
73/4 Petchkasem Road
Hua Hin, Prachuab Khirikhan 77110, Thailand
telephone: +66.32.536 536
reservation@chivasom.com
www.chivasom.com

Four Seasons Resort Chiang Mai (page 192)
Mae Rim–Samoeng Old Road
Mae Rim, Chiang Mai 50180, Thailand
telephone: +66.53.298 181
spa.chiangmai@fourseasons.com
www.fourseasons.com/chiangmai

i.sawan Residential Spa + Club (page 194)
5th floor, Grand Hyatt Erawan Bangkok
494 Rajdamri Road, Bangkok 10330, Thailand
telephone: +66.2.254 1234
isawan.bangh@hyatt.com
www.isawan.hyatt.com

Kamalaya Koh Samui (page 196)
102/9 Moo 3, Laem Set Road
Na–Muang, Koh Samui, Suratthani 84140, Thailand
telephone: +66.77.429 800
info@kamalaya.com
www.kamalaya.com

Pimalai Resort + Spa (page 198)
99 Moo 5, Ba Kan Tiang Beach
Koh Lanta, Krabi, Thailand
telephone: +66.2.320 5500
reservation@pimalai.com
www.pimalai.com

Pranali Wellness Spa (page 200)
Shinawatra Branch:
32nd floor, Shinawatra Tower III
1010 Vibhavadi–Rangsit Rd, Ladyao, Chatuchak
Bangkok 10900, Thailand
telephone: +66.2.949 2400-4
pranali@pranaliwellness.com
www.pranaliwellness.com

directory

Siam Paragon Branch:
Unit 334 Siam Paragon, 3rd floor
989 Siam Paragon Tower, Rama 1 Road, Pathumwan
Bangkok 10330, Thailand
telephone: +66.2.610 9596-8

Salus per Crystal® (page 202)
189/5–6 Moo 7, Liangmuang Road, Bangtarad, Pakkret
Nontaburi 11120, Thailand
telephone: +66.25.844 804
info@saluspercrystal.co.th
www.saluspercrystal.co.th

Shangri-La Hotel, Bangkok (page 204)
89 Soi Wat Suan Plu, New Road
Bangrak, Bangkok 10500, Thailand
telephone: +66.2.236 7777 ext 6072
chi.bangkok@shangri-la.com
www.shangri-la.com

Shangri-La Hotel, Chiang Mai (page 204)
89/8 Chang Klan Road, Muang
Chiang Mai 50100, Thailand
telephone: +66.53.253 888
chi.chiangmai@shangri-la.com
www.shangri-la.com

Six Senses Destination Spa–Phuket (page 206)
32 Moo 5, Tambol Paklok
Amphur Thalang, 83110 Phuket, Thailand
telephone: +66.76.371 400
reservations-naka@sixsenses.com
www.sixsenses.com/Six-Senses-Destination-Spa-Phuket

THANN Sanctuary Gaysorn (page 208)
3rd floor, Gaysorn, 999 Ploenchit Road, Lumpini, Patumwan
10330 Bangkok, Thailand
telephone: +66.2.656 1424
thannspa@thann.info
www.thann.info

The Racha (page 210)
42/12–13 Moo 5, Rawai
Muang, 83130 Phuket, Thailand
telephone: +66.76.355 455
reservation@theracha.com
www.theracha.com

DESTINATION SPAS + MEDISPAS

MALO CLINIC Spa Macau
Level 5, The Grand Canal Shoppes
The Venetian® Macao-Resort-Hotel
Estrada da Baia de N Senhora da Esperança, s/n
Taipa, Macau, China
telephone: +853.2882 8888
inquiries@venetian.com.mo
www.venetianmacao.com/en/

SPAS IN CHINA

Aman at Summer Palace, Beijing
1 Gongmenqian Street, Summer Palace
100091 Beijing, China
telephone: +86.10.5987 9999
amanatsummerpalace@amanresorts.com
amanresorts.com/amanatsummerpalace/home.aspx

Bliss Spa
W Hong Kong
1 Austin Road West
Kowloon Station, Hong Kong, China
telephone: +852.3717 2797
www.blissworld.com

Six Senses Spa at MGM Grand Macau
3rd floor, Avenida Dr Sun Yat Sen NAPE, Macau, China
telephone: +853.8802 3838
reservations-macau-spa@sixsenses.com
www.sixsenses.com/six-senses-spas/mgm/

SPAS IN INDIA + THE INDIAN OCEAN

Ananda–In The Himalayas
The Palace Estate
Narendra Nagar, Tehri Garhwal
249175 Uttaranchal, India
Telephone: 91-1378-227500
Facsimile: 91-1378-227550
Email: sales@anandaspa.com

Lime spa
The Fortress
PO Box 126 Galle, Sri Lanka
telephone: +94.91.438 0909
info@thefortress.lk
www.thefortress.lk

Lime spa at Huvafen Fushi Maldives
PO Box 2017, North Malé Atoll, Maldives
telephone: +960.664 4222
info@huvafenfushi.com
www.huvafenfushi.com

The Rock Spa
PO Box 330, Victoria, Mahé, Seychelles
www.fregate.com

Spa at Aman New Delhi
Lodhi Road, 110003 New Delhi, India
telephone: +91.11.4363 3333
amannewdelhi@amanresorts.com
amanresorts.com

The Spa
Four Seasons Resort Seychelles
Petite Anse, Baie Lazare, Mahé, Seychelles
telephone: +248.393 000
www.fourseasons.com/seychelles

Ulpotha
Near Embogama, Kurungala District, Sri Lanka
www.ulpotha.com

SPAS IN INDONESIA

Kayumanis Spa
Kayumanis Ubud
Sayan Village, Ubud 80571, Bali, Indonesia
PO Box 777, Ubud
telephone: +62.361.972 777
ubud@kayumanis.com
www.kayumanis.com

Kriya Spa
Grand Hyatt Bali
PO Box 53, Nusa Dua, Bali, Indonesia
telephone: +62.361.771 234
bali.grand@hyatt.com
bali.grand.hyatt.com/hyatt/pure/spas

SPAS IN JAPAN

The Spa
Mandarin Oriental, Tokyo
2-1-1 Nihonbashi Muromachi, Chuo-ku, Tokyo 103-8328, Japan
telephone: +81.3.3270 8300
motyo-spaconcierge@mohg.com
www.mandarinoriental.com/tokyo

Tobira Onsen Myojinkan
8967 Iriyamabe, Matsumoto-shi, Nagano-ken 390-0222 Nagoya, Japan

SPAS IN MALAYSIA + SINGAPORE

Spa Village Tanjong Jara
Tanjong Jara Resort
Batu 8, off Jalan Dungun
23000 Dungun, Terengganu, Malaysia
telephone: +60.9.845 1100
travelcentre@ytlhotels.com.my
www.spavillage.com/tanjongjara

SPAS IN THAILAND

Sareerarom Tropical Spa
117 Thonglor Soi 10, Sukhumvit 55
Wattana, 10110 Bangkok, Thailand
telephone: +66.2.391 9919
info@sareeraromspa.com
www.thesareerarom.com

SPAS IN THE PHILIPPINES

Amanpulo
Pamalican Island, Philippines
telephone: +63.2.759 4040
amanpulo@amanresorts.com
www.amanresorts.com

spa glossary

A glossary of common spa, treatment and fitness terms. Variations may be offered, so it's best to check with the respective spas when you make your booking.

Abyhanga Ayurvedic gentle, rhythmic massage in which therapists work warm oil into the body to help enhance the body's immune system and encourage the removal of accumulated toxins.

Acupoints Points along the meridian channels where the life force—*qi* (Chinese), *prana* (Indian) and *ki* (Japanese)—accumulates. Also known as *sên* (Thai).

Acupressure Application of fingertip (and sometimes palm, elbow, knee and foot) pressure on the body's acupoints to improve the flow of *qi* throughout the body, release muscle tension and promote healing.

Acupuncture Ancient Chinese healing technique in which fine needles are inserted into acupoints along the body's meridians to maintain health and correct any imbalance that causes illness.

Aerobics Fitness routine that involves a series of rhythmic exercises usually performed to music. Promotes cardiovascular fitness, improves the body's use of oxygen, burns calories and increases endurance.

Aerobics studio Area used for floor exercises.

After-sun treatment Treatment that soothes skin that has been overexposed to the sun, and cools the overheated body. Treatment may include a cooling bath and a gentle massage with a lotion of soothing ingredients such as cucumber and aloe vera.

Aikido Japanese martial art that uses techniques such as locks and throws, and focuses on using the opponent's own energy against himself.

Alexander Technique Therapy developed by Australian FM Alexander in the 1890s that retrains you to stand and move in an optimally balanced way. Helps reduce physical and psychological problems brought on by bad posture.

Anti-stress massage Typically a 30-minute introductory massage, or one for those with limited time and who suffer from high levels of stress. Focuses on tension areas such as the back, face, neck and shoulders.

Aquaerobics Aerobic exercises performed in a swimming pool where the water provides support and resistance to increase stamina, and stretch and strengthen muscles.

Aquamedic pool Pool with specially positioned therapeutic jets for benefits such as relaxation and improving muscle tone.

Aromatherapy Ancient healing art that dates back to 4,500 BC. Refers to the use of essential oils from plants and flowers in treatments such as facials, massages, body wraps, foot baths and hydrobaths.

Aromatherapy massage Massage in which essential oils—either pre-blended or specially mixed for your needs—are applied to the body, typically applied with Swedish massage techniques.

Asanas Yoga postures.

Ashtanga A fast-paced form of yoga.

Ayurveda Holistic system of healing in India that encompasses diet, massage, exercise and yoga.

Ayurvedic massage Massage performed by one or more therapists directly on the skin to loosen the excess *dosha*. Promotes circulation, increases flexibility, and relieves pain and stiffness. Applied with herbal oil.

Back treatment Deep cleansing skin treatment for the back, neck and shoulders that removes impurities and excess oils, eases tension, and leaves the skin soft and smooth. Also known as clarifying back treatment or purifying back treatment.

Balinese *boreh* Traditional warming Balinese mask made from herbs and spices which improve circulation and skin suppleness. The paste is lightly applied to the body, which is then wrapped in a blanket. The spices produce a sensation of deep heat.

Balinese coffee scrub Exfoliating scrub in which finely ground Balinese coffee beans are applied to the skin.

Balinese massage Relaxing traditional massage of Bali that uses rolling, long strokes, and finger and palm pressure. Applied with oil.

Bath Soaking or cleansing the body in water that is typically infused with salt, flowers, minerals or essential oils. May serve as a prelude to, or conclude a treatment.

Bikram Hot yoga, where yoga is practised in a room heated to 29°C–38°C (84°F–100°F).

Beauty treatment Treatment provided by spas to enhance beauty and overall well-being. Includes facial treatments, makeovers, manicures, pedicures and waxing.

Body composition analysis Evaluation of lean body mass to determine the percentage of body fat for the purpose of tailoring a nutrition and exercise programme.

Body mask Regenerating treatment in which the body is slathered with clay. The minerals in the clay—which may be mixed with essential oils—detoxify and hydrate the skin, leaving it radiant.

Body scrub Exfoliating body treatment, using products such as salt or herbs, that removes dry, dead skin cells and improves blood circulation. Scrubs soften the skin and give it a healthier glow. They are often used for preparing the skin to receive the benefits of massages and wraps. Also known as body polish.

Body treatment General term that denotes treatments for the body.

Body wrap Treatment in which the body is wrapped in linen, soaked in a herbal solution for about 20 minutes, and sometimes kept under a heated blanket. May be preceded by an application of fruit, herbs, mud or seaweed, and accompanied by a face, head and scalp massage. Detoxifies the system, soothes tired muscles and hydrates the skin.

Chakra The seven energy centres in the body that are associated with the flow of the body's subtle energy.

Champissage Head massage that was developed by blind Indian therapist Nehendra Mehta, who popularised his technique in London in the 1980s.

Chi nei tsang Internal organ massage that focuses on the navel and surrounding abdominal area where stress, tension and negative emotions accumulate. Relieves illnesses, and releases negative emotions and tensions, bringing relief to the abdomen and vital energy to the internal organs. Effective in eliminating toxins in the gastrointestinal tract, promoting lymphatic drainage and treating digestive problems such as irritable bowel syndrome, bloating and constipation.

Coconut mangir Exfoliating and hydrating Indonesian scrub made from a paste of flowers, spices, ground rice and grated coconut.

Cold plunge pool Small pool filled with chilled water to stimulate blood and cool the body quickly, especially after a sauna.

Colour therapy Use of colour to bring about balance and well-being.

Complementary therapy Health care system not traditionally utilised by conventional Western medical practitioners, and which may complement orthodox treatments. Also known as alternative therapy.

Crème bath Hair and scalp conditioning treatment in which a rich cream is applied to the hair section by section. The hair may be steamed before being rinsed. Treatment sometimes includes a neck, scalp and shoulder massage.

Cupping Chinese treatment where small glass cups are attached to the skin by a vacuum that is created by placing a lit match inside each cup to burn the oxygen. The suction increases the circulation of *qi* and blood.

Dance movement therapy Dance as a therapy, with or without music, to help those with emotional problems. The therapist may suggest movements and encourage the participants to innovate their own to express themselves.

Dead Sea mud treatment Application of mineral-rich mud from the Dead Sea. Detoxifies the skin and body and relieves rheumatic and arthritic pain.

Deep tissue massage Firm and deep massage using specific techniques to release tensions, blockages and knots that have built up over time. Believed to release emotional tension. May be adapted to a specific area of tension.

Dosha In Ayurveda, the three humours that make up the physical body. Also describes the three constitutional types.

Energy balancing General term to describe a variety of practices aimed at balancing the flow of energy in and around the body. Practitioners generally try to remove blockages, and balance and amplify this energy flow.

Essential oils Oils, extracted from plants and flowers, that have specific characteristics that determine their use. They may be sedative or stimulating, and have antibacterial and therapeutic qualities. Usually inhaled or used in treatments such as massages, where they are absorbed by the skin.

Exfoliation Removal of dry, dead skin cells and impurities that impede oxygenation, using products such as salt or herbs, or techniques such as dry brushing.

Eyebrow shaping Grooming of the eyebrows, typically by tweezing, to suit the facial features.

Eye treatment Treatment that focuses on the delicate eye area, generally to combat signs of premature ageing, relieve tired eyes, and reduce puffiness and dryness.

Facial Treatment that cleanses and improves the complexion of the face using products that best suit a specific skin type. May include gentle exfoliation, steaming to open pores for extractions, application of a facial mask and moisturiser, and a facial massage. Types of facials include aromatic, oxygenating, whitening and deep cleansing facial treatments.

Facial mask Cleansing facial treatment where products are applied on the face and left on for a period of time to cleanse pores and slough off dead skin.

Facial scrub Exfoliating face treatment that uses products with abrasive ingredients to remove dry, dead skin cells and improve blood circulation. Softens the skin and gives it a healthier glow.

Fitness facial for men Facial that addresses men's skin types and needs, including shaving rash. May include a face, neck and shoulder massage.

Flotation therapy Treatment where you float on salt and mineral water at body temperature in an enclosed flotation tank (also known as an isolation tank). The feeling of weightlessness, and the isolation from external sensations and stimuli provide a deep feeling of relaxation and sensory awareness. May be done in complete silence and darkness, or with music and videos. A two-hour treatment is said to be the equivalent of eight hours sleep.

Floral bath Bath filled with flowers and essential oils.

Four-handed massage Massage performed in complete tandem by two therapists. Often uses a blend of massage techniques.

Gymnasium Workout room with weights, and a range of high-tech cardio and variable resistance equipment.

Hair services Services for the hair, including cutting, styling, deep conditioning, hair colouring, and washing and blow drying.

Hammam Arabic steam bath.

Hatha Common form of yoga, focuses on control through *asanas* and breathing techniques.

Herbal *bolus* treatment Treatment where a heated muslin or cotton parcel of herbs and spices are placed on various parts of the body to relieve sore muscles, boost circulation and refresh the skin. The herbal packs are also used in place of hands to massage the body. Also known as herbal heat revival.

Herbal medicine Use of medicinal herbs and plant-based medicine to prevent and cure illnesses. Some healing systems, traditional Chinese medicine for instance, use mineral- and animal-based ingredients in herbal medicine. Herbal medicine is used by many complementary health disciplines including ayurveda, homeopathy, naturopathy, and Chinese, Indonesian and Japanese medicines. It may be prepared for internal and external uses through various forms such as pills, teas, oils or compresses. Also known as herbalism.

Herbal steam infusion Steaming with herbs. The heat, moisture and fragrance of the herbs help to open the skin's pores and promote relaxation.

Herbal wrap Treatment where the body is wrapped in hot cloth sheets that have been soaked in a herbal solution. Eliminates impurities, softens the skin, and detoxifies and relaxes the body.

High-impact aerobics High-energy aerobics involving jumping, jogging and hopping movements where both feet loose contact with the ground.

Hilot Indigenous Filipino massage treatment that uses banana leaf strips and extra virgin coconut oil. It can be followed with Filipino coco-cocoa scrub and coconut milk bath.

Holistic approach Integrated approach to health and fitness that takes into account your lifestyle, and mental, physical and spiritual well-being.

Homeopathy Holistic health care practice, based on the concept of 'like cures like', that treats diseases by using minute doses of natural substances that in a healthy person would produce symptoms similar to what is already being experienced. Developed by German physician Dr Samuel Hahnemann (1755–1843).

Hot plunge pool Pool of hot water that helps open the capillaries.

Hotspring Natural, sometimes volcanic, spring of hot mineral water.

Hot tub Wooden tub of hot or cool water to soak the body.

Hydrobath Bathtub with water jets that pummel all parts of the body. Seawater may be used, or the water may be infused with essential oils or mineral salts. Relaxes, and stimulates muscle tone and circulation.

Hydromassage Underwater massage in a hydrobath equipped with high-pressure jets and hand-manipulated hoses to stimulate the blood and lymphatic circulations.

Hydropool Pool fitted with various high-pressure jets and fountains.

Hydrotherapy Therapeutic use of water which includes baths, steam baths, steam inhalation, in- and under-water massage, soaking in hotsprings, and the use of hot, cold or alternating shower sprays.

Indonesian massage Traditional massage of Indonesia that uses deep pressure and specially blended massage oils to ease tension and improve circulation.

Jamu Traditional Indonesian herbal medicine.

Javanese *lulur* Traditional fragrant scrub originating from the royal palaces of Java. A blend of powdered spices, including turmeric and sandalwood, is rubbed on to the body. After the vibrantly coloured paste dries, it is removed with a gentle massage. The skin is then moisturized with yogurt. The *lulur* is often used to clean and pamper the bride during the week leading up to her wedding.

Jet-lag treatment Treatment that eases travel-associated aches, pains and stiffness, and helps the body to adjust to the new time zone.

Kanpo Japanese traditional herbal medicine. Less commonly used to refer to the Japanese traditional healing system.

Ki The life force that sustains the body. Known as *qi* in traditional Chinese medicine.

Lap pool Swimming pool with exercise lanes. Standard lap pools are 25 metres in length.

Light therapy Use of natural or artificial light to heal.

Lomi Lomi Massage originating in Hawaii that uses the forearms and elbows, rhythmical rocking movements, and long and broad strokes.

Low-impact aerobics Form of aerobics with side-to-side marching or gliding movements which spare the body from excessive stress and possible injuries.

Lymphatic drainage massage Massage that uses a gentle pumping technique to stimulate lymphatic circulation, and thus reduce water retention and remove toxins from the body. Lymph drainage can be achieved through manual massage or hydromassage. May be performed on the face and neck, or on the body.

Macrobiotics Diet that aims to balance foods by their *yin-yang* qualities and according to your needs.

Malay massage Traditional massage that uses pressure and long, kneading strokes that focus on the body. May be applied with herbal oil.

Manicure Treatment that beautifies the hands and nails. Hands are soaked and exfoliated with a scrub to remove dead skin cells, cuticles are groomed, and nails are trimmed and shaped. Nails may be buffed to a shine or coated with a polish. May include a hand massage.

Marma point massage Ayurvedic massage in which the *marma* points are massaged with the thumb or index fingers in clockwise circles. Focuses on the face, neck, scalp and shoulders.

Marma points In Ayurveda, these are the body's vital energy points. It is believed that the dysfunction of any of these points leads to illness.

Massage Therapy that uses manipulative and soft tissue techniques that are generally based on concepts of the anatomy, physiology and human function. Relaxes, creates a sense of well-being, eases strain and tension, mobilises stiff joints, improves blood circulation, improves the digestive system, and encourages the removal of toxins from the body. Generally delivered by hand, though machines and high-powered water-jets are also used.

Masseur Male massage therapist.

Masseuse Female massage therapist.

Meditation Method of deep breathing, mental concentration and contemplation. During meditation, breathing, brain activity, and heart and pulse rates slow, encouraging the body to relax and achieve a greater sense of inner balance and peace. Relieves stress, removes pain and reduces blood pressure.

Meridians Pathways or channels through which the vital energy circulates throughout the body. All illnesses are believed to result from an imbalance or blockage of this flow.

Meridian stretching Stretching exercises designed to encourage physical and mental flexibility, for the body and mind to perform at their peak. Combines exercise, yoga and traditional Chinese medicine.

Microdermabrasion Clinical skin-resurfacing procedure where a jet of fine crystals is vacuumed across the surface of the face to remove the topmost layer of skin.

Moxibustion Burning of the dried herb moxa around the acupoints to relieve pain. Applied using cones of moxa directly on the skin, or indirectly with an insulating layer of other herbs.

Mud pool Pool with a central pedestal of volcanic mud. The mud is self-applied to the body and left to dry in the sun before being rinsed off.

Mud treatment Mineral-rich mud used to detoxify, loosen muscles and stimulate circulation.

Mukh Lepa An ayurvedic facial treatment.

Nail art Beautification of the nails with patterns, paintings or other decorative motifs.

Naturopathy Holistic approach that believes in the body's ability to heal itself. Uses treatments not to alleviate symptoms, but to encourage the body's self-healing mechanism. Symptoms are viewed not as a part of the illness, but as the body's way of ridding itself of the problem. Also known as natural medicine.

Nutritional consultation Consultation with a qualified nutritional practitioner to review eating habits and dietary needs. Taking into account your lifestyle, food intolerance, appetite control and weight goals, the nutritionist may compile a nutritionally balanced programme to help you attain optimal health and weight.

Onsen Japanese natural hotsprings.

Organic food Food grown without the use of pesticides or other chemicals.

Panchakarma Ayurvedic therapy (*vamana*, *virechana*, *vasti*, *nasya* and *raktamokshana*) that helps rid the body of its toxins.

Pedicure Treatment that beautifies the feet and nails. Feet are soaked and exfoliated with a scrub to remove dead skin cells, cuticles are groomed, and nails are trimmed and shaped. Nails may be buffed to a shine or coated with a polish. May include a foot and calf massage.

Personal fitness assessment Programme that assesses your current fitness levels to recommend a suitable exercise programme. May include tests for aerobic capacity, body composition, blood pressure, heart rate, and muscular endurance and strength.

Personal training One-on-one personalised workout with a qualified instructor.

Physiotherapy Rehabilitative therapy that helps recovery from injury, surgery or disease. Treatments—which include massage, traction, hydrotherapy, corrective exercise and electrical stimulation—help relieve pain, increase strength and improve the range of motion.

Pilates Exercise comprising slow, precise movements with special exercise equipment that engage the body and mind, and increase flexibility and strength without building bulk.

Purvakarma Two Ayurvedic treatments (*snehana* and *svedana*) that soften and cleanse the skin in preparation for *panchakarma*.

Qigong Chinese physical exercise of working with or mastering *qi*. Uses breathing and slow body movement to help develop a powerful *qi*.

Qi 'Vital energy' or 'life force' of the universe and the body. Also known as *ki* (Japanese) and *prana* (Indian).

Reflexology Application of finger-point pressure to reflex zones on the feet—and to a lesser extent, hands—to improve circulation, ease pain, relax the body and re-establish the flow of energy through the body. Its underlying theory is that specific areas on the feet and hands correspond with specific body parts, organs and glands, and that the manipulation of specific areas can bring about change associated with the corresponding parts.

Reiki Healing technique based on ancient Tibetan teachings. The practitioner places his palms over or on various areas of the body for a few minutes each to energize and balance the body, mind and spirit. Helps treat physical problems, heal emotional stresses and encourage personal transformation.

Samana Ayurvedic herbal medicine that works to balance the *dosha*.

Sauna Dry heat, wood-lined treatment room. The heat brings on sweating to help cleanse the body of impurities and relax the muscles. Usually followed by a cold plunge or shower.

Shiatsu Massage that uses finger pressure—and also the hands, forearms, elbows, knees and feet—on acupoints. Calms and relaxes.

Shirodhara Ayurvedic massage in which warmed medicated oil steadily drips on the forehead. Relieves mental tension and calms the mind.

Signature treatment Treatment specially created by a spa or spa group, often using indigenous ingredients.

Sivananda A form of yoga based on the 12 sun salutation postures.

Shirovasthi Ayurvedic treatment in which warm herbal medicated oil is massaged on to the head after which a closely fitted cap is worn for a while to retain the therapeutic benefits.

Snehana Ayurvedic oil therapy in which a mixture of herbs, oils and natural ingredients are massaged on to the body. The oils may also be taken orally or introduced as enemas. One of the two preparatory treatments in *purvakarma*.

Spa Term, originating from the name of a town in Belgium where people flocked to in the 17th century for its healing waters, that refers to anything from a mineral spring to an establishment which provides facilities and services that helps you achieve a sense of well-being. Many spas also provide fitness activities, classes on well-being and spa cuisine. Types of spas include day spas (spas for day use); hotel or resort spas (spas located within hotels or resorts); destination spas (spas with an all-round emphasis on a healthy lifestyle, and include on-site accommodation, treatments, programmes and spa cuisine); and mineral springs spas (spas with a natural source of mineral or thermal waters, or seawater).

Spa cuisine Light, healthy meals served at spas. Typically low in calories, fat and salt.

Spa menu Selection of treatments and therapies offered by a spa.

Spa package Two or more treatments offered together. Often longer in length and good value.

Sports massage Deep tissue massage directed at muscles used in athletic activities to help the body achieve its maximum physical efficiency. Before physical exertion, it buffers against pain and injury; after, it helps remove lactic acid and restore muscle tone and range of movement.

Steaming Use of hot steam—often infused with essential oils or herbs—to relax the body, soften the skin, and open up the pores to prepare the face or body for treatment. Hair may also be steamed by wrapping it in a hot towel or exposing it to steam.

Steam room Tiled room with benches in which steam is generated at high pressure and temperature. The steam opens the pores, eliminates toxins, cleanses the skin and relaxes the body.

Step aerobics Aerobic sessions done with a small platform for stepping up and down.

Stone therapy Massage where hot, warm or cold smooth stones are rubbed in long, flowing strokes on to the oiled body, then placed on energy points to ease away tension. Also known as hot stone massage or la stone® therapy.

Stress management Techniques to deal with stress and anxiety.

Stretching Flexibility workout where various parts of the body are stretched by assuming different positions. Helps increase flexibility, and relieve stress and tension.

Svedana Body purification method to cleanse and relax through sweat therapy. One of the two preparatory treatments in *purvakarma*.

Swedish massage Massage in which oils are applied to the body with techniques such as gliding, kneading, rubbing, tapping and shaking. Relieves stress, tension and muscle pain; improves circulation; increases flexibility; and induces relaxation.

Tai Chi Graceful movement that combines mental concentration with deep, controlled breathing. Regular practice brings about relaxation and good health. Stimulates the body's energy systems and enhances mental functions.

Tantra A form of yoga that includes visualisation, chanting, *asana* and strong breathing practices.

Tapik Kawayan Filipino therapy that uses a short bamboo stick to tap specific areas of the body to unblock flow of energy.

Thai herbal massage Massage using a warmed pouch of steamed Thai herbs pressed against the body's meridians.

Thai massage Traditional massage of Thailand, influenced by Chinese and Indian healing arts, that involves a combination of stretching and gentle rocking, and uses a range of motions and acupressure techniques. The massage is oil-free, and performed on a traditional Thai mattress on the floor. Loose pajamas are worn.

Thalassotherapy Treatments that harness mineral- and vitamin-rich seawater and seaweed for curative and preventive purposes. True thalassotherapy centres are located no more than 800 metres (2,625 feet) from the shore, and constantly pump fresh seawater filtered through large canals for use in the treatments.

Thermal bath Therapeutic use of thermal water rich in salts and minerals.

Traditional Chinese Medicine (TCM) Holistic system of care that sees the body and mind as a whole. Treatments include herbal medicine, physical and mental exercises, and therapies such as acupuncture and moxibustion.

Treatments for couples Typically treatments that a couple can enjoy together with a therapist pampering each person. Treatments specially designed for couples usually use an aphrodisiac blend of essential oils.

Tui na Chinese system of manual therapy used to treat specific illnesses of an internal nature and musculoskeletal ailments. Principal hand strokes include pushing (*tui*), grasping (*na*), pressing (*an*), rubbing (*mo*), rolling (*gun*), pulling (*qian*), beating (*da*) and shaking (*dou*). The hands, arms, elbows and feet may be used.

Turkish bath Series of hot and humid steam rooms, each of which increases in heat. You spend several minutes in each room and finish with a cool shower.

Vamana The consumption of potions to induce vomiting to treat bronchitis, and throat, chest and heart problems. One of the five purification techniques in *panchakarma*.

Vasti Use of enemas to calm nerves and treat fatigue, dry skin and digestive imbalances. One of the five purification techniques in *panchakarma*.

Vegetarian Person who consumes mainly vegetables, fruit, nuts, pulses and grains, and who does not eat meat or fish, but eats animal products such as butter, cheese, eggs and milk.

Vichy shower Spray of water from five micro-jets fixed to a horizontal rail which rain down on you while you lie on a table below. May also include a massage. Also known as affusion shower or rain shower.

Virechana Drinking a herb tea to help flush out elements that may clog the digestive tract. One of the five purification techniques in *panchakarma*.

Visualisation Technique that involves focusing the mind by consciously creating a mental image of a desired condition to bring about change. May be self-directed or therapist guided. Also known as imaging.

Watsu Therapy where you float in a swimming pool, supported by a therapist who manipulates your body with stretches, rhythmic movements and pressure point massage to bring deep relaxation.

Waxing Temporary hair removal method. Warm or cool wax, usually honeycomb blended with oils, is applied on to areas of unwanted hair. A cloth is smoothed on to the area and quickly whisked off, pulling the hair off with the wax.

Wet area Area in a spa where Jacuzzis, saunas, cold tubs, hot tubs, steam baths and pressure showers are located.

Whirlpool Tub of hot water with high-pressure jets on the sides and bottom that circulate the water. Massages muscles and relaxes the body.

Whitening treatment Treatment that brightens the skin, restores lost radiance and tones pigmentation marks.

Yin and yang *Yin* is the universal energy force whose characteristics are feminine, cold, dark, quiet, static and wet. *Yang* is masculine, warm, bright, dynamic and dry. In traditional Chinese medicine, true balance and health are achieved when these two opposing forces are in balance. Also known as in and yo (Japanese).

Yoga Ancient Hindu practice comprising focused deep breathing, and stretching and toning the body using various postures. The ultimate goal is to reach full physical, mental and spiritual potential. Relaxes and improves circulation, flexibility and strength.